JOEY
DUNLOP

JOEY
DUNLOP

THE DEFINITIVE BIOGRAPHY OF THE GREATEST ROAD RACER

STUART BARKER

JB

First published in the UK by John Blake Publishing
an imprint of Bonnier Books UK
4th Floor, Victoria House
Bloomsbury Square,
London, WC1B 4DA
England

Owned by Bonnier Books
Sveavägen 56, Stockholm, Sweden

www.facebook.com/johnblakebooks
twitter.com/jblakebooks

First published in hardback in 2021
This edition published in paperback in 2022

Paperback ISBN: 978-1-78946-508-2
Hardback ISBN: 978-1-78946-505-1
Trade paperback ISBN: 978-1-78946-506-8
Ebook ISBN: 978-1-78946-505-7
Audio ISBN: 978-1-78946-509-9

British Library Cataloguing-in-Publication Data:

A catalogue record for this book is available from the British Library.

Design by www.envydesign.co.uk

Printed and bound in Great Britain by Clays Ltd, Elcograf S.p.A.

1 3 5 7 9 10 8 6 4 2

Every reasonable effort has been made to trace copyright-holders of material
reproduced in this book, but if any have been inadvertently overlooked the publishers
would be glad to hear from them.

John Blake Publishing is an imprint of Bonnier Books UK
www.bonnierbooks.co.uk

For Joey

CONTENTS

FOREWORD

BY CARL FOGARTY, MBE

SEVEN-TIMES WORLD CHAMPION, TT WINNER, AND FORMER

OUTRIGHT TT LAP RECORD HOLDER

It's an honour to be asked to write the foreword for this book because Joey Dunlop was a bit of a hero to me when I was younger, and I didn't have many heroes. All my best childhood memories are of being on the Isle of Man for the TT and the Southern 100 races and Joey was always around and always seemed to be winning. I was at those races with my dad whom, obviously, I wanted to win but there was just something about Joey that made you like him – his scruffy appearance and the fact that his early bikes always looked like they were going to fall apart and not finish the race, although they somehow always did. So, to go on to effectively become team-mates with Joey in 1988, and to travel around with him, was something very special to me.

I liked Joey's scruffy appearance. I was like that back then, too, and my dad would always have a go at me, telling me I would never get any sponsors or get anywhere unless I tidied myself up, but my response was always, 'Well, Joey doesn't tidy himself up, does he?' There wasn't much my dad could say to that.

I always felt a bit nervous around Joey for some reason, especially in the early days. I was quite shy and was an awkward kind of kid in some ways. I would often stand by the side of Joey's bike while my dad was talking to him, but we were never really introduced properly because I was only twelve or thirteen, so it wasn't until I started racing at the North West 200 and the TT that I got to know Joey a little better.

He was a man of very few words, but I was a bit shy and mumbled a lot myself back then. Joey kept himself to himself and was quite a shy person; he certainly didn't go looking for the spotlight or media attention. I was a bit like that in the early days, but then I became the complete opposite once I started winning world championship races and gained more confidence in myself. I kind of opened up then and completely changed, but Joey always remained the same.

Most of my best Joey memories are from 1988 when we both competed in the TT Formula One world championship and I won my first world title. Joey would drive to the foreign racetracks in his van – places as far away as Finland, Portugal and Sicily – and he often had just one friend helping him, so that gave me a chance to get to know him better. I remember at Pergusa in Sicily that year, Joey turned up and parked his van next to mine. When he opened the back doors of his van there were tins of baked beans rolling around everywhere and this beautifully prepared Honda RC30 race bike sitting in amongst them all, tied to the side of the van! I put my big awning up and, to my surprise, Joey asked if he could put his bike under it along with mine. He was number 3 and I was number 4 and I looked at the bikes side by side and thought, 'Wow! I'm team-mates with Joey Dunlop!' And when he later invited me to have a few drinks in his van, I thought, 'Fuckin' hell! I'm drinking with Joey Dunlop – and in his own van, too!' I felt so cool.

I also shared a garage with him at the final round of the TT Formula One championship at Donington Park that year, and once again I was pinching myself and thinking, 'I'm team-mates with Joey and we're proper factory Honda riders!' That's how I saw it in my own head, anyway, even if it wasn't actually the case – in reality we were both riding Hondas, but in our own teams.

At the end of the 1988 season, I went over to Northern Ireland for the Neil Robinson Memorial meeting at Kirkistown. After I had won the main race Joey invited us all back to his pub and he got me really pissed. I don't usually drink much but he was making me drink this stuff called poitín (a devastatingly strong home-made brew that can be up to 90% proof). It was fucking horrible. I don't remember a lot about the evening, but I do remember nearly passing out and being carried out by Joey and some others and dumped in the back of my van to sleep it off.

Joey had won the Formula One, the Junior and the Senior TTs that year and had the three huge trophies on display in the pub. They were priceless but there they were, just sat on the floor in a corner of the pub. Before I got too drunk, I was staring at them and reading all the famous names on them when Joey came over and said, 'Hey, boy, they're not yours yet – you're not getting your hands on them just yet!' I told him that one day I would win them and, two years later, my name was on those very same Formula One and Senior trophies. That's something I'm still proud of to this day.

Joey really was something else at the TT. He was so smooth round there and I can't remember ever seeing him getting out of shape. Irish racers have always been fast at the TT because they're brought up on those kind of road circuits, but Joey always seemed so safe too, just pinpoint accurate, and he knew every part of that circuit like the back of his hand. Knowledge is second to none round the TT course and Joey had more than anyone else.

As to Joey winning the Formula One TT in the year 2000 at the age of forty-eight, that was just mad. I had been injured in April that year and my career was over, so I was sitting at home not feeling too brilliant, mainly because of my head injury. I was always tired and was sleeping a lot, but when I heard the news that Joey had won the Formula One TT, I just thought, 'Wow, that's fucking fantastic! That is just incredible.' It really cheered me up.

I sincerely hoped he would retire after that. I hoped he would just walk away, but, instead, he did what Joey Dunlop always did – he jumped in his van and headed off to some obscure, far-flung race. While that's how I felt at the time, over the last twenty years I've seen how hard it is for so many road racers to retire and I'm sure that, if Joey was still alive today, he'd still be racing bikes of some kind. There's something different and unique about road racers – they just don't ever want to stop. Whether they switch to smaller bikes or classic bikes, they just want to keep going because they absolutely love it, and Joey was the same.

I usually try to steer away from conversations about who's the best rider of all time because you really can't compare riders from different eras. But as far as all-time greats go, Joey has to be right up there, whether you mention Mike Hailwood or whoever else. As a road racer, Joey was one of the best ever – and I get goosebumps just by saying that. So, while it's impossible to say who was the greatest of all time, on the roads or anywhere else, Joey is the most successful TT racer ever and that's a hard fact, so you can't argue with that.

And to have a twelve-year gap between winning big bike races at the TT? That will probably never happen again. I can't see anyone else winning a Superbike TT at forty-eight years old, either. So, Joey Dunlop is one of the greatest road racers ever, if not *the* greatest, and I'm extremely proud to have raced against him and to have gotten to know him a little when so few people did. He was such a unique character and is still greatly missed. One thing's for sure: there will never be another Joey Dunlop.

Carl Fogarty
Blackburn
February 2021

PROLOGUE

A NOT SO GOOD FRIDAY

'PEOPLE WAS LAUGHING AT ME, TELLING ME TO FORGET ABOUT IT.'

Joey Dunlop

'I remember finishing twentieth at the Ulster Grand Prix and, another half lap, and I'd have been lapped… People was laughing at me, telling me to forget about it, that I was finished – could I not content myself and give it up?'

It was painful to watch the greatest road racer of his era struggling to even stay on the same lap as the race leaders. Many knowledgeable Northern Irish spectators exchanged knowing looks, others simply shook their heads as the once great Joey Dunlop went past them, desperately trying to avoid the humiliation of being lapped. Contrary to Joey's belief, however, few people were laughing; he was the most popular road racer there had ever been, and no one wanted to see him struggling and in pain, a shadow of his former self.

The new road-racing hotshots, Steve Hislop and Carl Fogarty, were miles ahead in the 1989 Ulster Grand Prix and setting a pace so fast that Dunlop, even had he been fully fit, might have struggled to match. It seemed his time was over. Joey was thirty-seven years old. He had been racing for twenty years and was already a veteran in what had always been a young man's sport. Hislop was ten years his junior and Fogarty was thirteen years younger than him. He had already achieved more than most could even dream of and had nothing left to prove. Five consecutive TT Formula One world titles, 13 Isle of Man TT wins, 13 wins at the North West 200, and 13 wins at the Ulster Grand Prix at Dundrod. Yet now he was struggling to finish inside the top 20 at the circuit where he had long been considered the undisputed master. Perhaps it was time to call it quits and hang up the famous yellow helmet. Perhaps he should concentrate on running the pub he had bought as a post-retirement investment five years earlier. Perhaps, for such a superstitious rider, there were just too many thirteens in the equation.

It wasn't ability that was lacking – it was fitness. Five months earlier Joey had been racing in the Eurolantic Match Races at Brands Hatch in the south of England. A somewhat farcical successor to the once prestigious Transatlantic Match Races (which had pitted the UK and the USA's best riders against each other over a series of races around Easter weekend), the Eurolantic instead featured a British team taking on a mismatched group of riders from various other countries. Few were known names and the prestige of the original series had long since evaporated.

Although he would later become known as a pure roads specialist – racing on closed public roads rather than much safer, purpose-built short circuits – Joey had also been a great short-circuit racer earlier in his career, which is why he was picked to be part of the British team. But this meeting at Brands Hatch would change all that. It would change many things. It would prove to be a watershed in the life of Joey Dunlop. And the man who was unwittingly involved in that watershed moment was Belgian rider Stéphane Mertens.

Mertens was an experienced rider and a fast one, too. He had been Belgian road racing champion before moving up to race in 250cc Grands Prix and had finished fourth in the inaugural World Superbike championship in 1988. He would finish second to Fred Merkel in the same series by year's end in 1989 and would eventually become a double World Endurance champion. He was good; of that there was no doubt.

The crash happened on the tenth lap of the third match race, held on Good Friday, 24 March 1989, on the approach to Paddock Hill bend, the fast and fearsome downhill right-hander after the start/finish straight. Mertens was having his first ride on his new Honda RC30 and was using the Good Friday race to get used to his bike before the first round of the World Superbike championship at Donington Park on Easter Monday.

'I started very carefully, just to learn the bike,' Mertens says. 'Joey and me were not very fast and were probably around eighteenth position. I was following Joey then, towards the end of the race, I decided to overtake him at the end of the start/finish straight before Paddock Hill bend. He was on the right side of the track and I went on the left side to overtake him. When I tried to enter Paddock Hill bend he was on my right, and then I don't know what went wrong, really. I couldn't make the turn because Joey was there, and he didn't enter the corner. So, we went straight ahead and off the track towards the tyre wall. There wasn't enough run-off area before the tyre wall, so it was a pretty bad accident. We were probably doing around 160kmh [100mph] at the time of the crash, and we didn't really get a chance to brake.'

Joey got buried under the tyre wall and broke his left femur and his right wrist while Mertens suffered a dislocated pelvis. According to photographer Don Morley – who witnessed the crash and photographed it – things could easily have been much worse. 'Several people have been killed in very similar crashes at Paddock Hill bend,' he says. 'I really don't know whose fault it was because I was about 100 metres away. As I recall it, Joey's bike just slid away, as has happened so many times to so many riders, but Joey was thrown from the bike and badly injured.'

Dunlop and Mertens were transferred to nearby Sidcup hospital in the same ambulance. 'We were together in the ambulance and Joey was crying in pain and also I was in a lot of pain,' Mertens says. 'We went together to the same hospital, but we were put in different rooms.'

While Mertens has often been blamed for causing the crash, he doesn't see it that way. 'Some people said I closed the line so he couldn't take the corner but, for me, we weren't really going fast, and we weren't fighting hard. My feeling is that I overtook him. I don't know why he was so surprised, but he failed to make the turn and he was in my way to enter the corner. Maybe he was surprised because I tried to overtake him on the left side rather than the right, as this is not always the best way to do it. But when he went straight ahead, then I had to go straight ahead too, and we both hit the tyre wall very hard.'

Despite having raced for twenty years at that point, this was the first time Joey had suffered a serious injury. 'I knew I was hurt and hurt bad, like, and didn't know what to really expect,' he later said. 'I never was hurt before, seriously, and it was so quick an accident, and so serious an accident, that I thought it was all over, like.'[1]

Dunlop underwent an operation to insert a pin in his broken femur but had to then undergo a second operation when surgeons realised the pin wasn't long enough. Graham Sanderson was the press and media man for Honda UK at the time. He remembers visiting Joey in Sidcup Hospital and arranging to spring him. 'He looked so grey – the colour of a paving slab,' Sanderson says. 'He looked absolutely awful and, even though he had always been slim, he looked very thin and wasted and completely de-tuned. He didn't quite beg me, but he did say quite strongly, "Graham, you've got to get me out of here." He gave me the impression that the level of care he was receiving was not quite what he expected. He was known at hospitals in Northern Ireland and knew he would get the very best treatment there and could also be closer to his family.'

There may have been another reason why Joey was so keen to get back to his local hospital in Belfast – his wife Linda was in the same building, having just given birth to their fifth child, daughter Joanne.

'I assured Joey that I would sort it out, but at that time I was just a PR man and didn't have a huge budget for things like air ambulance transfers,' Sanderson continues. 'So, I arranged it off my own bat and then presented my bosses with a fait accompli, more or less. I don't remember the exact cost of the air ambulance transfer, but it certainly ran to thousands of pounds, and I had to get a purchase order signed for it by my boss at Honda. But the people back at HRC [Honda Racing Corporation] in Japan held Joey in the highest regard and Honda has a good reputation for reciprocating loyalty when it's shown to them. So, even though I didn't have the authority to organise such a thing, I knew I would have the backing and support of Bob McMillan [then general manager of Honda UK] and Honda. Joey had to be taken into an environment where he was going to be more comfortable and able to make a quicker recovery.'

'I remember getting the call from Graham Sanderson and we

decided to fly Joey home because he was threatening to leave the place, he was that unhappy,' Bob McMillan says. 'He was threatening to get in his van and drive back to Belfast!'

What Joey thought of the helicopter ride can only be guessed at, but he certainly wasn't keen on flying, as Don Morley remembers. 'Joey wouldn't fly – he was petrified of flying. The only time he ever flew, during the years I worked with him, was when we had to go to the launch of Honda's VFR750 at Jerez in Spain in 1986, and there wasn't enough time for Joey to drive there. He was so terrified he held my hand all through the flight, never said a word, and was as white as a sheet. Here was a man who had won all those TT races and Formula One world championships, yet his knees were knocking, and his knuckles were white when he had to fly in that aeroplane.'

Back home in Northern Ireland, Joey began the long, strenuous battle to regain full fitness. But he wasn't the only one: Stéphane Mertens also suffered long-lasting effects from the Brands Hatch crash. 'For me, this accident was a big shame because, otherwise, I would have been World Superbike champion that year. I was in hospital for about four weeks after that crash and I was in a lot of pain when I started racing again because my pelvis had opened up – the same thing that happens to women when they're pregnant. The bone wasn't really broken, it was the ligaments of the pelvis which were damaged, and I had to wear a special belt for a while to hold my pelvis together. As it turned out, I lost the championship by just seven points to Fred Merkel that year. I had a lot of pain for many years, and I still have some pain in my pelvis now from that crash. I have suffered for many years.'

Joey's recovery was also hampered by complications. 'I'd broken my leg, up at the top, but I had a lot of trouble with it, and they couldn't get it straight,' he said. 'They pinned it and then they operated again, and they re-pinned it and they re-pinned it, and they had to put it in traction for a long time.' [2]

The eighteen-inch pin inserted in his leg would later be taken out as doctors feared another crash could bend it and cause the femur to snap. Joey kept the pin and admitted that it was 'the hardest trophy I ever got'.

The crucial factor in Joey's decision to return to racing was the belief that he hadn't been to blame for the accident. 'I'd been talking to a lot of people that saw the accident and, like, it wasn't my fault at all. Once I got back and got going again and got on my feet, got my wrist working, got out on the road bike, I wanted to try and go out and do it again.' [3]

Asked how he would have felt had he been to blame for the crash, Joey said, 'Oh, that would have been me finished. I wouldn't even have dreamt of coming back again.'

Dunlop and Mertens never did get the chance to meet up after the crash to discuss who was to blame. Instead, each did their best to recuperate and get back to full strength so they could concentrate on the rest of their respective careers. It was part of racing after all: these things happened. But while Mertens soon got back to winning ways, for Joey it took an awful lot longer. On returning to the Ulster Grand Prix some five months later, he could do no better than struggle round in twentieth position, trying desperately not to be lapped. It looked like the greatest career in road racing was over.

It wasn't. The Good Friday accident proved to be a watershed in Joey Dunlop's career, but it did not signify the end of it. He would no longer race on short circuits in the UK, for one thing, as there was too great a chance of falling victim to someone else's crash. Nick Jefferies, Joey's Honda team-mate at the time, says Joey's attitude towards English short-circuit racing changed after the Brands Hatch incident. 'Joey was very fussy about who he would share track time with – he wouldn't dice with you if he didn't know you,' he says. 'I think that was a result of his big crash at Brands Hatch. He was far more cautious about who he diced with after that.'

Joey would also be forced to concentrate on much smaller, lighter and less powerful 125cc machines as he was no longer able to handle the big, heavy and fiercely powerful 750cc superbikes. He was approaching forty years of age and had another baby to consider but, despite all this, he refused to give up on his racing. It was, after all, his life; it was all he had ever known and he determined that, no matter how long it took, and no matter how much humiliation he had to endure along the way, he would get back to winning ways.

The knowing looks continued, however, even amongst loyal fans. 'Joey's finished,' they were forced to admit. 'He'll never win on a superbike again – he's too badly injured, and he's too old. He'd be better just packing it in.'

Don Morley admits to being one of those who thought Dunlop's career was over. 'He was very badly injured,' he says. 'He couldn't ride a big bike properly for a long time after that and, I must admit, I pretty much wrote him off – I didn't think he would ever come back to the big stuff.'

Joey at least had Honda's promise of support in whatever kind of racing he chose to do. Bob McMillan took it upon himself to help his rider in any way he could. 'After he got out of hospital I decided to look after him,' he says. 'We didn't yet have Neil Tuxworth [future Honda race team boss] at that point, so there was no team manager to look after Joey. I decided that he was going to get bikes for as long as he needed them, because he deserved that for what he had already achieved for Honda. It almost didn't matter what he might achieve in the future, it was reward for all he had already done.'

McMillan, who would become a great friend of Joey's over the next decade, still had belief in his rider and knew how highly thought of Joey was back in Japan. 'I don't think I felt his career was over at that point,' he says. 'He was so highly revered within Honda UK and amongst the old bosses at Honda, Japan, like Mr Kawashima and Mr Kawamoto. They knew Joey was a TT man and Honda was a TT company, in a way, and they had put a lot of store on winning at the TT since the 1960s.

'And I think that, because Joey was in a mould with the likes of Mike Hailwood, and was such a legendary-type character, I was supported by Japan whenever I needed support for Joey. So, I just thought I would look after him as best I could, until such time as he could get back to where he was at before – but I never dreamt he would go on to achieve the things he did.'

Joey did admit to considering retirement, but none too seriously. He would later say of the accident, 'I did actually think about giving it up… but when I discovered it wasn't my fault, I wanted to get back again. I didn't really think I'd ever win races again, but once I got going and I got back to the TT again… I started off on a wee 125 and I'd never rode a 125 but I went well… and then I rode the 750.'[4]

Even though the ride on the 750cc Honda RC30 at the 1989 Ulster Grand Prix ended in him almost being lapped, Joey still refused to give up: he desperately wanted to prove his doubters wrong. 'If Joey opened a newspaper and read that somebody was putting him down or said he was no use, he would go out and beat everybody,' admits his younger brother, Jim Dunlop. 'He did that once at Aghadowey, whereas, the week before, at the same circuit, he'd been nowhere. He could do it when he wanted to – or when he had to.'

Joey's comeback was a struggle and, at times, an embarrassment, as he himself admitted. 'It annoyed me a little at the start… I did a lot of short circuits and was struggling to qualify and all that sort of stuff. Once I started getting going and started coming up through the field again…. Like, they were putting me on the front row of the grids [at a time when riders had to push-start their machines] and I couldn't even run alongside the bike, I had to pedal [paddle] it and that annoyed me, and other riders was complaining about me.'

Joey raced on through the second half of the 1989 season, but the results were poor, and he was written off by most pundits. But by the time the Ulster Grand Prix came around again in August of 1990, the quiet publican from Ballymoney shocked the racing world. 'I rode on, and the next year I was a wee bit fitter again,' he told Irish sports presenter Jackie Fullerton. 'I went to the TT and I was lying second to [younger brother] Robert on the 125. I broke down, but I came back to the Ulster Grand Prix [on the 750] and I won it. They weren't laughing then.'

For the one and only time in his life, the famously undemonstrative Joey Dunlop punched the air with his fist as he crossed the finish line to win the Formula One race at the 1990 Ulster Grand Prix. That's how much it meant to him.

They weren't laughing then.

The King of the Roads was back. And the best was yet to come…

CHAPTER 1

A BOY FROM NOWHERE

Ballymoney is a sleepy and unremarkable little town in County Antrim, Northern Ireland. Situated some forty-eight miles to the north-west of Belfast, it has a population of around 10,000 and its name in Irish means 'Townland of the moor'. Situated on the A26 that runs between Ballymena and Coleraine, it would most likely have remained relatively unknown outside of Northern Ireland had it not been for the birth of one William Joseph Dunlop. As the child grew to be a man, his fame would ensure that every motorcycle racing fan the world over would know the name of Ballymoney – and the name of Dunlop – even though Joey didn't actually hail from the town itself.

At 8am on Monday, 25 February 1952, Mary 'May' Dunlop gave birth to the second of her seven children – her first boy – and named him after his father. Weighing in at a healthy seven pounds,

William Joseph Dunlop was born into a semi-detached stone cottage that stood within the small townland of Unshinagh, a mile outside the hamlet of Dunloy and some six miles south-east of Ballymoney, the closest town of any size. Townlands are an ancient Irish measure of land and they range in size from just a few acres to several hundred acres.

The birth had taken place at home, as was traditional at the time. A midwife had been called for, but young William Joseph beat her to it and was delivered by his auntie Peggy and a helpful neighbour. 'He was a straightforward birth and was born at home because that was the custom in those days,' May Dunlop later recalled.[5]

William Joseph was born into a Northern Ireland that was still affected by post-war rationing. Jobs were scarce and money was tight for most families. The boy who would become Joey Dunlop certainly wasn't born into luxury: the family cottage on the Bravallen Road had no running water and no electricity. This wasn't particularly unusual – mains electricity had not yet reached every house in Northern Ireland – but it was a humble beginning nonetheless, and one that would play a big part in determining the character of William Joseph for the remainder of his life. 'We weren't the poorest family in the country, but not far off,' his father admitted.[6] The family wouldn't even own a television set until the young Dunlop was well into his teens.

A motor mechanic by trade, William, or 'Wullie', Dunlop had a canny knack for making do and mending and would eventually provide his growing family with power by linking a windmill to a generator and rigging the windmill in a treetop some sixty-five feet off the ground. This knack for technical improvisation would ultimately be passed on to his eldest son and William Joseph would put it to extraordinarily good use.

Instigating a family tradition of calling their children by their middle names, William Joseph soon became known as Joe. It would be many years before he became known by millions as Joey and it was distinctly against his will; for years, anyone attempting to call him Joey would be angrily corrected. 'He hated being called Joey. Wouldn't have it at all,'[7] his father testified. Only with time would he come to accept the name.

Joey had been born two and a half years after his sister Helen and would in time be joined by younger siblings Jim, Virginia and Linda, and twins Robert and Margaret. Another sibling, Shirley, died of cot death at just seven months old. It was a lot of mouths to feed, and the post-war austerity years didn't help Wullie Dunlop's plight. The family relied on the age-old Irish custom of digging peat for fuel to stay warm in winter and the young Joey was always on hand to help. 'We used to cut a lot of turf, about one and a half miles from the house,' his mother said. 'And even when he was tiny, he'd insist on coming with us.'[8]

In the first of a series of moves around the countryside south of Ballymoney, the Dunlop family soon relocated to another townland known as 'The Leck', just three miles away, and settled into a house that belonged to Joey's grandmother. Situated as it was on a farm, there may not have been much room in the house for the ever-growing family, but the surrounding area at least allowed for plenty of room to play – and playing with engines began early. With Wullie Dunlop being a mechanic, there were always engines and parts lying around the house and, according to the cousin who would later become one of Joey's most trusted mechanics, Jackie Graham, Joey could strip and rebuild an engine at a very early age. 'I was down seeing his father and he [Joey] came out and he was as black as your boot,' Jackie explained years later. 'He had an engine pulled out and had stripped it completely and had it rebuilt. I would say he'd have been about ten at the time.'[9]

The make-do-and-mend attitude of Wullie Dunlop rubbed off on Joey and gave him a solid grounding in the skills he would later need to tune, develop, and improve his racing bikes.

There were chores to be done too, as elder sister Helen explained in 2019. 'My father kept pigs and Joey and I had to feed the pigs and muck them out before we went to school and after we came home.' The young Dunlop would also have to check the makeshift windmill every night and start up the generator if the batteries were low. He understood machinery, and how it worked, from infancy.

Joey had initially attended Garryduff Primary School but, after the family moved yet again – this time to nearby Culduff, close to the site where Joey would later build his own house on the Garryduff Road – he went to Lislagan Primary School. By the time he was fourteen, Joey's family had moved on once more and took up residence in the quiet little hamlet of Killyrammer, just three and a half miles east of Ballymoney.

Fitting nine people into a three-bedroom house was no easy task and personal space was not a luxury any of them were afforded. With three boys and four girls, the easiest solution was to have the boys sharing one bedroom, the girls sharing another, and Mum and Dad the third. 'There was usually a bit of fighting going on, like with all families,' Helen admitted. 'But, ach, we mucked in and got on pretty well.'

Growing up in out-of-the way places meant Joey was never a natural socialiser. With brothers and sisters to play with, there was no real need to go seeking out gangs of other kids, not that there were any around anyway – the various homes of Dunlop's early years were all out in the countryside, and a bus ride away from the nearest decent-sized town of Ballymoney. It was this very fact that helped instil self-reliance in the young Dunlop, and perhaps it was the lack of personal space offered by a small house hosting nine people that made him value quiet time on his own as he grew older.

Even family days out were calculated to avoid towns because 'they cost money,' according to Wullie Dunlop. Instead, there would be trips to the wide-open spaces of the north Antrim coast – trips that would imbue a love of remote, rural places that never left Joey. In his later years, he would make many trips to the mountains of Donegal when he needed to be alone. This deep-seated need for personal space would later make him extremely uncomfortable under the gaze of television cameras and the attentions of the press. 'Even when he was a nipper, he was a wee, shy thing,' Jackie Graham recalled in 2000. 'Didn't like to meet strangers at all.'[10]

By the time the family moved to Killyrammer, Joey was attending Ballymoney Secondary Intermediate School – or at least he was most of the time; it wasn't unknown for him to get on the school bus then jump back off before it reached the school. He was far happier messing around with engines than he was learning English literature. While he was never troublesome at school, neither was he very interested in it. After all, if he was going to be a mechanic (and, despite toying with the idea of joining the army at one point, he was fairly certain his future would involve working with engines) then he could learn a lot more in his father's shed than he could in a classroom.

'He was quiet and a bit shy, but he would have got up to a bit of devilment at school,' Helen has said. Like all kids, Joey found himself in the odd scrape. His mother was once called to school to explain why her son had tipped a pot of black paint over a fellow pupil and, on another occasion, Helen managed to break her little brother's nose when she accidentally pulled a tractor harrow on top of him. There was also a lucky escape when the young Joey threw a beaker of paraffin onto an open fire and singed his hair and eyebrows so badly he had to be hidden from his mother until his hair grew back.

Younger brother Jim Dunlop remembers Joey being a fun-loving kid, at least when he was around people he knew and trusted. 'There was always a bit of devilment in him,' he says, agreeing with Helen. 'We used to go down on the beach and Joey would egg me on to jump between the rocks. If you couldn't jump far enough, you landed in the sea. He was older than me, so he cleared the gaps, but I often landed in the sea. There was always a bit of carrying-on with Joey. Robert was four years younger than me, but he was a bit of a devil as well. I don't think I was as bad as them two.'

Like many in Northern Ireland, Wullie Dunlop had an interest in riding motorcycles and watching the local road races. Jim Dunlop remembers being taken the two and a half miles to Garryduff Primary School (without a crash helmet) on Wullie's old Norton or BSA, himself sitting on the fuel tank while elder sister Linda rode on the pillion seat. Helen remembers her dad performing the same taxi duties with Joey propped on the tank and herself on the back seat.

Jim believes Joey's interest in motorcycles was ignited by his father. 'I would imagine that it was my dad that got Joey interested in bikes. He had always a bike or two around the house. I would say if he [Joey] wasn't given permission, he usually would have sneaked it [a bike] out and went up and down the lane on it. My dad never raced properly, but he raced up and down the road and ran into a car one time. It was a bad smash. So, there were always old bikes about when we was growing up.'

From a very young age, Joey Dunlop, along with the rest of the family, was taken to the annual North West 200 road race that runs between the coastal towns of Portrush, Portstewart and Coleraine, just a short drive north from the Dunlop family home.

In the absence of most other luxuries, a day out at the seemingly glamorous and glitzy North West was a real treat, and one that the young Joey Dunlop particularly enjoyed. First held in 1929, the North West is now Northern Ireland's biggest outdoor sporting event and, along with the Ulster Grand Prix, staged on the Dundrod circuit just outside Belfast, was one of the big two international bike racing events in the province where local Irish heroes would get their chance to take on the world's best riders. By 1964, a twelve-year-old Joey Dunlop would have witnessed the triumph of local rider Dick Creith in the feature 500cc race and realised that it *was* possible for a local boy to defeat the glamorous Grand Prix stars on their exotic machinery.

But such thoughts were far from Joey's mind when he first moved to Killyrammer: he was far more interested in a fifteen-year-old schoolgirl called Linda Paterson who lived a few doors down in Hillcrest Gardens. Joey was sixteen at the time and Linda lived with her family just a few doors down in the same small estate. As shy as he was, Joey readily accepted the notes Linda passed to him via his sister and before long the pair had started 'going steady' and Joey would climb up a neighbour's drainpipe to get to Linda's window for late-night trysts. Having caught Joey in the act one on occasion, the neighbour whose drainpipe he used was shocked at such behaviour and began to spread the story around the village, hoping to create something of a scandal. In retaliation, the next time Joey clambered up the drainpipe, he continued onto the neighbour's roof and blocked her chimney with sods of earth and moss, literally smoking the hapless woman out of her house. Severely unimpressed, the neighbour saw to it that the young Dunlop appeared in court for the prank, but the judge found the story too amusing to inflict any more damage on Joey than a caution.

Around the same time he was mastering the art of climbing

drainpipes, Joey started his first job as an apprentice at Jim Wallace's Ballymoney car dealership, working alongside his father Wullie. After serving his apprenticeship, he then took up the position of diesel fitter at Danny McCook's coal yard in Ballymoney. As well as working on engines, Joey also had to help with delivering coal. 'He was a mechanic then – or he came to be a mechanic,' McCook recalled in an interview in 2000. 'He probably wasn't the most orthodox mechanic in the world... Joey might have worked all night or, the next day, he might not have come to work at all. He wasn't the most orthodox chap in the world.'[11]

Had he not discovered a passion for racing motorcycles, Joey would, in all likelihood, have ended up in a similar kind of job, married his sweetheart Linda, and settled down to a quiet and unremarkable life. But when his sister Helen met a young man at the 'Pop In' fish and chip shop in Ballymoney one night in 1967, Joey's destiny was to change. It was a meeting that would have profound consequences for him, because the young man his sister had met was called Mervyn Robinson – and he raced motorbikes. And as Helen herself has said, 'If there hadn't been Mervyn Robinson, there would have been no Joey Dunlop.'

o

Joey and Mervyn got along instantly when Helen brought her boyfriend home to meet the family. While Joey had never shown any inclination to race before, Robinson's enthusiasm for the sport was contagious and it soon began to rub off on Joey. 'Mervyn Robinson had raced before but given it up,' Jim Dunlop explains. 'When he started courting my sister Helen, he started racing again and he got Joey into it. They both had road bikes and the two of them used to race each other coming home from work. There was some S bends on a local road, and we used to go up after school and lie on the bank to watch Joey and Mervyn come round flat out. Merv would win sometimes, and Joey would win sometimes. They were pretty evenly matched.'

Joey bought his first road bike – a 250cc BSA – in 1968 and took it on its first trip to the seaside town of Portrush for a day out. The only problem was that he failed to attach L-plates and was stopped by the police on the way home. It was enough to land Joey in court again and this time he was ordered off the roads for three months.

Jim Dunlop remembers another troublesome encounter on bikes not long afterwards. 'Me and Joey raced down the road one time. I had a 200cc Suzuki and Joey was on our dad's Honda Super-Six. I followed Joey down the wee back roads, just sitting on his back wheel. We stopped and turned round, and Joey said he'd follow me on the way back. I went as fast as I could and at the very first corner I ran onto the grass and crashed. I threw myself down in a ditch because I thought Joey was right on my back wheel and would crash into me, but he made it round the corner safely. Then the big problem was getting home with just one bike. I wouldn't sit on the back with Joey, and he wouldn't sit on the back with me, so we were stuck. We eventually came to an agreement that he would ride half-way home and I'd ride the other half. When we got to the house my dad was waiting in the drive, shaking his head, saying, "I knew this was going to happen."'

Joey bought another road bike – this time an Ariel Arrow – from Merv Robinson but, by now, road riding was losing its appeal. It seemed a racetrack would be a safer place to play and to evade the police, so when Robinson took up racing again, Joey also took a serious interest. So serious, that he bought his first race bike (a 199cc Triumph Tiger Cub making about 10bhp) from Robinson with a view to trying his hand at the sport he had now heard so much about. The bike cost him the princely sum of £50, and he had to borrow money to buy it (he and Merv would even pick potatoes in the early summer as a means of making a few precious extra pounds), but it set him on a career path that would bring success and fame beyond his wildest dreams.

Speaking of Merv, Joey later said, 'We ripped about on road bikes and scramblers round fields – or, actually, *road* bikes round fields – and we just happened to be talking one day and he says to me, just whenever I came of age, "You're very good at riding these motorbikes. You know, I used to race – you should try it," and that's how it came about. Him and me started in the wintertime and worked at a Triumph Cub and bits and pieces for me to race.'[12]

Joey being Joey, he didn't simply buy the Triumph Cub and go racing on it straight away – he had to first strip it, refine it, and rebuild it to make it faster. Since the house at Killyrammer didn't have a garage, Wullie Dunlop helped his son to floor the loft space to give him somewhere to work on the bike. The difficulty of lifting a motorcycle into the loft of a three-bedroom house clearly presented no impediment to the young Dunlop. It would become Joey's sacred space, and for the remainder of his life he would never be happier than when he was tucked away figuring out how to make a motorcycle go ever faster. Merv joined him most nights too, often at the expense of his girlfriend. 'There were times when Mervyn came to see me and promptly disappeared up into the loft and I never saw him again that night!' Joey's sister said.[13]

Joey Dunlop entered his first-ever race at the former airfield circuit of Maghaberry (now the site of HM Prison Maghaberry) in April of 1969. Still without a driver's licence, he provided the Motorcycle Union of Ireland with his sister's driving licence number to get his racing licence. He didn't trouble the results sheets that day but enjoyed the experience enough to know he wanted more. But racing costs money, even at the lowest level, and Joey could only afford to fund occasional outings in his first year. There were entry fees to take care of, tyres to buy, fuel for the race bike and for getting to the racetrack (Joey had a bright yellow Mini Traveller and would take the wheels off his bike to fit it in the back of the car), oil, lubricants, spares and other consumables – not to mention the cost of crash damage, should he fall off the bike. Money was so tight that Dunlop and Robinson came up with a unique system to see them through: while Merv also had a Tiger Cub, the pair often only had enough parts to build one bike between them, so they would enter different heats at race meetings (both using the same bike) and, whoever qualified best would get to race it in the final. It was far from ideal, but it was better to take turns racing than not be able to race at all. It also meant that Joey was in direct competition with a very good rider right from the start of his career and, in trying to out-qualify one another, both riders improved their performances.

Joey was a slow burner on a racing motorcycle, and it would be some time before he started threatening the top six in the results sheets. It was, in those early days at least, Robinson who looked like being the future star.

Despite later becoming known as a roads specialist, Joey's career began on short circuits like Maghaberry, Kirkistown and Bishopscourt (all former airfields) and not between the stone walls, trees, and hedges of closed-off public roads. While he would later become far more comfortable on the roads, Joey was, initially, a very good short-circuit racer.

As the 1960s drew to a close, success was still a long way off, but the roots of it were formed in those early years when, without any sponsorship or formal backing, Joey would learn to do everything by himself: preparing his bike, tuning his bike, repairing crash damage, and learning how to race it. Wullie Dunlop was roped in as a mechanic, as was Joey's cousin, Jackie Graham, and Merv Robinson helped, too, just as Joey helped him in return. It was very much a family affair and as far removed from the glitz and glamour of the modern-day MotoGP paddock as it was possible to be. 'There was no awnings and no big vans – just cars and trailers,' Jim Dunlop says of those early meetings. 'And you didn't need three or four sets of tyres for every meeting. You had a set of intermediates for all weather and that was it.'

A windswept, disused airfield, a Mini Traveller, his dad, his cousin, and his soon-to-be brother-in-law, Mervyn Robinson. This was Joey Dunlop's first experience of racing and, despite all the success that would later come his way, he always attempted to maintain a similar gathering of friends and family around him and always preferred to work on his own bikes out of the back of a van. Essentially, he never changed, nor did his work ethic. 'He never gave up, even if people were laughing at him,' Linda later said. 'They were very poor days – Minis and trailers, doing without to pay for the bike. There was no sponsorship.'[14]

There were no results either. Joey's younger sister, Virginia, recalled having to wait for 'about fifteen minutes' after the winners passed the finish line before Joey and Mervyn would finally finish their races. It might have been an exaggeration on Virginia's part, but it didn't matter anyway – a race meeting was as much a family gathering as anything else and that was reward enough in itself. It was a social thing, with a bit of fun on the bikes thrown in; where they finished didn't matter, for now, at least.

Joey made his road-racing debut at the Tandragee 100 on Saturday, 3 May 1969, and finished in tenth place in the 200cc class. Road racing, as its name suggests, takes part on closed public roads rather than on purpose-built short circuits or converted airfields. By its very nature, it is much more dangerous, as the tracks are surrounded by walls, houses, trees, and all manner of other roadside hazards. There are no run-off areas and there's very little in the way of tyre walls or straw bales to protect crashing riders from these solid objects. Yet this is the environment in which Joey would later excel and where he would feel most at home. 'I took to the roads very, very quickly,' he said. 'I think that's one of the reasons why I did so well on the roads. There's people takes to scramblers and can't ride road racing bikes, but I took to road racing and I took to roads. I remember riding my first road race – it was Tandragee and I couldn't believe it.'[15]

When the motorcycle Grand Prix world championships began in 1949, many rounds were held on public road courses, so riders had to be able to perform on both short circuits and closed public roads. But from the 1970s onwards, increasing concerns over safety led to most – and eventually all – world championship rounds being staged on short circuits. Road racing still co-existed with short-circuit racing, but it became a more specialist thing and it would be the route that Joey Dunlop would later choose to go down.

But in 1969, riders quite happily mixed the two and Dunlop was no exception. The Tandragee 100 was just another chance to race, and it didn't bother Joey that it was staged on a more dangerous circuit than the likes of the old airfield at Maghaberry.

After the Tandragee, Joey took part in another road race, the Cookstown 100, later in the month, and finished eighth in the 200cc class. By the time he competed in his third roads event at the Carrowdore 100 in September, his results were improving, and he came home in fifth place. He was starting to get the hang of it.

The following season he added the Temple 100 meeting to his repertoire. The Temple was the oldest road race in Ireland (it is no longer held), having been established in 1921 but, by 1970, had been reduced from its original length of around twenty-five miles to just over five miles. But it was still held on real roads with real jumps and real trees, walls and hedges surrounding it. Joey was becoming more accustomed to the 'roadside furniture' and started using trees and walls as reference points and braking markers. The richness and proximity of the surroundings at a road race provide far more visual cues than the wide-open spaces of a converted airfield and, rather than scaring Joey, seemed to comfort him and give him an advantage. Speaking in 1983, he would say of the Ballacraine-to-Ramsey section of the TT course (which is particularly hemmed in by trees, walls and bankings), 'I can really make a lot of ground on people… I think it's because it's more like the road races back home; it's all in among trees, houses, walls, everything. I can really pull a lot of ground… It's just being able to judge it, you know, without seeing round the corner. I can judge it without seeing round it.'[16]

Joey only competed in a handful of races in 1970 after suffering a financial setback on the way home from an Easter Monday meeting at Kirkistown. Travelling in his faithful Mini, with his bike in a trailer on the back, his car was hit from behind by another car which then launched itself right over the Mini and came to rest on the road in front. There were no serious injuries, but the damage sustained to his bike and car meant funds for racing were severely restricted and it would be 1971 before Joey had the finances to put together a full season of racing. By then, Mervyn had become Joey's brother-in-law, having married Helen Dunlop, and moved to the small village of Bushside. When Joey married Linda Patterson on 22 September the following year at Ballymoney Register Office, they also took up residence in Bushside. Just two miles away was another village that would soon become famous amongst motorcycle racing fans. It was called Armoy.

CHAPTER 2

THE GURK

'ROAD RACING WAS VERY, VERY HAIRY IN IRELAND BACK THEN.'
Nick Jefferies

Between his job as a diesel-fitter-come-coalman, and his constant tinkering with bikes, not to mention his inherent disregard for his appearance, the young Joey Dunlop was rarely squeaky clean. With his extremely gaunt face and his long, tangled hair, combined with his ultra-casual dress sense (a pair of heavily soiled overalls or old jeans and a T-shirt were the preferred options), Joey cut quite a figure in the racing paddocks of Ireland: he was as black as a miner and soon became known locally as 'the black Gurk' or just 'the Gurk', a name that stuck with friends and local race fans alike. 'He was always covered in oil and dirt, from head to foot,' says Hector Neill who Joey would later ride for. 'He was known as the black Gurk, which basically just meant "dirty". He was known as that for years – I think it was Mervyn Robinson that started it.'

By 1971, Joey had replaced the Triumph Tiger Cub with a

200cc two-stroke Suzuki Invader. Like the Triumph, it was a road bike rather than a purpose-built racer, but with Joey and Mervyn's engineering skills, it was soon stripped and tuned and faster than the Cub had ever been. But it was still clearly going to be an uphill battle against grids full of pukka racing machinery. Yet it was fast enough to earn Joey his first-ever podium finish (second place) at the Tandragee 100 that year.

Joey felt the 200cc class was the ideal one in which to start racing as it was relatively cheap and the bikes were not too powerful. For this reason, as late as 1989, he was still sponsoring the 200cc class in Ireland as a way of helping young, underfunded riders to break into the sport.

A dire lack of funds meant Joey could only afford to take in five race meetings in 1971 (at Kirkistown, Bishopscourt, Tandragee, Cookstown and Maghaberry) but another podium finish at the Cookstown 100 had been encouraging and an early sign that perhaps he might become quite a good motorcycle racer, given some time and, more importantly, some money.

There was one upside to this lack of funds, however. Throughout his career, Joey Dunlop was never a frequent crasher, and at least part of the reason for this was that he simply couldn't afford to crash in those early years, as his father attested. 'I was always thinking how much it would cost to fix if he fell off or blew up the bike,' Wullie Dunlop said. Not being able to afford a blow-up, Joey instead exhibited a high level of mechanical sympathy in his riding and would never over-rev or abuse a bike. This was another trait he would maintain throughout his career.

With not much more money at his disposal than the year before, 1972 was something of a disappointment and Joey's upwards trajectory tailed off somewhat. But he did at least impress his boss, Danny McCook, with his speed and, by doing so, laid the foundations for his first bit of sponsorship. But Joey being Joey, rather than inviting McCook to a race to witness him in action decided to put on a display on the roads near his home. 'Joey rode the bike away up the mountain at 30mph then raced back down again – *really* raced,' McCook said in a BBC Northern Ireland tribute to Joey in 2000. 'When I saw Joey going round corners coming down this [hill], that's when I was really impressed by him…. That's when I first realised he was something.'[17]

By this point, Joey and Mervyn had met up with local Armoy garage owner Hugh O'Kane, who was another bike-racing fanatic and who also happened to own an ex-Bob McIntyre 350cc AJS 7R. McIntyre was a Grand Prix and Isle of Man TT winner who had set the first-ever 100mph lap at the TT in 1957. O'Kane had allowed Joey to try the bike on the open road and Dunlop had been thrilled by its speed but, when he raced it at Kirkistown, it was clear that it was now hopelessly outpaced by the more modern competition.

There was at least one podium in 1972 (a third place at Maghaberry) but fifth and sixth places were more usual, and it was clear that without better machinery Joey had little prospect of bettering his results. His season ended with his first trip to the Mid Antrim road race where he finished fifth in the 200cc class. It was a respectable enough result, though not enough to attract the attentions of a major sponsor. But Danny McCook, encouraged by Joey's speed on public roads, had by now attended an odd race to watch his employee in action and decided he deserved a bit of help.

For the 1973 season, McCook secured a 350cc Aermacchi to complement Joey's little Suzuki twin and to enable him to race in the highly competitive 350cc class. With some of the financial constraints eased, Joey was also able to enter more races and spend a bit of money on tuning the Suzuki, so the 1973 season promised to be a much more successful one. He had two bikes, a little financial support, and a far greater number of races in which to prove himself. Things were looking more promising.

The problem was, by 1973, more and more riders were turning up with new Yamaha two-stroke twins, which were much faster than the Aermacchi, and Joey was forced to spend most of the season dicing for the lower leader board places. It was, however, a significant year for another reason, as it marked the first time Joey raced in Ireland's two biggest road races – the North West 200 and the Ulster Grand Prix. Neither outing could be considered a great success (his chain snapped on the start line at the North West, and he could only manage nineteenth place on the Aermacchi at the Ulster) but it was an important first step and allowed him to race against some of the big names from England for the first time.

One of those riders was Neil Tuxworth, who would become Joey's team boss many years later. 'I first encountered Joey when I went over to ride at the Ulster Grand Prix in 1973,' he says. 'I was out in 250cc practice and this guy passed me with "DUNLOP" on the back of his old green leathers, which I thought meant Dunlop tyres. He was pretty quick; I followed him for a while and learned quite a lot. When I got back to the paddock, I told someone that this guy who rides for Dunlop tyres had passed me and was going quite quick and left me behind and he said, "Oh, that's Joey Dunlop – one of our local riders."'

It would be another two years before Tuxworth actually got talking to Joey, however. 'I first got to know him when I went to ride in the Southern 100 on the Isle of Man in 1975. Me and Joey ended up camping next to each other in a little field near the circuit. I think I won the 250cc race and he won the 350cc race and we just got talking and spent a bit of time together.' It was the beginning of a relationship that would eventually reap huge rewards for both men.

The year 1973 was also the one in which many of the work practices Joey would maintain for the rest of his life became embedded. 'Joey preferred to work on the bikes the night before a race, rather than go to bed and lie awake thinking about the race,' Hugh O'Kane explained to Dunlop biographer Jimmy Walker.[18] Even when he later had full factory support from Honda, and teams of mechanics to do the work for him, Joey would continue this practice.

Joey's 'gang' was starting to take shape, too. As well as his father Wullie and his cousin Jackie Graham, Joey's outfit was bolstered by Mervyn 'Curly' Scott who also worked for Danny McCook as a diesel fitter. He would help Joey as a race mechanic while Andy Inglis tagged along as a general helper. Along with Joey's wife Linda – who attended every race until she became pregnant for the first time in 1974 – it was quite an entourage, and a guarantee that any race weekend, no matter what results were achieved, would be a fun social outing and a 'bit of craic'.

Joey also developed a unique way of learning road courses around this time. Because they are normal everyday roads used by the public, he was free to drive on them whenever he liked, and his preference was to do this at night because the headlights from his car would highlight bumps and surface variations that were much more difficult to see in daylight. On top of this, the narrow, limited view of the road ahead – as picked out by the headlights – replicated the tunnel vision view that a racer gets at speed when his focus is aimed solely at the apex of the next corner. It all made sense and Joey would later put this technique to great use when learning the daunting 37.73-mile Isle of Man TT course.

By now, Joey and Mervyn had struck up a firm friendship with another man who raced an Aermacchi – Frank Kennedy. A giant of a man standing at six foot three, Kennedy owned a small car showroom in Armoy and shared Dunlop and Robinson's passion for racing and tuning bikes. The trio soon became inseparable friends as well as great on-track rivals. 'Frank Kennedy came upon the scene and the three of them had a bit of craic, a bit of drinking, and a bit of racing,' said Robinson's son, Paul, who would himself later enjoy a long and successful racing career. The nucleus of the gang that would become the Armoy Armada had formed, and the impact they would have on Irish road racing would be tremendous.

There would be some decent results for Joey in 1973, though nothing spectacular. He started the season on his Suzuki, as his Aermacchi was not yet ready, and took a sixth place at Maghaberry, one position clear of the man who would later become his manager and right-hand man, Davy Wood. He took another sixth place, this time on the Aermacchi, at Tandragee, and he beat Merv Robinson (who was mounted on a similar bike) to fourth place at Mondello Park, proving he was now every bit as good as his racing mentor.

After the disappointment of his debut at the North West 200, Joey suffered his first broken bone following a crash at Maghaberry. But a broken collarbone didn't stop him from taking seventh place at the Mid Antrim 150 just three weeks later. In what was by far the busiest year of his career to date, Joey also took in races at Kirkistown and Fore and usually finished as the top four-stroke on his Aermacchi in fields increasingly dominated by much faster, 350cc Yamaha two-strokes.

Joey also made his racing debut on the Isle of Man in 1973, though not on the world-famous TT course. Instead, he raced at the former airfield circuit of Jurby in the north of the island and took a second and two third places. It was Joey's first time racing away from home and it was a significant trip for one particular reason – he made the journey in a converted fishing boat. This unorthodox method of transport to and from the Isle of Man would soon become a tradition and would have serious consequences in 1985.

A second place at Maghaberry rounded out Joey's 1973 season, and his dogged determination to grind out results on his underpowered Aermacchi was enough to persuade Danny McCook to buy Joey an air-cooled Yamaha TZ350 for the following year. It would make all the difference. Finally armed with a competitive machine, in 1974 Joey Dunlop would really start to prove his worth on a racing motorcycle.

On the Yamaha, Joey finally started taking race wins: one at Maghaberry early in the season and another at the same venue in September. It wasn't a huge haul but even when he wasn't winning, Joey was now always in the fight, and was starting to impress the established riders of the day like Tom Herron and Ray McCullough. 'I knew he was gonna be good, for you can tell when a rider's gonna be good, like,' McCullough later recalled. 'I knew he'd got something special for he'd a lot of go in him, although his machinery wasn't that good then.'[19]

There was to be another trip to a 'foreign' race in 1974, this time to Knockhill in Scotland, where Joey finished second to Merv Robinson in the 350cc race. The pair had now become competitive enough to attract a following of fans and, in Joey's case, the attentions of a serious sponsor. John Rea owned a successful haulage company, Rea Transport, and he was obsessed with motorcycle racing. Having enjoyed little success with his rider Gordon Bell, Rea was on the hunt for an up-and-coming, hungry young rider who could really deliver results. And, despite being a rival, Ray McCullough wasn't slow in trying to secure some help for Joey. 'Joey, whenever he started, hadn't had good motorbikes – they weren't really top-class stuff. So, I said to John Rea, "There's a man who, with good motorcycles, he'd win all the races." And John went ahead and got him the bikes and Joey became the best.'[20]

Hector Neill, who now owns the Synetiq BMW British Superbike team, and provided Joey with a Suzuki RG500 to ride in the late 1980s, also played a part in landing Joey his first major sponsorship deal. 'I sponsored a fella called Norman Dunn on a Yamaha and we were at a race at Maghaberry, not racing, just having a look. I was talking to John Rea and he told me he was thinking of getting more involved in racing. Norman pointed out a wee man who was in midfield in the race, battling away for all he was worth. He said, "That's Joey Dunlop – nobody's heard of him yet but he's going to be good," so I watched him. He was well down the field and had a poor bike and poorly leathers, but I saw the style of him and said, "Aye, right enough – that wee boy, on the right bike, he would be good."'

John Rea joined them after the race. 'When I asked where his own rider was, he said "Oh, he never turned up, as usual," Neill continues. 'I said, "Come with me" and I took him down the paddock and introduced him to Joey Dunlop. Joey was sitting in the back of an old van. He was very shy to start with when I introduced them, but then I left them to it. Two weeks later, we were at Aghadowey and Joey was out on John's bike and that was the start of Joey Dunlop and Rea Racing.'

John Rea sadly passed away in 1993 but his son, Johnny, remembers how his father came to sponsor Joey in the first place. 'Ray McCullough had a lot to do with it – and Hector Neill, too. My father and his two brothers were sponsoring a fella called Gordon Bell, but he wasn't putting a lot of effort into it and would just pick and choose where he wanted to race. So, my dad and his brothers thought, "Well, we've bought this bike – we want to see it out there, racing." Ray had mentioned to my father before that Joey could do with a bit of help, so that's how it started. Basically, my father and his brothers ran things for Joey in 1975. They got a Yamaha TZ350 Cantilever, but Joey said he wanted a Seeley frame, so they bought that for him too, and anything else he needed, and they turned that bike into a Yamsel. They also bought Joey a big-bore 351cc Yamaha so he could race in the 500 class.'

Joey's first sponsor, Danny McCook, was happy to see his rider progress and get more support than he himself could offer. 'Joey said to me that John had asked him if he wanted to ride on this particular bike and he asked me if I would mind and I said, "No, certainly not." I was only too glad that he could further himself or get a ride on more machinery than I had.'[21]

Johnny Rea – who would later enjoy a hugely successful racing career himself and would then watch his son Jonathan become the most successful World Superbike rider in history – was not yet a teenager when he first met Joey. 'The first time I met him was at the Tandragee, the first time he rode for my dad in 1975. I would have been about twelve at the time. He went out and finished second to Ray McCullough and I was just in awe of them both.'

Rea remembers witnessing that odd character trait of Joey's of seeming to be lost in his own world and his own thoughts, almost obsessively avoiding any contact with others on occasion. 'Joey would have talked to you for ages one time and then the next time you saw him he wouldn't talk at all – he was a strange wee man, you know. He always was quiet, but he would talk away to my father. They were very close, and he did treat Joey like another son – maybe better than another son!'

For the 1975 season, with the full backing of John Rea, Joey had both a 350cc and a 500cc Yamaha at his disposal. He made his debut in Rea Racing colours at the Tandragee 100 where he finished second to Ray McCullough. Although Mervyn Robinson was Joey's earliest racing rival, the two were related and were effectively racing out of the same camp. McCullough was another matter. He was the man to beat in Ireland at the time and had a hugely impressive pedigree. Unwilling to travel outside of Ireland to race (with the odd exception like the Southern 100 meeting on the Isle of Man), McCullough could only prove himself against the world's best riders at the Ulster Grand Prix which, up until 1971, had counted as a round of the Grand Prix world championship. That year, he beat the great Jarno Saarinen in the 250cc world championship race by some 90 seconds. Most people believed that if McCullough had decided to race further afield, he would have been a world champion and multiple TT winner: he was that good. But, in 1975, Joey Dunlop started harassing him at every opportunity.

'The racing was good then,' McCullough said of the mid-seventies scene in Ireland. 'Everybody sort of had the same motorcycles – there was no works motorcycles, so everybody had the same bike, basically. Like, Joey just come from nothing to be really good in a short space of time.'

The second-place finish behind McCullough at the Tandragee delighted Joey as much as it did his new sponsor, and he would always credit John Rea for his later success. 'John made my career,' Joey said. 'I had nothing at all. The very first race I did for John, I led for most of the race, and Ray McCullough beat me on the last lap and John spent anything I wanted after that!'

After Tandragee, Joey took wins in both the 350cc and 500cc classes at Aghadowey, but the North West 200 was a huge disappointment, just as it had been the previous year, with the 500 blowing up in practice and the 350 seizing on the first lap of the race. After this, the Rea brothers bought a 350cc Yamsel (a Yamaha engine in a Seeley frame) for their rider and Joey's results started to improve immediately. He was crowned 'King of Kirkistown' on the bike's debut at the former airfield circuit and then took more race wins at Mondello Park in the south of Ireland, before taking his first-ever win on a public roads circuit at the Temple 100.

With John Rea's backing, Joey finally started to believe in himself as a rider. 'I remember everybody telling me that I was brilliant to watch, and I just couldn't believe this, like,' he would later say. 'Then, whenever John Rea started sponsoring me and I had got something decent to ride, I realised then that I was as good, or better than, most of the other riders that I was riding up against.'[22]

John Rea also provided Joey with his first manager, Victor Freeman. From Coleraine, Freeman had been race secretary at the North West 200 for ten years and was a good friend of Rea's. While he left Joey to get on with the bike preparation and racing, Freeman helped out with the administrative side of things, an aspect of racing that Dunlop had absolutely no interest in. Freeman, like so many others, found his charge to be one of the most laid-back and honest men he ever had the pleasure of working with. 'He was one of the straightest fellows I ever met,' he said. 'He kept nothing hidden from you... He was as honest as the day is long.'[23]

There were further wins for Joey at the Mid Antrim, at Aghadowey, at the Leinster 200 and at Carrowdore, and another head-to-head with Ray McCullough at the prestigious Embassy Final at Kirkistown. McCullough again got the better of Joey, but he had years more experience and Joey's time was clearly coming.

Nick Jefferies would become Joey's team-mate in the late eighties but clearly remembers his first encounter with him at the Skerries in 1975. 'He was so ragged-looking and was constantly smoking – and he was just totally incomprehensible to me when he spoke!' he says. 'I wasn't posh, but I'd been to a public school and I knew my

"Ps and "Qs". I probably seemed like an alien from another world to Joey!'

The Irish road-racing scene was just as alien to Jefferies, and worlds apart from the short-circuit racing scene in England at the time. 'It seems surreal now, but at the Skerries the race secretary invited us into his tent for drinks *before* the big race!' he says. 'I went in and they were pulling pints for the riders. I refused a full pint, but I had a half pint of Guinness and then set off to race. That was typically Irish back then. I had so many piss-ups over there.'

The Skerries was unlike anything Jefferies had encountered before and health and safety clearly weren't high on the agenda. 'Road racing was very, very hairy in Ireland back then,' he says. 'The lack of practice time was ridiculous. You got to the Skerries circuit on Friday afternoon about 2pm, got settled in the paddock and went through scrutineering, and at 5pm we all got a couple of laps of practice and then we went racing. We didn't have tents or awnings or anything – we just parked our bikes next to our vans and worked on them outside.'

In what was Jefferies' road-race debut, and only his second year of racing (he was known as a very successful trials rider before taking up road racing), he found himself lining up on the Skerries grid with the biggest names in Ireland. 'I was an absolute novice in my first-ever road race, but there I was lining up on the grid with Sam McClements, Mervyn Robinson, Ray McCullough, and Joe Dunlop – he was called "Joe" back then, never "Joey". There weren't a lot of straw bales or any other kind of protection around the track either. I finished fourth in the last race behind McCullough, Robinson and Joey. Sam McClements was so angry at me for cutting him up on the last lap that he ran straight into the back of me after we crossed the finish line and knocked me off my bike!'

Mervyn Robinson stole all the headlines at the Ulster Grand

Prix at Dundrod the following month when he beat all the top English riders to take victory in the 500cc race. It was by far his most important win to date and it underlined the belief that, in those early years at least, Robinson was a more promising prospect than Joey.

But Joey had shown great promise throughout the 1975 season, too, particularly in his first race on English soil at Croft, where he finished third in the 350cc race behind future world champion Kork Ballington and English star Roger Marshall.

Never a prolific crasher, Joey managed to slide off his Yamaha as he exited the hairpin in the 350cc race at the 1975 Ulster Grand Prix. He broke his collarbone, leaving Ray McCullough to lead the rest of the field home by 42 seconds. If ever proof was needed that McCullough could have gone all the way in the sport, had he been prepared to travel, this was it. Amongst the riders he so easily defeated that day was Tom Herron, who had won the Junior and Senior TT races just two months previously and would later become Barry Sheene's Suzuki team-mate in the 500cc Grand Prix world championship. Herron is considered one of the greatest road racers Ulster has ever produced, yet McCullough completely outclassed him on that day, and on many others. This was the calibre of the competition that Joey Dunlop faced as he fought his way up the Irish racing ladder.

Jim Dunlop made his racing debut in 1975 aboard Joey's old 200cc Suzuki twin. He would soon prove to be a good rider but not so good at crashing. With Jim picking up injuries all too frequently, Joey took it upon himself to teach his little brother how to crash properly. 'We took a car down to the beach and I sat on the bonnet while Joey drove,' Jim explains. 'He said he'd brake hard, and I'd fly off and learn to roll to a stop on the sand. The first time he braked I slid off but was still able to run alongside the car because we weren't going fast enough. The next time he went a wee bit quicker, and I slid off and landed on my head and broke my collarbone! I thought, "Fuck there's something wrong here" and Joey said it looked like a broken collarbone. I hadn't a clue what a collarbone was back then, but we went straight to Coleraine hospital and they tied me in a figure of eight and sat me on a chair. A doctor put his knee on my chest and pulled at me to get the bone back into place and I just passed out with the pain. They don't do that anymore – they just strap you up and leave it to heal, or pin and plate it if you're desperate to race.'

Big Frank Kennedy was by now firmly established as part of Joey and Mervyn's 'gang' and the three had started to build up a fiercely loyal following amongst race fans. At some point during 1975 or 1976, the trio became known as the Armoy Armada. Despite the fact that only Frank was an actual resident of the village itself, the name had a certain ring to it and gave an identity to this rag-tag group of grass roots racers. 'A man called Mel Murphy started it all,' Jim Dunlop explains. 'He was a mechanic for Joey and knocked about with him a lot. He had a motorbike shop in Ballymoney and him and a few friends used to drink in the Railway Tavern – which later became Joey's Bar – and they dreamed up the Armoy Armada in there.'

The Armoy Armada banner wouldn't have worked half as well had there not been another gang of opposing riders to do battle with, so it was fortunate that several riders from County Down – namely Ray McCullough, Trevor Steele, Ian McGregor and Brian Reid – had formed a gang of their own. They called themselves the Dromara Destroyers and, over the next few seasons, the rivalry between the two groups of riders and their associated fan bases would lift road racing in Northern Ireland to new heights. A golden era was about to begin: the road racers had arrived.

CHAPTER 3

THE ROAD RACERS

'WE WERE COMING DOWN INTO BARREGARROW ABSOLUTELY
FLAT OUT, AS FAST AS THE CAR WOULD GO, AND JOEY SWITCHED
THE HEADLIGHTS OFF. I NEARLY FAINTED.'

Hector Neill

David Wallace was an aspiring filmmaker from just outside Dunloy who was working for the BBC Schools Department making short, educational films. Now a double BAFTA-winning director, in 1976 Wallace was desperate to make his first feature-length documentary and he chose as its subject Joey Dunlop, Mervyn Robinson and Frank Kennedy. He would call it *The Road Racers* and it would not only become a classic of the genre, it would also introduce Joey Dunlop to the wider world.

'I met Mervyn first,' Wallace says. 'He was the most open and the most humorous and impish of the three. He was a lovely warm character. Frank was a bit more serious but fantastically friendly and helpful. Mervyn took me along to meet Joey because they were related and Joey was quiet, as you would imagine.'

While he wasn't exactly uncooperative, neither was Joey terribly keen on the idea of attracting attention to himself. 'He didn't speak a great deal,' Wallace adds. 'He never said anything negative, but you got the impression that being in a film was probably the sort of nuisance he could live without. To be honest, I think that Joey thought the others wanted it to happen, so he went along with it. He probably didn't realise just how much of an imposition it is, having a film made about you. But he managed to keep the nuisance value down by keeping a bit of distance, though he was never unfriendly.'

Joey's professionalism and perfectionism soon became apparent to the aspiring director. 'If you said you wanted to come and film in his garage the night before a race, that wasn't a problem. You could film what you liked and stay as long as you liked but, for example, if you were shooting something and you missed something happening and asked if you could shoot it again, he'd say, "Look, it'll make all our lives easier if we just get it right first time, every time." With the other riders you could do as many re-takes as you liked, but with Joey you just had to be that bit more efficient. He always got his part right first time, so it was almost as if he was saying, "Look, I can do it, why can't you?" Of course, he would never have said that, but it was difficult to ever really know what Joey was thinking.'

Wallace was given a budget of just £4,000 by the Northern Ireland Arts Council but, with additional sponsorship from Moira County Council and a large injection of cash from his own pocket, the overall budget ended up being more like £9,000. Research work on the project began in 1976 and this included Wallace taking promotional photographs of his riders at the Mid Antrim that year. Even on a bike travelling at great speed, and with a helmet completely obscuring his face, Joey wasn't keen on being photographed and viewed it as a distraction. 'It was an issue with Joey,' Wallace admits. 'I remember saying to the riders that I would be out there with a camera but I'd be hidden in a hedge and they wouldn't see me. At the end of the race Joey came back and said, "You were in the hedge behind the jump after the stone bridge on laps two and three, but you'd gone by lap four." You have to remember that, on that part of the circuit, Joey would have been in the air doing over 100mph and, when he landed, he had to get straight on the brakes to make the next turn. Yet he still had time to see me hiding – and I *was* hiding, because I knew Joey was sensitive about being photographed.'

It was an early indication of just how much Joey disliked being in the limelight. 'Some people just get embarrassed when you point a camera at them, and Joey was one of those people,' Wallace says. 'I'm sure that if I had tried to make a film about Joey Dunlop that year, and not the Armoy Armada itself, I would not have been able to do it. It was the other two that made it happen. Joey knew that the village liked it, and Merv and Frank enjoyed it, so he went along with it. I'm not going to say Joey enjoyed making the film – that would be crazy. How would I know? He never said a single aggressive word the whole time we were there, but he did say exasperated things like, "How long's this going to take?" or "Can I get on now?"'

The opening shot in the film captures the spirit of the Armoy Armada perfectly. It shows Mervyn, in T-shirt and jeans (but at least with his helmet on), firing up his bike on a narrow country lane, overtaking a tractor, and startling a flock of sheep in a nearby field. Testing their bikes on public roads was common practice for the Armoy boys, but it presented a slight problem in terms of committing it to film. 'I had asked Joey what it was like testing a race bike late at night on country roads and was he worried about the police? He said, "I'm far more worried about the sheep," so that's where the idea for the opening shot came from. We set the shot up, so it was just a timing thing. We had to be sure the farmers could get the sheep off the road before the bikes arrived at speed. I think the health and safety brigade would have had something to say about that now!'

Over the coming decades, Joey would make a habit of testing his race bikes on the country roads near his house and the police would usually turn a blind eye. They could not, however, be seen to be encouraging such behaviour. 'If we'd asked the police for permission to film Joey testing on open roads, they would have had to refuse us, so we had to just say nothing and go ahead and do it,' Wallace explains. 'There were quite a few occasions when the cops did stop the riders during test sessions, but they tended to just stop them and say, "Look, you can't do this while we're in the area." So, they just waited until the police had gone and carried on. But the police were very sympathetic to the riders. We're talking about country roads that very few people used, and it was always done at dusk when it was even quieter. But the people who live in that part of the world weren't that surprised when they saw those bikes flying along at 100mph.'

It wasn't just the police who were sympathetic to Joey's illegal testing – the locals helped him out too, as photographer Don Morley remembers. 'He would take the bikes out to test them on the public roads near his house and, almost miraculously, without anyone making a single telephone call, farmers in tractors would appear and block all the side roads so that Joey could do his plug-chops and flat-out runs. The police turned a blind eye, too. It was astonishing. He just had that aura about him that got everybody on his side. He had such an effect on people.'

Despite Joey's reticence, David Wallace did manage to persuade him to show some aspects of his life, as humble as it was, away from the bikes. 'Joey was living in a council house at the time and I think he may have been on the dole. I wanted to shoot something of him away from the racetrack and he volunteered the peat-digging scene [where Joey and his family dig peat for fuel to keep themselves warm in winter]. He was happy to do that, but he probably regretted volunteering – not because of how it would make him look, but because he had to take a couple of hours away from his bikes to do it!'

While Wallace continued work on the film and dipped in and out of Joey, Merv and Frank's lives, the serious business of racing continued. By now, the trio had started receiving a bit more financial support, thanks in part to the efforts of the official Armoy Armada Supporters' Club. Set up by Mel Murphy, the members regularly met in the Square Peg pub in Ballymoney (which Joey would later buy and rename the Railway Tavern) and dreamt up novel ways of raising funds for their riders. They included sponsored walks (Joey, Merv and Frank walked the ten miles from Armoy to Ballymoney), auctions (at one, the winner of a loaf of bread donated it back to the club and it was then auctioned off slice by slice), and even joint fund-raising evenings with the Dromara Destroyers who, despite being racing rivals, were also good friends. Jim Dunlop remembered one such evening. 'We had to eat raw onions, or see who could get changed into a boiler suit the fastest – just different bits and pieces, you know? Drinking a pint of Guinness with a sausage in it – it looked like someone had crapped in your pint! There might have been a bit of needle just for the craic, but there was nothing serious about it. It was all good fun.'

It was a bit more serious out on track though, with each Armoy or Dromara rider determined to get one over on the opposing 'team' as well as each other. It was big Frank Kennedy who stole the early limelight with a second place in the premier 500cc race at the international North West 200 behind Englishman Martin Sharpe – a race Frank would undoubtedly have won, had his Sparton not developed a misfire while he was leading on the last lap.

Ray McCullough evened out the score by winning the 350cc race for the Dromara Destroyers, while Joey took his first international podium placing with third in the 250cc race behind two other English riders – Ian Richards and Tony Rutter.

The 1976 season would prove to be an outstanding one for Joey. He would take the 500cc Irish championship by winning every round he entered; he would be completely unbeaten in every race held at Mondello Park; he would take wins at Tandragee, Fore, the Skerries, Aghadowey, Kirkistown and Dundrod; and he would set new lap records almost everywhere he raced, including at Jurby and the Southern 100 meetings on the Isle of Man. He took his first Isle of Man win at the Southern 100 (the first of a record-breaking 40 on the 4.25-mile Billown course), beating Ray McCullough fair and square in a road race for the very first time. He even started winning on the UK mainland, with victories at Croft in England and East Fortune in Scotland.

Yet, despite all his success, Joey wasn't exactly getting rich. 'The prize money in the local races is very small – maybe twenty or thirty pounds for a win,' he said in *The Road Racers*. 'It's not very much for risking your neck for an hour.'

By season's end Joey would be presented with the 'Best Road Racer of the Year' trophy back home in Ireland, but perhaps the most significant event of the 1976 season – at least as far as Joey's future was concerned – was that he made his debut at the Isle of Man TT races.

First held in 1907, the TT (the initials stand for 'Tourist Trophy' as the event was originally held to prove the prowess of 'touring' motorcycles) grew in stature year-on-year and from 1949 until 1976 it counted as the British round of the motorcycle Grand Prix world championships. The TT circuit is made up of 37.73 miles of closed public roads and includes more than 300 corners. Unlike purpose-built racing circuits, it has all the hazards associated with everyday roads – tram lines, humpback bridges, and notoriously bumpy surfaces. Rather than being surrounded by safety features like gravel traps and air fences, it is surrounded by stone walls, houses, lamp posts, street signs, and bankings. There is, quite simply, no room for error. And with the course being so long, it takes years for riders to learn it well enough to be able to attack it at racing speeds - and racing speeds these days mean over 200mph. It is, without doubt, the most dangerous racecourse in the world and by 1976 it was deemed to be just *too* dangerous for world championship racing by many of the top riders, including Giacomo Agostini, Phil Read and Barry Sheene. The event was stripped of its world championship status following the 1976 races and was replaced by the British Grand Prix at Silverstone in England. But the TT carried on and riders were free to participate, or not, without the pressure of chasing championship points on such a dangerous course. Joey Dunlop made his debut at the TT in its last year as a world championship round but, by then, practically none of the regular Grand Prix contenders raced there. In short, it had become more of a specialist event; a standalone race meeting that represented the very pinnacle of pure road racing. Ireland might have had a far greater number of road races than the Isle of Man, but the TT was the daddy of them all, and a win there was like a Grand Prix win for a short circuit racer – it simply didn't get any better.

Another unique aspect of the TT is the emphasis that is put on holding the outright lap record. While most race fans wouldn't know the lap record at any other circuit, they're all aware of who holds the outright lap record at the TT. In 1976, when Joey first entered the event, the outright lap record was held by Mick Grant at 109.82mph (although it would be raised to 112.27mph by John Williams that same year). To hold the outright lap record at the Isle of Man TT is a real badge of honour in motorcycle racing and one that commands a great deal of respect.

There would be no lap records for Joey in his debut year, however. It usually takes a very good rider at least three visits to the TT before he can think of winning, since the course takes so long to learn. Nowadays, there are various aids to help new riders learn their way around, from onboard video laps to highly accurate computer games. The organisers even lay on 'Newcomer' trips to take new riders over and teach them the course with the help of more experienced competitors. But in 1976 Joey was simply let loose on the course to find his own way round. 'It was wet, and I rode a 250, and I never was round it before, even in a car, and I didn't know where to go to,' he later explained. 'I remember coming up to Ballacraine and I didn't know whether to turn, left, right or straight ahead.'

With absolutely no knowledge of where the course went, Joey would slow down and wait for another rider to pass him, then follow him for as long as he could before tagging onto another rider. He would also complete lap after lap of the course in a car at night. Johnny Rea remembers using the same tactic. 'I always did the same at the road races at home and at the TT. I did as many laps as I could at night-time. To start with, you knew the road was going to be quiet and, because you could see the headlights of any oncoming traffic, you could use the proper racing lines. It definitely helped.'

By the time Rea made his TT debut in 1983, Joey was a multiple winner and knew exactly which way the course went, and Rea will never forget Joey taking him round the course at night in his car. 'The first year I went to the TT, Joey took me round and showed me a lot of things to watch for – watch this, watch that. He would take me round after every practice session and show me a wee bit more and a wee bit more. I wasn't racing on the Saturday that year but Joey was, so I went out and had a few beers and I was walking back towards my hotel when Joey came out and said, "Right, come on with me," and we jumped in his car – which I think was a Ford Mondeo – and he took me round on a lap, and he drove round that TT course as if he was riding it.'

Rea learned more on that one lap than he had all week. 'Before, he had told me that this corner or that corner was "maybe" flat out on a race bike, but now he was saying they WERE flat out. He wasn't mincing his words anymore, and he had the pedal to the metal the whole way round. In fact, we had to stop as we were coming down the mountain [the TT course rises to 1,400 feet over the shoulder of Snaefell mountain] because the brakes were smoking! I was holding on in that car, I can tell you.'

Hector Neill was another man who got the late-night-lap treatment. 'We were in the pub at the TT one night drinking vodka – Joey liked vodka – and he says, "Hey, Heccie, you want to do a lap?" This was about two or three in the morning. We were coming down into Barregarrow [a fearsomely fast, narrow, downhill section with walls and a house at the apex] absolutely flat out, as fast as the car would go, and Joey switched the headlights off. I nearly fainted. I says, "Joey, what the hell are you doing?" and he told me that he wanted to show me that he knew the course so well he could drive it blindfolded. I would never do it again, I can tell you!'

The 1976 TT was a steep learning curve and Joey finished the fortnight (one week of practice and one week of racing) with two retirements, an eighteenth place in the Senior (500cc) and sixteenth place in the Junior (250cc). He also managed a best average lap speed of 102mph. It was as good a start as he could have hoped for and Joey had loved the experience. He would be back – of that there was no doubt.

Back home in Ulster, the Armoy Armada had become so popular that Joey's sponsor, John Rea, had taken to laying on a bus for the supporters to travel to race meetings. It was invariably a rowdy and beer-soaked trip with an atmosphere more akin to a group of football fans on their way to a match, though there was no hostility or ill will towards the Dromara Destroyers – it was just friendly rivalry and 'good craic', as the supporters themselves have testified.

In 1977, Joey would give the Armada fans plenty to cheer about. The timing of the filming of *The Road Racers* could not have been better, as far as Joey's career was concerned, because the 1977 season was when he really started to look like someone special. Now in his eighth year of racing, he had the experience and, with John Rea's continued support, the best machinery of his career to date. And David Wallace was there with his film crew to capture the season (or at least, part of the season) in which Joey Dunlop came of age.

Joey's pinpoint accuracy was already known amongst race fans, as Wallace remembers. 'When I was taking photos at the Mid Antrim, I asked a spectator where the bikes would land after the jump as I needed to get my camera focused. He said, "Well, they land all over the place – except Joey. Wherever you see Joey land on lap one, you could put a coin down on the spot and he'll hit it on every lap after that." That summed Joey up. He was disciplined. He was very fast, and he was very fearless, but he didn't fall off that often. Merv and Frank did most of the falling off.' Frank and Merv *did* spend a good part of the 1977 season on the sidelines due to injury, but Joey carried the flag for the Armada.

Filming for *The Road Racers* began in earnest at the Cookstown 100 where Joey beat Ray McCullough fair and square in the premier 500cc race. Joey had been in awe of McCullough for several years and, despite having some close races with him, had never felt entirely comfortable being in front of his hero. 'I'd get ahead and get frightened – feel like I must be going too fast,' he would say. But at the Cookstown in 1977 he finally found his self-belief and the confidence to face up to McCullough. But such was the rivalry between the two by now, Joey felt it was getting dangerous. After a particularly fierce encounter with McCullough at that year's Temple 100 he said, 'I have never ridden like that before or been involved in such madness. But one thing's for sure – I will never do it again.'

He *would* do it again though. Many times.

Joey carried his good form into the North West 200 where he briefly led the 250cc race before eventually having to give second best to visiting English star, Tony Rutter. He did manage to beat McCullough again though, this time into third place, but his rival had suffered an appalling start, so it wasn't exactly a fair fight.

Shortly after the North West, Joey and his motley crew of helpers made their way to the Isle of Man for a second attempt at the TT. After losing its Grand Prix world championship status the TT now faced an uncertain future and many feared it would sink into oblivion. Desperate to save the event, the ACU (Auto Cycle Union – the governing body of motorcycle sport in the UK) devised a new concept with the full backing of the FIM (Fédération Internationale de Motocyclisme – the governing body of world motorcycle sport) and announced three brand-new world-championship classes, which they named Formula One, Formula Two and Formula Three. The Formula Three class would be for two-stroke motorcycles over 125cc and up to 250cc, and for four-stroke bikes over 200cc and up to 400cc. Formula Two would cater for two-strokes over 250cc and up to 350cc, and four-strokes over 400cc and up to 600cc, while the premier Formula One championship would be for two-strokes over 350cc and up to 500cc, or for four-stroke machines over 600cc and up to 1000cc.

If the classes were a trifle confusing for some, the nature of the championships, at least in the first year, was nothing short of farcical. While the Grand Prix world championships at that time tested riders over thirteen rounds all around the globe, the new Formula championships would be held over just one round at the TT. Win the race, and you were entitled to call yourself an FIM world champion. Mick Grant, a double-TT winner at the time who would set a new outright lap record in the 1977 event, did not approve. 'How can you take a world championship seriously when it's only one round?' he says. 'It wasn't a world championship, in my opinion, in the early days. I took every race I entered seriously, but to sit there with a smug look on your face thinking you were a world champion after one round? I think that would have been embarrassing. If that was my only claim to fame, I'd certainly be embarrassed. But everything's got to start somewhere, and once it got going and had a lot more rounds, it was a different ball game.'

In time, the championship would grow, not only in the number of rounds involved, but also in terms of the level of support from manufacturers and the prestige attached to winning it. The TT Formula One world championship was, essentially, the forerunner to today's World Superbike championship – a multi-round, international series catering for production-based machinery, as opposed to the thoroughbred prototype machinery raced in Grands Prix. And it would be Joey Dunlop who gave the series the credibility and fanbase it needed to expand. In the 1980s, Joey would make the Formula One championship his own.

With hindsight, it's clear that the launch of the TTF1 championship was a seminal moment in motorcycle racing history. 'It was the beginning of the move away from pure racing bikes towards production-orientated machines,' says Barry Symmons, then manager of the Honda Britain team. 'One of the issues was cost, but the TT was also looking for something to replace the loss of its Grand Prix status, so staging an F1 world championship seemed a useful alternative. It was based on road circuits so that the TT could have something to hang a championship on.'

Joey didn't race in the inaugural Formula One TT in 1976, which was won by a returning Phil Read (one of the men who had been at the forefront in calling for the TT to be banned from the Grand Prix calendar), much to the chagrin of many fans, marshals and even Manx garage owners, who felt Read had betrayed the event and was now a hypocrite for returning just to make some money. 'When I arrived, I parked my van outside the hotel on Douglas seafront,' Read explains. 'A policeman tapped on the door and said, "Mr Read, I advise you to move your van out of the way, round the back, because there's a bit of a feeling here." I also had a Rolls-Royce at the time and was going round the circuit with a friend. When we stopped for petrol, they refused to serve me. The marshals threatened to go on strike too. I thought, "My God, I didn't think I was so important."'

Such was the strength of feeling about his apparently cynical comeback, Read was even pelted with stones during practice sessions. It was an ugly, and dangerous, beginning to the new championship.

Joey stayed out of it and quietly went about his business. Having travelled over to the TT for a second time – again by manhandling his bikes onto a fishing boat – he was not on anyone's radar for a win, and that was just the way he liked it. Motorsport filmmaker David

Wood was working at that year's TT but took very little notice of the diminutive Irishman. 'He really hadn't been mentioned in pre-race talk of the favourites,' Wood says. 'We were filming that year but couldn't film every rider, so I had a list of my top ten and I'm embarrassed to say Joey wasn't on it.'

He soon would be.

In what was the Queen's Silver Jubilee year, soft-drinks maker Schweppes put up a first prize of £1,000 for the Schweppes Jubilee Classic race (the term 'classic' did not mean older bikes, as it does in today's Classic TT), and Joey Dunlop, to the astonishment of almost everyone watching, won it. 'It was on a 750 Yamaha and to keep that 750, four-cylinder, two-stroke going for four laps round there was pure luck,' Joey reflected in a 1997 documentary for BBC Northern Ireland. 'I had wee bits of trouble during the race, but I just used my head and kept my fingers crossed. Tom Herron took me round the course before and he said if he couldn't win it, I was to win it, cos he wanted an Irishman to win it! It did me a lot of good cos, to sit me in my second year on a 750 round the TT was… it was scary, put it that way.'

Incredibly, Joey briefly considered throwing the race on the last of the four laps because he was acutely aware of what lay in store if he did cross the line as the winner. 'I remember coming down [the mountain] and I knew that I could near enough free-wheel to the line if anything went wrong, and I was that afraid of opening the bottle of champagne. I had never opened one in my life before, and I didn't know how you would open it, or what you do with it, or anything about it! I remember thinking to myself, "I wonder if I should win this, or should I break down?" But I kept it going anyway.'

In the end, Joey did manage to open the champagne, and also walked away with the biggest payday of his career to date. Up to that point, the most he had earned for winning a race was £100 plus 50 gallons of free petrol. Now he was presented with a cheque for £1,000 – a huge sum to a man who had spent much of 1977 on the dole.

David Wood, like so many others, was both surprised and impressed by Dunlop's win. 'I didn't know much about Joey at that point but took a few pics of him in the paddock after the race. He was just a young Irish road racer. He looked so smooth out on track though, rather than out of control. He looked as though he'd been riding the TT course all his life, yet it was only his second TT. His win was a big surprise.'

Joey won the race by 51.6 seconds from George Fogarty and also set the fastest lap at 110.93mph – the third fastest lap ever recorded at the TT. That same year, Mick Grant raised the outright lap record to 112.77mph on his factory Kawasaki, but Joey had been mounted on John Rea's privately owned Yamaha TZ750 and, in only his second visit to the TT, he was already posting lap times that were making the big boys take notice. They would ignore him again at their peril.

The only downside to Joey's first TT win was that most of the top men had already left the island before the Jubilee Classic was staged on the final day of race week. The race had been hastily put together at the last minute as a way of marking the twenty-fifth anniversary of Elizabeth II ascending the throne, so it didn't attract the very best riders. But it hardly mattered: Joey's pace was such that they would have struggled to match him even if had they been there. He had proved his point.

A twelve-year-old Carl Fogarty literally had a grandstand seat as he watched his dad trying to chase Joey down. 'I think my dad is now quite proud to have finished second to Joey when he got his first TT win,' he says. 'I remember being there watching. My dad always seemed to have a bit of bad luck at the TT and he was trying to catch Joey but, round there, he was never going to catch him. I was in the grandstand and I remember the commentator saying: "Joey's stopped – he's pulled in and stopped at Parliament Square on the last lap!" I think something was hanging off his bike, so he stopped to check, but he was that far in front he still managed to win the race.

'To be honest, his bike looked like it could have fallen apart at any time during the race. Me and my dad were on the grid at the Southern 100 next to Joey one time and we're looking across and thinking, "Bloody hell, that thing's not gonna last round here – there's some rope holding the exhaust pipes on!" The next thing we knew, he had won the race.'

To prove his win was no fluke, Dunlop backed it up with tenth place in the Junior 250cc race, seventh in the Classic TT and, most impressively, fourth place in the Blue Ribband Senior TT, behind Phil Read, Tom Herron and Eddie Roberts and ahead of America's Pat Hennen, who would go on to finish third in the 500cc Grand Prix world championship that year.

Joey credited Herron for his top four placing. The night before the race he had taken Joey for a lap of the course in a car and instructed him on all the correct lines to take, what gears to be in, and what hazards to be aware of. It was a lap that finally allowed Joey to string everything together. 'If it hadn't been for Tom, I would never have been able to reach such a high placing,' he admitted. 'I will always be grateful to him because he showed me how to get among the quick boys round this track.'[24]

Joey was now racing in some serious company and he returned home to Northern Ireland a conquering hero. He would never again enjoy the anonymity that he so cherished. As a 1977 TT winner, he had reached the very top in pure road racing and the adulation began immediately. And Joey didn't disappoint his native supporters back home that year either: in total he took thirty-three race wins in Ireland that year, as well as sixteen second places and five thirds. He also won three Irish national championships in the 250cc, 350cc and 750cc classes and, in what would prove to be something of a transitional year, he travelled more often and took in several meetings in England where he challenged established stars like Barry Sheene, Ron Haslam and Roger Marshall.

Sheene won his second 500cc world championship in 1977 and was by far the biggest star that motorcycling had ever produced. With a playboy lifestyle, a glamourous model wife, a Rolls-Royce, and a cheeky, cocky personality that made him a natural on television, he was about as far removed from the nature of Joey Dunlop as it was possible to be, yet the two got on surprisingly well. 'I think Joey's great – I've always liked Joey,' Sheene said in a 1998 interview. 'He's down to earth and he's a good laugh and, riding-wise, you can't fault him – he's very fast. He's not frightened of a bit of hard graft and he's not frightened to get his hands dirty – and he's s true sportsman, like myself, who smokes cigarettes! I like Joey.'

If 1977 had been a breakthrough season for Joey, the following year was largely one to forget. After making the long trip to Daytona, Florida in 1978 he suffered a blown engine on his Rea Yamaha TZ750, though he did at least finish a respectable eighth in the 250cc race, which included such greats as Greg Hansford (a 250cc Grand Prix winner later that year) and Randy Mamola (a future multiple 500cc Grand Prix winner).

There was also a trip to France to take part in the Formula 750 series which was being contested by the likes of future 500cc champion Kenny Roberts and 500cc GP race winner Johnny Cecotto, but Joey could only finish midfield.

The promise he had shown at the 1977 TT wasn't backed up in 1978 and Joey finished the fortnight with a best result of fifth place in the TT Formula Two race, thanks to a series of breakdowns in the other classes. The event had attracted global headlines that year as the great Mike Hailwood returned after an eleven-year retirement to win the TT Formula One race. For many, Hailwood was the greatest motorcycle racer of all time, and his fairy-tale comeback win only enhanced his legendary status. Joey did at least manage to finish one place ahead of Hailwood in the Lightweight TT, although eleventh was nothing to write home about.

The TT attracted further criticism in the press following the deaths of Sidecar racers Mac Hobson and Kenny Birch and another crash which left American 500cc Grand Prix ace Pat Hennen with permanent brain damage. Hennen would prove to be the last current 500cc Grand Prix star to compete at the TT, his injuries seeming to act as a warning to others who might otherwise have been tempted. From now on the TT would be for specialist road racers, and there would be none more specialist than Joey Dunlop.

But if the fatalities at the TT in 1978 were hard enough to deal with, Joey would suffer a tragedy much closer to home the following year; one that would truly test his resolve to keep on racing in such a lethal sport. Black Saturday was just around the corner.

CHAPTER 4

THE PRICE

**'WHEN I LOOK BACK AT SOME OF THE OLD PICTURES IN MY
SCRAPBOOK, THERE'S ONLY HALF OF THE GRID LEFT ALIVE.'**
Roger Marshall

**North West 200 course, County Antrim,
Saturday, 26 May 1979**

Tom Herron's black, yellow and red Texaco Heron Suzuki emerged
from a wall of flame and churning smoke that covered the entire
width of the road that formed part of the North West 200 course. It
was the opening lap of the opening race of the day – the International
Match Race for Superbikes – and Kevin Stowe, a promising young
English rider who had been attracting the attentions of Suzuki,
suddenly raised his hand to alert the riders behind him that his chain
had just broken. Dennis Ireland had time to react and managed to
slip past him, but Australia's Warren Willing was unsighted and

smashed into the back of Stowe's bike, causing an instant explosion and fireball. Frank Kennedy also crashed into the wreckage and his Suzuki RG500 – now effectively a fireball – catapulted itself into the air, flying over Herron's Kangol-helmeted head, and narrowly missing the Grand Prix star. Burning motorcycles law strewn across the track, which itself was ablaze with furiously burning fuel and oil. Such was the extent of the blaze that the roadside hedges caught fire. Pieces of twisted motorcycles lay strewn across the road. Bodies lay inert amongst the carnage. It looked like the aftermath of a plane crash. Yet the race went on.

Herron was team-mate to Barry Sheene in the Texaco Heron Suzuki squad and was contesting the 500cc Grand Prix world championship in 1979. He had no need to be at the North West 200 and, in fact, some said he shouldn't have been there because of the broken right thumb he had suffered in the Spanish Grand Prix the previous week. Herron's wife begged him not to race in his condition, but he insisted that he owed it to his home fans to put on a performance. He had asked his close friend Hector Neill to remove the plaster before the first race: 'Tom was so determined to ride he had me cut the plaster cast from his hand with an angle grinder.'

Herron managed to avoid the tragedy that was unfolding all around him, on this occasion at least. He would survive the race, but he wouldn't live to fight another day. Ashen-faced and badly shaken by what he had seen, Herron would say to reporter Jimmy Walker after the race, 'There's been a bad accident. I went under Frank's bike, which was flying through the air. It was like riding into a wall of flame.'

After pulling out of the race, complaining that his bike was 'wobbling all over the place' Herron stated he did not intend to race again that day.

Joey Dunlop passed English stars Steve Parrish and Mick Grant to win the race – his first ever North West 200 win – and was elated as he crossed the finish line, completely unaware of the tragedy that had unfolded behind him. As he celebrated, Warren Willing, Kevin Stowe and Frank Kennedy were being taken to hospital. Willing and Stowe were so badly injured that they were never able to race again, and Joey's close friend Frank Kennedy was left battling for his life.

More tragedy was to follow when young Scottish rider Brian Hamilton was killed in the 350cc race. And yet the racing continued.

Later in the day, Tom Herron changed his mind and decided to compete in the final race, the feature Superbike race, in order to get some practice in for the upcoming TT. He was also due to start filming in two days' time for David Wickes' bike racing movie *Silver Dream Racer*, standing in to do the riding for the film's lead actor, David Essex. Herron's star was most definitely on the rise.

Although they were radically different characters, Tom Herron and Joey Dunlop got along well, according to Hector Neill who was great friends with both men. 'They got on rightly, but Tom didn't take any prisoners,' he says. 'Tom was Tom, and he had to be number one. Tom and me were the best of mates and he knew that Joey was a friend of mine, so he helped him as best he could. They were two very different people – Joey was rough and ready while Herron was always well dressed and immaculate. Nice leathers, all the gear, and far more comfortable in front of cameras than Joey ever was.'

Flushed by his success in the earlier Superbike race, Joey was untouchable in the second and cleared off to take an impressive double, once again completely unaware of the tragedy that was playing out behind him. On the last corner of the last lap, as Herron entered Juniper Hill bend, he parted company from his bike and struck a concrete post. He was still conscious at the hospital when his wife, Andrea, arrived but died two hours later when blood entered his lungs. He was thirty years old.

Frank Kennedy clung precariously to life for almost six months, unable to communicate with family and friends, but tragically succumbed to his severe head injuries on Wednesday, 14 November 1979. Joey Dunlop and Mervyn Robinson had been regular visitors to their friend's bedside in Coleraine hospital throughout those six months. Frank Kennedy, at just thirty-one years old, was buried in Ballymoney cemetery. He was survived by his wife and baby daughter.

Roger Marshall, who had ridden in that fateful North West meeting, soberly sums up the unforgiving nature of road racing when he says, 'When I look back at some of the old pictures in my scrap book, there's only half of the grid left alive.'

The 1979 North West 200 would become known as Black Saturday.

o

Despite the all-too-recent tragedies, Joey still went to the TT after the North West, but it was another disappointing year for him on the island, and that was partly down to machinery. Benelli UK had loaned him a 900 Sei for the Formula One race, but it proved to be both slow and unreliable and he retired from the race on the second lap. The bike that Benelli loaned him for the TT Formula Two race wasn't much better, and Joey could only manage a lowly thirteenth place in a race that had just nineteen finishers.

He then ran out of fuel in the Lightweight TT but learned a valuable lesson from the experience: he made sure it would never happen again, as he did every time he suffered this kind of failure.

Over the years, Joey would refine his race strategies and pre-race checks to the point where he could almost eliminate the potential for anything to go wrong, other than his actual riding – and that was rarely below par. By the time he was racking up win after win at the TT in the 1990s, Joey had long since made every kind of mistake and knew how to avoid most of them.

He broke down while riding Hector Neill's Suzuki RG500 in the Senior TT and could only manage sixth place in the Schweppes Classic that he had won two years previously. The difference this time around was that the purse had been raised to an impressive £30,000 so the race attracted all the top riders, including race winner Alex George and second placed man Mike Hailwood, in what would prove to be his last TT.

Hailwood did, however, win the Senior TT that week to take his overall tally to fourteen wins. It was more than any other rider had amassed in the long history of the event and it was considered highly unlikely that his record would ever be matched, let alone broken. Hailwood was, and still is, widely regarded as one of the greatest, if not *the* greatest, motorcycle racer of all time. As well as his fourteen TT wins, he also won nine world championships in the 250cc, 350cc and 500cc classes and took the TT Formula One world title with his win in the one-round series in 1978. Tragically, he was killed in a road accident while taking his children for fish and chips on 21 March 1981. A lorry driver had performed an illegal U-turn in front of him and Hailwood had no time to react. His nine-year-old daughter, Michelle, was also killed in the crash. The lorry driver was fined £100.

While Joey only managed sixth place in the Schweppes Classic while Hailwood was battling out front, he did post a lap just short of 110mph, which was about the only encouragement he could take from the 1979 TT. It had not been an easy fortnight, coming so soon after he had lost Tom Herron, and he was also worried about the condition of his close friend Frank Kennedy, who was still uncommunicative in Coleraine hospital at that point. The fact that he had raced at the TT at all was testament to his dogged determination, willpower and full acceptance of the risks he was taking.

As the season progressed Joey's results improved and he would take four wins at the Southern 100 in July, once again riding Hector Neill's Suzuki in the 500cc races. Having won both Superbike races at that year's ill-fated North West 200, Joey then went on to complete the gentleman's set by winning his first Ulster Grand Prix. The North West, the TT and the Ulster had always been the three biggest road races on the calendar and Joey had now won all three.

At the Ulster he won both the Superbike and 500cc races, the two main events, beating big names like 500cc Grand Prix winner John Newbold and multiple British champion Roger Marshall. The wins didn't come easy as practice had been badly affected by weather and he had a coming together with Newbold, who was making his Ulster GP debut. According to Hector Neill, whose bike Joey was riding at the time, Joey feared he had lost a finger in the crash. 'After about two laps of practice the word came through that Joey had crashed at Ireland's bend,' Neill says. 'We went along the back roads to collect the bike and a first aid man told us Joey was sitting with his hand inside his leathers and wouldn't let anybody look at it, cos, he said, his "wee finger's aff". Joey was sat smoking a fag and I asked to see his hand, but he wasn't keen. I told him to look away and I removed his glove and saw his finger hadn't come off, it was just dislocated and sticking out at a weird angle. I could have pulled it and snapped it into place again, but if anything had gone wrong, he would have went berserk. So, I took him back to the paddock and off he went, telling me he wouldn't be riding the next day.'

It was with some surprise that Neill saw his rider back in the paddock the following morning, dressed in his leathers and ready to race. 'He turned up and showed me his hand, all fixed up. I said, "How did you get that fixed?" and he told me "I had it charmed – a man up the road charmed it for me and it went back into place again." Apparently, he used this faith-healer-type fella quite often. It was just one of the funny wee ways he had about him.'

The faith healer was called Matt Gibson and Joey would turn to him again and again over the years. Barry Symmons, who would later be Joey's team manager in the Honda Britain squad, says Gibson was indirectly responsible for the nickname Joey would come to be affectionately known by amongst his legions of fans. 'I remember Joey using this guy for various remedies but I never did hear his name mentioned – Joey just always referred to him as "my man". In fact, that's how we started calling Joey "yer man". We nicknamed him that and it stuck.

'He would go and see this guy whenever he was injured,' Symmons continues. 'He damaged his shoulder one year and this guy would turn up to treat him. He had a bottle with a crucifix on it that was supposedly filled with some kind of elixir to heal Joey's injuries. I dread to think what it was, but Joey believed in it.'

Something was clearly working as Joey notched up a spectacular double at the 1979 Ulster. Most impressive was his performance on Neill's two-year-old Suzuki against a field of faster, newer models. Due to the incident in practice Joey had failed to complete enough laps and had to start from the fifth row of the grid, but astonished everyone by cutting right through the pack and eventually winning the race comfortably by over 8 seconds from Barry Sheene's factory Suzuki team-mate John Newbold. It was a performance that made

Suzuki sit up and take notice. Joey Dunlop was now on their radar: if he could beat Suzuki's top riders on a privately owned, two-year-old machine, what could he do on one of its latest thoroughbred factory bikes?

Joey's win in the 1000cc race was just as emphatic. He had exited the last corner of the last lap side by side with Roger Marshall but had taken a wider line around the outside of the track and managed to get the drive to the line, beating Marshall by a tyre-width.

The 1979 season saw Joey pick up win after win at home in Ireland; he took a triple and set three new lap records at the Killinchy 150, as well as another four wins at Kirkistown and the same again at Aghadowey.

There were some good performances further afield in 1979, too. He would take part in his first British Grand Prix at Silverstone, finishing fifteenth in the 350cc race on a day that will be long remembered for the ferocious battle between Kenny Roberts and Barry Sheene in the 500cc race (Joey would race against both men later in the season in the Race of the Year at Mallory Park and finish tenth). The French Grand Prix at Le Mans resulted in a highly credible ninth place before Joey and his road-trip gang went on to take in Formula 750 races in the Netherlands, Germany, Yugoslavia and Austria. While he took an international win on his Yamaha TZ750 in Austria, results were mixed at the other circuits, often due to detonation problems with his Yamaha. But those races gave Joey a real love of driving around the continent and it was a love that never left him. He may have hated flying but the freedom of driving the open road with a gang of close friends, camping rough on any old scrap of spare ground, and racing his bike on the weekends, was irresistible to Joey. That was how he liked to go racing, and the offers of five-star hotels and luxury travel that would come later were almost always shunned.

Tony 'Slick' Bass, who would mechanic for Joey in 1987, remembers the kind of antics that occurred on such road trips. 'Joey and his gang were staying in a tent in Portugal while the rest of us were in a five-star hotel,' he says. 'A mole burrowed its way up into the middle of the tent during the night and they absolutely flattened the tent trying to batter the mole with their shoes. Joey couldn't get any sleep, so he went to sleep in the van, but ended up getting so badly bitten by mosquitoes that both his eyes were practically closed with the swelling. He could barely see – but he still won the race.'

Results-wise, it had been a good year, aside from the TT, but it was bookended in tragedy. Early in the season, Joey had lost his friend Tom Herron and by November, when the season had ended, he would lose Frank Kennedy too. But it wasn't over yet: there was more tragedy just around the corner, and this time it would be even closer to home.

○

One year on from the darkest North West 200 anyone could remember, Joey Dunlop and Mervyn Robinson lined up on the same grid without their great friend Frank Kennedy. There can be no doubt that both men were equally determined to win a race in honour of Frank, but Robinson was already unsettled as he took to the grid. Most motorcycle racers are superstitious due to the dangers of their chosen sport, and many cling to any belief that might help them compartmentalise their fear. Mervyn Robinson was no exception. When he was allocated the number 31 for the race, he didn't want to ride. Frank Kennedy had been killed while riding with the same number and, to those who are prone to holding superstitions, it also seemed foreboding that 31 is the mirror image of the number 13. Against his better judgement but desperate to race, Robinson eventually but reluctantly agreed to take his place on the grid.

No one really knows what caused Mervyn Robinson to crash in the 500cc race, which was the second event on the day's programme. There were strong crosswinds on the day and a sudden gust might have been enough to cause a crash on a seriously fast corner like Mather's Cross. Then again, his bike may have suffered a partial seizure as evidence of this was found by a race scrutineer who examined the motorcycle afterwards, though there was, he said, every chance that this could have happened after the event.

Mather's Cross was a very fast corner in 1980. There's now a chicane immediately before the corner to slow bikes down, but it would have been flat out in top gear for Robinson. And he may have been pushing just a little too hard, given the situation he found himself in. The great irony is that the race organisers had adopted a new system in a bid to avoid further tragedies like those that had occurred the previous year. To allow more space for the riders on-track, they were set off in two groups, with the fastest men from qualifying in the front group. The second group would set off one minute later, but would have their race times adjusted accordingly, so there was no need for anyone in the second group to chase after the first group – they could, in theory, still win the race, despite starting one minute behind, as the final results would be based on corrected time. By rights, Robinson should have been in the leading group with his experience and pace, but he had endured a poor qualifying session and was forced to start in the second wave. Journalist and author Jimmy Walker is just one who believes Robinson's racing instinct took over and caused him to push even harder, in order to battle on the road with the fastest men in the front group.

Whatever the cause, Mervyn Robinson lost control of his machine at Mather's Cross and was thrown into the air when the bike hit a grass verge. His son Paul was watching his dad race that day from the side of the track, accompanied by his grandmother. 'Where the finish line is now was part of the paddock and I was a five-year-old watching my father going around and then he didn't appear,' Robinson told the *Belfast Telegraph* in 2019. 'I didn't think the worst, or anything like that at the time, and it wasn't until later, when I was sat eating my dinner at a neighbour's, that my mother came and told me what had actually happened. I was devastated.'[25]

Mervyn Robinson had sustained critical head and neck injuries in the crash and would die in hospital two days later. He was thirty-two years old. Incredibly, his son would later take up road racing himself and would enjoy a successful career on the Irish scene. He continues to visit his father's grave regularly, but only once did he take a set of winner's laurels to place on it. In 2010, exactly thirty years after his father lost his life at the North West 200, Paul Robinson won the 125cc race and proudly laid the winner's laurels on his grave.

Joey and Jim Dunlop, the last two surviving members of the Armoy Armada, immediately withdrew from the remainder of the race meeting and Joey announced he would not be taking part in his beloved TT. The price was just too high. He was finished. It was over.

CHAPTER 5

THE BIG ONE

'I REMEMBER LOOKING AT HIS PILE-OF-CRAP YAMAHA TZ750 AND THINKING, "WELL, HE'S NOT GOING TO BE A PROBLEM."'
Mick Grant

'When Mervyn was killed Joey just abandoned the whole thing,' Jim Dunlop says. 'We had a meeting and that was it finished.'

It was too much. Joey had lost his brother-in-law and two close friends within the space of a year. No sport was worth such sacrifices.

'As we were leaving the North West, Joey said to me "Hector, I'll no be at the TT",' recalls Hector Neill. 'I thought, "Right, fair enough," so we went over to the Isle of Man, anyway. On the first morning of practice, I went to the Walpole Hotel where Joey and his contingent always stayed, and there he was, stood at the wall overlooking the garage. I wandered over and said, "You've turned up then?" and he says, "Aye, I think Merv would have wanted me to come." I agreed and told Joey to go out there and win a race for Mervyn. When I asked him which race he would like to win, he said, "The big one," which, that year, was the Classic.'

It had been three years since Joey's win in the Schweppes Classic TT and even then he hadn't been racing against the very top riders, as it had, to all intents and purposes, been a support race. It would be different this time around; he would be up against men like Mick Grant and Ron Haslam on factory Hondas and Graeme Crosby on the factory Suzuki. There was nowhere to hide.

Joey was also at a huge disadvantage. Before they were outlawed in the interests of fairness, the teams that could afford them were permitted to use 'quick-fillers' to force-feed fuel into fuel tanks in seconds, rather than minutes, during a pit stop. While the top teams like Honda had such assets, most other riders, Joey included, couldn't afford them and had to rely on much slower gravity-fed fillers. No matter how fast he rode, Joey would lose the race during the two scheduled pit stops. Guaranteed.

But one of Joey Dunlop's greatest strengths as a rider was his cunningness. He could always figure out a way around problems and so turn them to his advantage. And in the 1980 Classic TT, he pulled a blinder.

Although Joey would be riding his John Rea Yamaha TZ750 in the race, and not Hector Neill's Suzuki, Neill still felt loyal to Joey and wanted to help. Joey had that kind of effect on people. 'I told him that, if he wanted to win the Classic, he would need all the gear,' Neill says. 'Of course, he had nothing. I told him he would need a quick-filler for a start, because the Honda team had the very latest ones. I told him that, without a quick-filler, he had no chance of winning the big race. He said, "What about a bigger fuel tank?" and asked if I had one. I didn't, but I had got one made on the Isle of Man at the previous year's Manx Grand Prix. I shouldn't even have been helping Joey, but I told him Sam McClements had a spare tank so he should borrow that and bring it to me – but he wasn't to tell Sam what we were going to do with it. I took the tank down to the same sheet metal workers who had enlarged the tank for me at the Manx and asked them to make it two inches bigger all round. They asked me who it was for and I said I couldn't tell them, so they refused to do it. It was only when I said it was for Joey that they agreed to make it. That cost me £47 and I'm still waiting for that money back from Joey!'

Joey's plan was to stop for fuel just once, rather than twice like all the other riders, thereby making up for all the time he would have lost by not having a quick-filler. So long as the other teams didn't discover his plan ahead of the race, Joey stood a good chance of outwitting them all. It was still a long shot, and he still had to beat riders of the calibre of Grant, Haslam and Crosby, but it was worth a try.

'The tank held exactly seven gallons, which is what he would need for three laps,' Neill continues. 'It was all above board though – there was nothing in the rules saying you couldn't use a bigger tank. I told him the tank would feel heavy for the first lap and that he was to take it easy until he'd burned off some fuel and dropped some weight. After that he could go faster, and then go as fast as he could on the third lap when he would be coming in for his only pit stop.'

What Neill didn't know was that two of the straps holding the huge, heavy fuel tank in place had broken just a few miles into the opening lap, forcing Joey to hold the tank in place with his knees for the remainder of the race. It seemed an impossible ask at race pace – especially when the TT course included jumps like the leap over the humpbacked Ballaugh Bridge – but then, Joey did have previous experience that may have helped him out.

During filming for *The Road Racers*, David Wallace had got hold of a World War II gun camera from a fighter plane that had been set up to record for a few seconds when the 'fire' button was pressed in order to confirm kills. It was with this ancient technology that he managed to break new ground with astonishing onboard footage at the North West 200 in 1977. 'The camera itself was quite small, about the size of a small paperback book, but the problem was that the 12-volt battery was quite bulky, so it had to be strapped somewhere else, like under the seat,' Wallace says. 'In Joey's case, we had a problem – and Joey didn't like problems. He didn't like complications, he just wanted things to work. When he came for his bike, we had the camera fitted but the battery still wasn't attached. and Joey didn't want to wait. I said we were going to have to forget it, but Joey asked what the problem was. When I told him we hadn't mounted the battery he said, "Is that all? That bit of metal?" When I said yes, he jumped on the bike and put the battery between his legs and rode off! The only thing that was holding that battery on during a lap of the North West 200 at racing speeds was Joey's knees.'

Now Dunlop found himself employing a similar tactic with an oversized fuel tank. 'Grant and Haslam were well ahead of Joey when they came in for their first pit stops after the second lap because Joey had been taking it steady, like I told him,' Neill continues. 'The commentator said, "There's Grant in, there's Haslam in – where's Joey? He must be in trouble!" Then he reported that Joey had gone straight through and missed his pit stop, but when people saw he was still going strong at Ballacraine, and actually making ground, they caught on and realised his tactics. I was in pit lane at Steven Cull's pit, and I looked over at Barry Symmons, the Honda team boss (who Grant and Haslam were riding for). He had a face on him like the devil and he knew straight away what I was at.'

Symmons, however, claims he knew exactly what Joey was up to and had even colluded, to a certain extent. 'What Hector didn't know was that I had actually helped Joey to find a welder to make his fuel tank bigger,' he says. 'Joey's manager, Davy Wood, came up to us and asked if we had a welder. We hadn't, but I knew of one in town, so I sent him off down there. So, to a certain extent, I was complicit in Honda being beaten!'

'The next thing I knew, Joey was in the lead,' Neill says. 'When he came in for his only pit stop at the end of the third lap, that let the Honda team get in front again, but when the Hondas came in for their second pit stop, Joey took the lead and never lost it again.'

Despite being manager of the mighty Honda Britain team, Barry Symmons was a sporting man and couldn't help but feel for the underfunded Dunlop and his shabby private bike, and says his heart went out to the Irishman as he came in to refuel. 'It was very close and we had one of these high-tech refuelling rigs. Mick Grant came into the pits and we refuelled him in about six seconds and Joey came in and they were still using the hand-filler. And I remember seeing my mechanics sort of… not quite cheering him on, but urging him on and wanting to dive in and help. We almost felt that we didn't deserve to win. Well, as it happened, we didn't – and Joey did.'

Joey Dunlop, on a privately entered, scruffy-looking Yamaha, had out-thought and out-raced the biggest teams and riders at the TT and his achievement wasn't lost on him. 'I broke the lap record, right enough, but it was the way I fooled Honda – because Honda knew they had it [the race], and they knew I couldn't do it. But I fooled them, for once!'

Despite running a two-year-old engine, Joey lapped the TT course faster than any man in history during that Classic race and became the first man to break the 115mph average speed barrier.

Such was the scruffiness of his machine Mick Grant hadn't even considered Joey a threat before the race. 'I remember looking at his pile-of-crap Yamaha TZ750 and thinking, "Well, he's not going to be a problem." But what we didn't know was that Joey had fitted a much bigger fuel tank, so he only had to stop once for fuel, and we just didn't expect that. Joey was tickled pink because he'd beaten the factory Honda team, so it was kind of ironic that he ended up riding for the same outfit!'

Neil Tuxworth also lined up alongside Joey for the 1980 Classic TT and he too remembers dismissing the Irishman as soon as he saw his bike. 'I remember being on the grid and that Yamaha 750 he had was leaking fuel all over the place,' he says. 'I thought, "Well, he's not going to last long," but he went out and won the race! I think he even stopped to check his back tyre during the race. He was just incredible.'

Less than three weeks after the death of his brother-in-law, Joey had won the biggest road race on the planet and dedicated his win to his late friend. In just over a year, he had experienced the ultimate highs and the ultimate lows that road racing had to offer. If he hadn't made the last-minute decision to travel to the Isle of Man just to see how he felt about continuing he may never have raced again, and the world would have been deprived of a career that enthralled millions. Nevertheless, Joey felt road racing was living on borrowed time after so many tragedies and was considering a switch to racing on much safer short circuits. 'I can't see much future for racing on public roads after all the accidents this year,' he had admitted ahead of the TT (and after there had been several further casualties at the Cookstown 100). 'I'm hoping to get a 500 Suzuki for UK meetings after the TT. If I get a Suzuki, I may concentrate on short-circuit racing.'

But there could be no going back after his famous TT win: Joey Dunlop was a road racer, through and through. As competent a short-circuit racer as he was, Joey always felt more at home surrounded by walls, trees and hedges. The roads were where he belonged. 'There's different techniques involved in road racing and short-circuit racing,' Mick Grant explains. 'I was brought up on short circuits, so I was good at stuffing it up the inside of someone at a hairpin. On the roads you're riding much faster corners. The fastest corners on most short circuits are taken at about 120mph. At the TT there are loads of corners that you take absolutely flat out in top gear, with the bike on its side, and Joey was particularly good at that. It's a different discipline.'

Grant also believes that, given the nature of the scarily narrow and bumpy roads circuits that Joey was brought up racing on, the TT course would have seemed less daunting for him. 'The TT course would have seemed like a big, wide-open space for Joey after racing on the much tighter Irish roads circuits. People have said to me you must be crazy to race round the Isle of Man, but if you were crazy, you wouldn't survive it. When I was at my best round there, if I did six laps and was more than two foot offline at any point during those six laps, I'd remember it. That's how accurate you have to be at the very top level. If you sat at any particular corner on the TT Course and watched Joey go round, he'd have been within an inch or two of the same line on every single lap.

'His level of skill, and feel for a bike, was superb,' Grant continues. 'One year when Phil Mellor was riding for my team, it started raining as the bikes were on the grid. Phil was on full wets and Joey was on slicks ['wet' tyres are heavily treaded to cope with heavy rain while 'slicks' are designed for dry conditions and have no tread whatsoever] yet Phil crashed, and Joey went on to win the wet race on slicks!'

It seemed that Joey could never turn his back on road racing, even if he'd wanted to. It was in his blood, and there was nothing he could do about it.

o

Due to a lack of budget, and having to persuade friends to edit the film in their spare time, David Wallace's documentary *The Road Racers* was not released until 1980. 'Joey wasn't a big name at the time, so there weren't exactly people banging on the door for the completion of the film,' he admits.

There had been other problems, too, mostly caused by the fast-talking, heavily accented Armoy clan. 'When we had finished filming, I sat down with a tape recorder and asked the guys lots of questions. I spent about three or four hours with each of them in a quiet room, and the answers they gave were used in the film. They kept using slang words in the interviews, so we had to keep stopping and go back and do it again because no one outside of Northern Ireland would have had any idea what they were saying.'

The problem was such that, at one point, Wallace even considered adding subtitles to his film. 'When I showed the film to people in the UK, they said they couldn't understand a word – they had no idea what Joey, Frank and Merv were talking about,' he says. 'I then had a difficult decision to make. I'm from Northern Ireland, and I really wanted the film to work in Ireland, not least because there was a sporting chance it was the only place it would ever be shown! On the other hand, I had access to the BBC and was in a position to sell the film to any number of people, but the advice I was getting from everyone was that the film wouldn't work anywhere else because of the riders' accents. So, what could I do? Spoil it by getting everyone to clean up their act voice-wise?'

In the end, he came up with a compromise: 'I explained the problem to the riders, and they all agreed to be interviewed again and would speak in what they called their "Sunday-go-to-meeting" voices. I spoke the local dialect, so they didn't feel they were speaking to an outsider, but they had to pretend they weren't speaking to me and so they spoke more slowly and more clearly. It's still their voices, but it would have been more fun for me if we could have used their natural accents.'

By the time the film was aired, two of the three featured riders were dead. Only Joey remained. And for that reason, according to Jim Dunlop, Joey never saw the film. 'I don't think Joey ever watched it because of what happened to Merv and Frank,' he says. 'I've only seen it a couple of times myself. *The Road Racers* is a good enough film to watch, but when you're involved in something maybe you don't look at it in the same way that other people do. I'm glad they made it, but I think Mervyn had most to do with it. He knew the man that made it and arranged a lot of things that they wanted to film. Joey wasn't too keen on getting involved in all that stuff.'

Whatever Joey's feelings about the film – and they were perfectly understandable – it proved a huge hit with race fans and has become a classic of the genre, perfectly capturing an era in a way that no other film did. 'It was a golden era for road racing and it was just nice to be a part of it,' says Hector Neill of the era Wallace so perfectly captured. 'The public loved it – the Armoy Armada and the Dromara Destroyers and all the fans with the badges and T-shirts. It never got nasty – it was just a bit of pure craic. That rivalry created a lot more interest in road racing. You'd get Armada fans on one side of the track at a race, and the Destroyers on the other side, but there was no bickering, it was just pure sport.'

Wallace was also shocked and saddened by the untimely deaths of two of his subjects. 'After Frank was killed, we talked about what we were going to do with the film. I don't think we ever considered *not* finishing it. I mean, it would have been easy to have had an instantaneous reaction and felt that it was no longer in good taste, but of course it *was* in good taste. I've met Mervyn's son, Paul Robinson, and lots of other people since then, and most of them consider that it was a good thing to have that recording of Frank and Mervyn.'

While Wallace rightly stands by his film, he found himself questioning the whole sport of road racing and his attitude towards road racing in general is now much more conflictive. 'I have had some second thoughts about road racing. I was young and gung-ho at the time and thought how wonderful road racing was – flying in the face of the nanny state and all that, but I don't know what I think about it now. I had dinner with the physician who treated Frank in the film, and he was quite firm in that he thought road racing should be banned. He felt it was an idiotic thing for anyone to do because it was so dangerous. And he said that, as a doctor, it was unfair that after every road race you could guarantee two or three beds were being taken up by people who had gone out there of their own free will and injured themselves. He was a terribly nice man, but you could see that he just didn't get it.

'I personally think it is still a very dangerous sport, even though they've cleaned it up as much as they can, but certainly back in 1977 it was very dangerous,' Wallace continues. 'I totally admire road racers, and part of me thinks it's wonderful, but there's another side of me that says it's illogical and that surely someone's going to put a stop to it sooner or later. I don't have a fixed opinion – I still can't make my mind up. I'm in two minds about road racing: one says it's completely daft and the other says it's absolutely wonderful.'

By the time of the film's first airing on BBC Northern Ireland, the Armoy Armada was no more. Joey was on his own. Jim Dunlop raced on until 1982, but never as seriously as his brother, and it wasn't until younger brother Robert began showing some promise on a race bike that Joey once again had a family ally to attend races with. Robert, some seven years younger than Joey, didn't appear to be a natural on a motorcycle. 'I remember when he started, I took him round Kirkistown and said, "Just follow me and I'll show you the way round,"' Jim Dunlop says. 'I was going as slow as I could, and after a lap or so I looked round and he was nowhere to be seen. I said to Joey, "He'll never make a racer – he's fuckin' useless." And so he was at that time, but he went on to prove me wrong!"'

He might have been a slow burner to start with, but Robert Dunlop shared his elder brother's determination and would one day become Joey's fiercest rival. But for now, he went about learning his trade and, despite all the tragedies he had already endured, Joey gave him all the support he could. He was family, after all, and if Robert was determined to race, then the best way to protect him was to arm him with as much knowledge as possible.

The rest of the 1980 TT didn't go particularly well for Joey, with only a twelfth place in the Junior and ninth in the Senior being notched up before taking his record-breaking win in the Classic. But it didn't matter – he had done enough to impress the factory teams who were now taking an interest in this scruffy, but clearly very fast, little Irishman. The first manufacturer to make an approach was Suzuki and Hector Neill acted as go-between. 'I knew Rex White from Suzuki very well and I got a phone call from him saying his rider, Graeme Crosby, had to win the Ulster Grand Prix to lift the TT Formula One world title, and they needed a rider to help him win it, and would I ask Joey if he would ride as Crosby's team-mate? I asked Joey and he agreed, even though he knew he would need to let Crosby through to win.'

In preparation for the event, Joey attended an official factory test session for the first time, and his modesty and humility were instantly apparent to Suzuki mechanic Martyn Ogborne, who had been Barry Sheene's mechanic for many years. Ogborne was given the task of tailoring Joey's bike to exactly suit his needs, but it proved no easy task. 'When Joey first rode the Suzuki, I said, "Right, tell me about the bike. What needs done?"' Ogborne remembers. 'He said it was perfect and nothing needed doing. He was just like Mike Hailwood in that sense – give him a bike and he'd ride it as it was [Ogborne had also worked with Hailwood when he rode a Suzuki in his last TT in 1979]. So, I started with the front end – the forks, the brakes, the tyre – and broke things down and we started getting somewhere. He'd just never had anyone to help him before, so he wasn't used to asking for changes. It took me hours, but I finally found out exactly what he needed to go faster.'

With the bike finally set up to Joey's liking, he turned up at Silverstone as a factory rider for the first time and finished second to Crosby, who would soon be a factory 500cc Grand Prix rider. To finish second to the flying Kiwi, at a short circuit and on his factory debut, was an incredible achievement, and one that again showed just how good Joey could be on short circuits. He also finished second to Crosby in an F1 race at Donington and was ninth at Cadwell Park before turning up at the Ulster Grand Prix, resplendent in the same Texaco Heron livery that the likes of Barry Sheene, Tom Herron, Pat Hennen and Steve Parrish had made so famous. Only, this time, he was hobbled by the knowledge that he would have to throw the Formula One race to allow Crosby to win.

For Crosby to win the championship, winning the race wasn't enough in itself. Honda's Mick Grant would take the title if he finished second to the Kiwi, so Joey's job was to get in behind Crosby and defend second place from Grant. If he could do that, he would gift Crosby, and Suzuki, the title.

No one likes team orders – neither fans nor riders – but at least, Joey reasoned, he could still prove a point while obeying them, as Hector Neill explains. 'With two laps of the race to go, Joey was miles in front and Rex White came up to me, shaking, and said, "When's he going to stop? When's he going to stop? Did you not tell him to stop?" I told him I didn't know, just to wind him up. But Joey knew to stop and, lo and behold, on the last lap at the hairpin, he pulled over to let Crosby through. Crosby won it, Joey finished second and Suzuki won the world championship.' Mick Grant could only finish third in the race. Had Joey not been drafted in by Suzuki, he would have finished second and won the title. So, while Joey had thrown the race, he had also proved that he could have easily beaten Crosby and won it himself. He had been leading by more than 20 seconds before slowing to allow his team-mate to pass and, under no team orders in any of his other races, Joey won the 250cc and 1000cc events that same day. But he was clearly playing the long game and thought that such a showing would convince Suzuki to sign him.

Hector Neill is still puzzled as to why Suzuki stalled. 'I said to Rex White, "For Christ's sake, Rex, get this man signed cos I know for sure that Honda's looking at him. You'll not get a rider better than this." But he footered about and said he had to speak to this person and that person and, the next thing, in the local paper about two weeks later, there was a picture of Joey, John Rea and Barry Symmons, and the news that Joey Dunlop had signed for Honda. That was one of Suzuki's biggest losses – they just dithered about too much. Joey won nearly everything for Honda, and he would have done the same for Suzuki.'

Martyn Ogborne believes it was all down to money and that Suzuki should have dug deeper to secure such a talent. 'We wanted to sign him, but Honda came in with a bigger offer that Suzuki GB couldn't match,' he says. 'Joey called me and asked what he should do, and I told him he should accept the biggest offer because it was up to Suzuki to come up with the cash and, if they couldn't, it was their loss. If someone at Suzuki Japan had woken up to this, Joey Dunlop could have achieved what he did on Suzukis instead of Hondas.'

Rex White *did* make Joey an offer to ride for Suzuki in 1981 but he claimed Joey didn't respond and he suspected that Honda had made a better offer, and that John Rea might have had some influence in Joey's decision. He was right. 'I had known John Rea for some time, so we went to his bungalow on his transport site just outside Belfast,' says Barry Symmons. 'He pinned me between the fridge and the cooker and said, "Now, are you going to sign this man?" I sort of waved a white flag and told Gerald Davison [director of Honda UK] about it and he put it all in motion and that was it. Gerald came to the arrangement and I took the contract over to Belfast and got Joey to sign it in front of us and several others.'

John Rea's son, Johnny, remembers his father's influence in both the Suzuki and Honda deals. 'My father arranged the ride with Suzuki for Joey when he was drafted in to help Graeme Crosby win the TT Formula One world championship at Dundrod. Then Honda approached Joey and my father went with him to do the deal. At that time, my father was running Rea Transport so he would organise Joey's ferries and stuff for him – things like that.'

Joey never forgot the kindness and support that John Rea had shown him as a privateer and Johnny Rea remembers a huge act of kindness that Joey later offered in return. 'Towards the end, my father's business went downhill – the Rea Transport part of it – and Joey offered my father the money to save it, but he never took it.'

Money was never a motivating factor for Joey, and Barry Symmons doesn't think it influenced his decision to sign for Honda. 'I don't think it was money, although I'm sure we offered Joey quite a bit more than Suzuki did.' According to Joey's manager, Davy Wood, John Rea secured a purse from Honda that was six times what Suzuki had offered.

'Davy Wood probably had quite a bit to do with it,' Symmons continues. 'Our relationship with John Rea definitely helped. We knew him through one of our sponsors, DAF trucks – John was a DAF agent and ran a fleet of them. Consequently, he told Joey what sort of an outfit we were, and I think that had a bigger effect on Joe than the bike we were offering. He was looking for a team he could get on with.'

Whatever the reasons behind his decision, Joey Dunlop was now an official factory Honda rider. He would have world-class motorcycles, a whole team of mechanics and helpers behind him, a handsome salary, and a new life in England, racing on famous circuits like Brands Hatch, Donington Park and Silverstone. And he hated every minute of it.

CHAPTER 6

ALIEN

'ONE THING HE DIDN'T LIKE WERE PEOPLE WHO WORE TIES.'
Barry Symmons

In the beginning, Honda didn't know how to deal with Joey Dunlop any better than Joey Dunlop knew how to deal with Honda. Both parties would have to learn how to work with the other. 'He was very shy,' Barry Symmons says. 'A team manager's job is not like being a crew chief – it's about getting people to work well together and creating an atmosphere in which they can perform at their best without having to wave big sticks around! I quickly sussed out that Joey was fairly quiet. He could be very serious at times, if he had something on his mind, but you could tell whether Joey was going to be chatty or not and we all got to know that, and made allowances for that, and treated Joey the way we felt he wanted to be treated. If he was in a quiet or thoughtful mood, we would leave him alone.'

Signing with Honda had turned Joey's life upside down. With

so much racing now to do in England he tried to base himself there but that didn't quite work out. 'We gave him a caravan to sleep in, but where he actually parked it up at night is anyone's guess,' Symmons says. Joey would sometimes stay with his new team-mate, Ron Haslam, who was very much cut from the same cloth as Joey himself. He too had come from a big family that had very little in the way of money, and he too had no time for sartorial elegance – he had the same long, greasy hair as Joey and wore a similar uniform of oil-stained jeans and T-shirts. The pair got on famously. 'I stopped at Joey's house a lot and he stopped at mine when we were going to Assen or the Suzuka 8 Hours race when we were team-mates,' Haslam says. 'I knew him not as just a rider but as a friend. As everybody says, he was so down to earth. What you saw was what you got with Joey, and I loved him for that. You didn't have to ask him for anything. I would just go to Ireland and turn up at his doorstep and I didn't even have to knock – I'd just walk straight in. He was that type of person.'

Even with a good friend like Haslam, being away from his family for extended periods was never going to work for Joey, and there were other problems too, like trusting his mechanics. Having always worked on his own bikes, Joey was extremely reluctant to trust their preparation to people he didn't know. 'At that stage we didn't know a lot about him, so we thought that if we could take all the responsibility off his shoulders for machinery etc., he would be well happy but, of course, that didn't work,' Symmons continues. 'Joey was always a hands-on man but, particularly, he needed to trust the people who were working on his machines. If he was back in Ireland all the time and didn't know who was going to turn up to work on his bikes... Nick Goodison, Wilf Needham, Dave Sleat – Joey didn't know any of them, so I realised very quickly that would be a problem.'

There was also the problem of exchanging his beloved Irish road races for the far more frantic pursuit of English short-circuit racing. 'English racing is a completely different type of racing,' Joey told David Wallace during filming of *The Road Racers*. 'They're all big, broad courses with no trees about them at all. It's very, very hard to adapt to that sort of circuit, where you really have to ride hard and not worry about falling off and hitting a tree or something like that. You would think, when you're riding against them [the short-circuit riders], that they're completely mad. I'm just starting to get it into my head now that you can afford to fall off in England – that's why they all go so hard.'

Then there were the promotional duties and appearances at motorcycle shows and other events. And on this issue, Joey put his foot down. 'Joey had spoken to Gerald Davison [Honda UK's general manager at the time] about that,' explains Symmons. 'Apparently, he said, "I dinnae want none o' them girls wi' no proper clothes." Gerald didn't understand what he meant, so Joey explained that he had a wife and family at home and didn't want them to see pictures of him at races and bike shows with models draped all over him, which I thought was lovely of him.'

There was also his appearance to think of. Never one to be fussed about how he looked, Joey did take it on himself to get a haircut in preparation for his new role, but he still felt uncomfortable in this new corporate world of suits, shirts, and ties. 'One thing he didn't like were people who wore ties,' Symmons says. 'I don't know why – I guess it made him think too much about office people or authority figures. He had his own ideas about who was trustworthy and who wasn't, and if you had a tie on, that sort of put you at a disadvantage.'

There have been those who have accused Honda – and Barry Symmons in particular – of 'changing' Joey, of trying to make him something he wasn't, but Symmons insists that's not the case. 'People said we changed Joey, but we didn't. Basically, if Joey wanted to do something, he'd do it, and there wasn't a lot you could do about it. But it was him who realised the position he was in with Honda and that he'd have to smarten himself up on occasion. I certainly never told him to put a shirt and tie on – I gave him the equipment, but he chose to wear it. The choice was down to him, and I was grateful when he did make the effort.'

And then there was the language barrier. Surrounded by English accents for the first time in his life, Joey struggled to make himself understood. It would be a problem for the remainder of his career. 'We always found him difficult to understand for the first few weeks of each season,' Symmons says. 'I've lived in Belfast for thirty-odd years now, but I still struggle to understand the way they talk in Ballymoney because they speak so fast. Once you got Joey to slow down a bit, he was alright, but it was tricky for all of us. I think after the first few weeks of each season he twigged that we weren't understanding him, so he made himself slow down a bit.'

Tony 'Slick' Bass would have communication difficulties even after Joey had been with Honda for six years. 'When I was eighteen, I was approached to work for the Honda Britain racing team and the first rider I was assigned to was Joey Dunlop – that was in 1987. I didn't understand a word he said to me the whole year! I remember he came into the pits midway through the British GP and was muttering something under his helmet. I just stood and looked at him because I couldn't understand what he was saying. I eventually shoved a paddock stand under him, looked busy for a minute, then pushed him off again. It took me two years of asking Joey to find out why he had actually stopped, and he eventually told me it was just "For a wee break" because he was knackered!'

Ferry Brouwer founded Arai Europe in 1983 and provided Joey

with his famous yellow and black Arai helmets from that year onwards. As a Dutchman, he also struggled with Joey's speech, at least in the early days. 'One of the first things he said when I handed him an Arai was, "Aw, it's a hanmaidyin" and I thought, "What in the fuck is a hanmaidyin?" I eventually realised he was saying "a hand-made one". You just had to have a broad mind, and a little bit of a creative mind, to understand him. But later, having spoken with Joey so often, I could understand what he was saying, no problem.'

Public schoolboy Nick Jefferies remembers having to endure a whole week of miscommunication. 'Me and Joey shared a garage together for a week in Macau one year and I had to *really* concentrate on what he was saying,' he says. 'I worked out it was best if I just nodded my head every now and then, as if I understood him!'

Scottish rider Ian Simpson was Joey's team-mate in the 1990s and never had a problem understanding him, as his native Galloway tongue is very similar to the Ballymoney accent. He could, however, see how tiring it was for Joey to have to constantly modify his accent. 'When he was around English people, Joey tried to slow down and speak more clearly, but it's hard to relax when you have to keep that up.'

This constant battle to make himself understood may partly explain why Joey preferred not to talk so much to the press or TV crews. He wasn't much of a talker anyway, but knowing that so many people struggled to understand him may have persuaded him to keep his words to a minimum.

As well as struggling to make himself understood when talking, Joey also struggled with written communications, according to Ferry Brouwer. 'Joey was partly illiterate,' he says. 'We were at the Arai booth at the Suzuka circuit one year and lots of people came to get Joey's autograph. Sometimes they would ask him to write a dedication, like "To so-and-so from Joey Dunlop", so I stood beside him and would write the people's names on the palm of my hand so that Joey could copy what I had written without people realising that he was illiterate. He never mentioned that it was a problem for him, and I never felt that he was embarrassed about it; for him, it was just the way he was.'

Joey's inherent shyness was another issue and another big barrier for him to get over. Removed from the close circle of Northern Irish friends he had known for years, he was now surrounded by strangers and was constantly meeting more people. 'He was such a shy guy,' says Neil Tuxworth. 'He didn't like the publicity and didn't like being in front of people. It was a hell of a job to get Joey to jump in the car and go to a Honda function. It wasn't that he was awkward or that he was a prima donna, he was just nervous about those kinds of things. He loved racing motorbikes, but he hated the fame that went with it. He wasn't a great mixer – he was a very private man and very much a family man.'

All these issues, both big and small, began to affect Joey's riding. There's an old adage in racing that says a happy rider is a fast rider but, in 1981, Joey wasn't happy and that meant he wasn't fast: his first year with Honda was a disappointment. He struggled in the new MCN/Shell Streetbike series, he struggled in the ITV World of Sport races, and he struggled in the Transatlantic Match Races that pitted a team of British riders against a team of hand-picked Americans. Joey's best result in the mini-series was a seventh at Oulton Park. Something was clearly amiss.

Despite his lacklustre performances, Joey's feedback during testing with the Honda RCB1000 was sound, right from the outset. 'A lot of riders, when they first ride a factory bike, try to make out that they know everything that's going on,' Barry Symmons says. 'So, one of the first things we would do with a new rider is find out exactly what they did know, so that we could make allowances. When Wayne Gardner had his first test with us at Cadwell Park, he was keeping a close eye on Ron Haslam because Ron had ridden the bikes and knew things about the offsets and the triple clamps. At one point, Ron asked if he could try a different-sized triple clamp so, sure enough, Wayne then asked to do the same thing. We didn't have any other triple clamps, so we took the one off of Wayne's bike and wrote a different number on it, pretended it was different, then put it back on. Wayne lapped slightly faster and said it was all down to the different triple clamp, so we knew then that he really didn't have much of an idea.'

Self-taught he might have been, but Joey knew exactly what he was doing in terms of bike set-up and feedback. 'Joe knew what he was doing,' Symmons testifies. 'He was a good development rider from the start.'

Joey also had his own unique way of working and was very guarded about all the knowledge he had so painstakingly garnered over the years. 'He was a true privateer in that he was very secretive,' Symmons says. 'He wouldn't tell his mechanics what setting he had his steering damper on, for example. Whenever he came into the pits, you would see him turning the steering damper back to zero. One day, Dave Sleat [one of Joey's Honda mechanics] got up on the pit wall as Joey came in, and he counted the clicks when Joey was returning the steering damper back to a neutral setting. The next time the mechanics were preparing Joey's bike, Dave said, "Set the steering damper to six," and Joey gave him a look like he was about to kill him! He didn't want his team-mates, or anyone else, to know his settings.'

Back on home turf for the North West 200 – and back with his family, racing on familiar street circuits, and in front of his adoring local fans – Joey seemed more himself and stormed to victory in the feature race. He clipped a dog during the race but was still so far ahead of Steve Parrish and Dennis Ireland on the last lap that he had time to stop and jokingly ask John Rea if he needed a lift back to the pits.

The next big road race was the TT, but instead of wearing Honda's traditional red, white and blue colours, Joey found himself wearing black and riding an all-black bike. The 1981 TT was the year of Honda's 'black protest'. In the opening race of the week, the Formula One TT, Suzuki's Graeme Crosby was scheduled to start at number 16. But, having decided to opt for a rear slick tyre at the last moment, he missed his starting position and was moved to the back of the grid. This gave him time to make the necessary adjustments, but it also meant the clock was ticking from when he *should* have started, even though he was still sat on the grid. The organisers clearly stated he would not be credited with any extra time to compensate for this and, with the clock already well underway, Crosby finally took the plunge down Bray Hill to give pursuit.

Mick Grant had now signed for Suzuki and was Crosby's team-mate, while the Honda team consisted of Joey Dunlop and Ron Haslam. Grant was closing in on race leader Dunlop when his Suzuki expired on the third lap, promoting Haslam into second place behind his Honda team-mate. When Dunlop opted for a wheel change during his fuel stop, Haslam took the lead and held it to the flag.

Crosby had ridden superbly to carve his way through the field and take third place at the flag behind Joey. His exploits had resulted in a new lap record but, for the Suzuki team, that wasn't enough. They protested and insisted that the clock should only have started ticking on Crosby when he left the start line – not when he was *supposed* to leave the start line, before he opted to change his tyre. After some debate, Crosby's time was adjusted and he was declared the winner, but the organisers failed to inform Ron Haslam or Honda – both of whom were to find out about the decision in the most galling manner.

Haslam takes up the story. 'That was the most excitement and disappointment in one hit that I've ever had. Neither me nor Honda had any inkling of it until the evening prize presentation. I got the champagne on the rostrum and all that stuff and then we went back to the hotel and got ready for the presentation. I was waiting at the side of the stage to be called up to receive the winner's trophy and they shouted me up for second place. I just thought they'd got it wrong, so I went up on the stage and thanked them but said they'd got it wrong because I'd won the race. They said, "No, no, no, we're giving it to Graeme Crosby." I just couldn't believe it – and Honda couldn't, either. That was the first time we'd been told we were second.'

Haslam and Honda naturally wanted to protest the decision but soon realised they were in a Catch-22 situation. 'In the rule book for that year it said if you don't start in your position, you'll get docked the time, so we decided to protest the decision,' Haslam explains. 'But the rules also said you have to protest any decision within thirty minutes of the race finishing and, since no one told us we had lost the race until hours later, there was nothing we could do.'

Haslam was relegated to second place and Dunlop to third, in what was one of the most controversial decisions in the history of the TT. By the time the Classic race came around, the Honda team had been fuming all week at the perceived injustice of the Formula One result. But time had not proved a healer in this instance, and it was in front of a bewildered paddock that the team rolled out its bikes. Rather than being painted in Honda's corporate colours, the machines were sprayed black. Even the riders – Haslam, Alex

George and Joey – turned up in plain black leathers to protest the organisers' ruling.

If anything, Joey went *too* fast to make amends in the Classic TT. Lapping at over 115mph from a standing start, he upped his speed on every circuit until he ran out of fuel at Hillberry on the third lap. Barry Symmons admitted his team had been caught out by Joey's sheer speed. 'We reckoned on 9.2 litres per lap,' he says. 'Even our most pessimistic calculations gave Joey enough fuel to complete three laps non-stop – but we didn't reckon on three 115mph laps!'

Dunlop pushed into the pits, refuelled, and set off at the same record pace until his Honda's cam chain broke and finally ended his race. Haslam fared no better and retired from third place with ignition problems leaving Crosby, ironically, to win.

Controversy aside, it was a disappointing Honda debut for Joey at the TT. He only had bikes for the Formula One and Classic races, so came away from the meeting with a solitary third place. The only encouragement was that he broke his own outright lap record and proved he could consistently lap at 115mph. It was something to build on, at least.

Things didn't go much better at the Ulster Grand Prix, where he could only finish fifth in the final round of the TT Formula One world championship to end up third overall. Crosby won the series for the second year, ahead of Haslam, before turning his back on road racing to concentrate solely on Grands Prix.

Joey's racing in England didn't go to plan either, and he ended the season with sixth place in both the 1981 MCN/Shell Streetbike series and the UK Formula One championship (a separate series to the F1 world championship, with all rounds held on short circuits).

By season's end, Honda was wondering what had happened to the Joey of old: the man who had beaten them on a shabby, two-year-old Yamaha at the TT. Between them, Davy Wood and Barry

Symmons came up with a plan. 'We had all the bikes at Honda Britain's HQ in Chiswick and brought Joey over to England, but it was fairly obvious that wasn't going to work, because Joey had been used to working on his own bikes with his own team of helpers,' Symmons says. 'So that's when we agreed to let Joey take some of the bikes back home to Ireland to work on himself. The only bikes he was never allowed to take away were the Formula One bikes because they were the pukka works bikes and were not allowed out of our control.'

In order to build up Joey's trust in his mechanics, Symmons arranged for them to live in Ballymoney for a period to build up a rapport with their rider. 'I sent some of our mechanics over to work with him so he could get to know them on a personal level, as well as a working level, and that gave him the confidence to trust what they were doing,' he says. 'One of them, Dave Sleat, even joined Rea Transport for two weeks and passed his HGV test so he could drive the race truck! That built the relationships that we needed between Joey and his mechanics. We then gave him his previous year's TT Formula One bike to tinker around with back at home – he understood that we couldn't lend him his current factory bike because there were things on it that even we didn't know about!'

He may not have been able to take his current factory bike home to work on but, according to Hector Neill, this didn't stop Joey getting hands-on with it whenever the opportunity arose. 'When Honda was getting its factory bikes ready for the TT, Joey wasn't allowed to touch them,' he says. 'But he used to go to the workshop at night where the bikes were kept and took his bike out of the workshop. I was coming out of the casino one night about 2am and the lights were on in the private garage Joey had rented behind our hotel, and there's his factory Honda sitting, completely stripped down. I says, "What are you doing, Gurk?" and he says, "I dinnae trust them boys – I'm putting this together for myself." So, he stripped the bike, checked it all over, put it back together again, and took it back to Honda's workshop before morning. That's the way he was.'

Former Honda UK press man Graham Sanderson believes Joey *did* regularly work on his factory machines, even though Honda never publicly admitted this. 'I believe I'm right in saying that, even though HRC might not have been too keen on the idea, I think they actually allowed Joey to work on the proper factory bikes too, although this was usually denied. He might not have been the smartest-looking, catwalk model-type person, but his machine preparation was of the highest quality.'

Based back in Northern Ireland again, surrounded by family and friends, now able to trust his Honda mechanics at least to some degree, and with some bikes to tinker on (Honda also agreed to support him with a 250cc machine), Joey once more grew comfortable in his own skin. He would operate this way for the remainder of his career. Joey now had everything he needed and, from this solid platform, he was ready to take on the world.

o

By 1982, the TT Formula One world championship had grown to become a three-round series, taking in the TT, the street circuit of Vila Real in Portugal, and the Ulster Grand Prix at Dundrod. At three rounds long, it was still a long way off being a full-blown 'world' championship in many people's eyes, but it was important to the manufacturers, nevertheless. 'Honda and Suzuki took it very seriously,' says Mick Grant, who would push Joey hard in the championship for several years. 'The bikes they ran in F1 were based on the world endurance racers – they were serious bits of kit, all hand-built. Bikes from the late 1970s got a bad reputation for having lots of power but inadequate chassis, but I think about 80 per cent of the poor handling was down to tyre technology. By the 1980s, the tyres were not a problem, and the chassis were good. The chassis on my Suzuki XR69 from 1982 was almost as sophisticated as any chassis now, as far as adjustment goes.'

Roger Marshall claims the series was so important to the manufacturers that riders were obliged to compete in it if they wanted to further their careers. 'If you wanted a factory ride, you had to race on the scary F1 road circuits,' he says. 'The Japanese thought as much of winning the F1 world title as they did of winning Grands Prix. So, if you wanted to get a factory ride in GPs, you had to go to these scary road circuits and do the business.'

As popular as the series was with manufacturers, riders and fans, there was still some unease about calling a three-round series a world championship. Rob McElnea would be a leading contender for the crown in the early eighties and he enjoyed every minute of it, but he also had his doubts about that moniker. 'It was a good series, but I don't think it should have been called a world championship with just three rounds – that was a bit of a joke. Each individual race was a great thing to be involved in, but I wasn't doing it to be called Formula One world champion – I wasn't hanging out to be world F1 champion with three fucking races!'

Grant and McElnea would sandwich Dunlop into second place in the feature race at the 1982 North West 200, with Grant taking the win. But it was a meeting that Joey very nearly didn't take part in, due to his superstitious beliefs. When he learned that he was to be on the cover of the race programme, Joey threatened to boycott the event if his picture wasn't removed. Both Frank Kennedy and Mervyn Robinson had been on the cover of the programme in the years they died. 'Joey was very superstitious,' Barry Symmons says. 'He didn't want his picture on the cover of the programme, and he wouldn't ride with number 31 either. That was because he had lost friends who had been on the cover or had ridden with that number.'

Neil Tuxworth also remembers this trait in Joey's personality. 'He was a very superstitious man,' he says. 'He didn't like it when he won thirteen TT races and he didn't like any combinations associated with that number. He would never ride with the number 31 because Mervyn Robinson had been killed while wearing that number and Joey always said 31 was 13 backwards.'

There were many other superstitions that Joey took very seriously. 'He always wore a lucky disc around his neck and one time he lost it, so Linda got him a replacement,' Symmons continues. 'I eventually found the original disc, but Joey said he couldn't switch back to wearing it as he had to wear the one Linda got him. But he told me to bring it to every race meeting just in case, so I attached it to my travel bag.'

The North West issue was resolved only when the publishers of the programme agreed to substitute the picture of Joey on the cover with one of Ron Haslam. Sadly, while Joey himself survived the 1982 meeting, John Newbold was not so lucky. A member of the factory Suzuki squad, Newbold was killed after colliding with Mick Grant and crashing out of the race. The North West had claimed yet another life.

Neither Grant nor McElnea would feature in the results of the Formula One TT in the first round of the 1982 world championship. Instead, it was Ron Haslam who won and took the lead in the series. But the F1 championship was not Haslam's priority – he was concentrating more on short-circuit racing as a route into 500cc Grands Prix and missed the second round in Portugal to race elsewhere. In his absence, it was another of Joey's Honda team-mates, Wayne Gardner, who dominated the race. The Australian would become 500cc world champion in 1987 and was devastatingly fast in the few road races he contested before breaking into Grands Prix. Joey finished in second place again, meaning that a fourth place in the third and final round would see him crowned champion. And to Joey's great advantage, that final round would be held in his backyard at Dundrod. He couldn't have scripted it better himself.

And by now 'Himself' had replaced 'the Gurk' as Joey's new moniker amongst Irish race fans. A term of reverence, Joey's presence was now so powerful, and the aura about him so strong, that wherever he appeared fans would nudge each other, nod in his direction and say, 'Look – it's Himself.' It did, at least, sound more respectful than 'the Gurk'.

That respect for Joey grew exponentially when he became the first Irishman to win a motorcycling world title since Ralph Bryans took the 50cc world crown in 1965. Joey took the F1 title with yet another second place, meaning it was consistency rather than race wins that saw him ultimately triumph. Haslam won the race at Dundrod, but Joey had done enough to win his first world title, and Honda breathed a sigh of relief that they hadn't made a mistake in signing him. Joey would later admit that the moment he crossed the line as world champion for the first time was one of his best memories in racing – but it was a memory that took a while to register. 'It's marvellous to win the title but it just hasn't sunk in' he said at the time. 'This is a day I will always remember.'.

And yet, world title or not, the season had been far from a complete success, with Joey failing to pick up a win at any of the major road races. He did win some rounds of the MCN/Shell Streetbike series on his Honda CB1100R, usually after ferocious tussles with Wayne Gardner and Ron Haslam. As a marker of how good Joey was on short circuits, both Gardner and Haslam would be racing in the 500cc Grand Prix world championship the following year yet Joey, on his day, could beat them. 'When Joey was team-mates with Wayne Gardner and Ron Haslam on the big street bikes, he and Ron were very closely matched' Barry Symmons says. 'Wayne was in a class of his own, but Joey and Ron were so close it was always touch-and-go who was going to come second.'

Ron would become Britain's most successful Grand Prix racer since Barry Sheene within the next few years. Had Joey really wanted to pursue a career in short-circuit racing, there can be little doubt he would have made a success of it. But the lure of the roads was always too great for him. For Joey, between the hedges was where the 'real' racing happened.

However fierce his rivalry with Haslam, the two remained firm friends and were forever daring each other with daft pranks, as Symmons remembers. 'We did a test at Donington once, and half of the day was allocated to cars, so Joey and Ron were bored and challenged each other to see who could walk the furthest round the concrete wall that surrounded the circuit. It was about fifteen feet high and four inches wide. George Turnbull [former managing director of Austin-Morris] had an office overlooking the Melbourne Loop and he got a bit of a shock when these two faces appeared at his window when there wasn't anything he knew of that anybody could stand on!'

It had been a happy alliance with Haslam before he set out for pastures new in Grands Prix. 'Joey and Ron were made for each other as team-mates,' Symmons continues. 'When the two of them got together they were hilarious. If you said to one of them, "I bet you couldn't climb that telegraph pole," they'd be fighting each other to be first up it. They used to egg each other on like a couple of kids.'

To round out the 1982 season, Joey made his second trip to the sweltering heat of Macau in the Far East. He had raced there the previous year but had collapsed after getting off the bike. Never one for staying in shape, racing in hot countries could often be a problem for Joey. At Macau, he was smothered in wet towels and given salt tablets to replace what he had lost through sweat, then went back out in the second leg and finished seventh. Paul Iddon, who would soon become a rival to Joey in the Formula One world championship, remembers racing against him at Vila Real in Portugal when conditions were even worse. 'Vila Real was suicide!' he says. 'I remember they held us on the grid for ages one year and it was 128 degrees. The sweat was pouring into my eyes when I was riding – I've never done a more physical race. People were actually collapsing, and after the race there were medical staff with stretchers and hosepipes to revive the riders. It was something like a two-hour race with pit stops.'

On his second visit to Macau, Joey didn't collapse, but neither did he score a race win; those went to Mick Grant and Ron Haslam, while Joey could only manage third and fourth places. Macau was one of the very few road circuits that Joey never took a win on, but there was a good reason for that, according to Nick Jefferies. 'He went round there like I did, just in holiday mode,' he says. 'We viewed Macau differently back then and just treated it as a holiday, rather than going all-out to win.'

A relaxing holiday it might have been but, results-wise, it was a mediocre ending to what had essentially been a mediocre year. Despite lifting his first world title, race wins had been few and far between. But that would soon change. In 1983 the world would finally see just what Joey Dunlop was capable of. Some fourteen years into his career, he would fully realise his potential and leave everyone else fighting over second place. Honda had built a new V-Four, and Joey would ride it to victory.

CHAPTER 7

V-FOUR
VICTORY

**'HE WAS VERY DETERMINED. VERY DETERMINED. BUT HE WAS ALSO
SO NATURALLY TALENTED, IT WAS UNREAL.'**

Johnny Rea

In 1983, Joey Dunlop once again found himself the subject of a documentary film and this time it was called *V-Four Victory* Directed by vastly experienced filmmaker David Wood, it would include a sensational and ground-breaking onboard lap of the TT course that left audiences stunned. 'In 1983 I filmed the Formula One race at the TT for Honda, Dunlop [tyres] and Shell,' Wood explains. 'After Joey won, and then picked up good points at Assen, it looked odds-on that he would clinch the TT Formula One world championship at the Ulster GP, so Honda asked us to go to Dundrod to capture the occasion on film.'

But it wasn't the race footage that made *V-Four Victory* such a huge success, it was the onboard lap that was the climax and highpoint of the film. 'Whilst we'd been in the Isle of Man, I'd been chatting to Peter Duke [son of six-times world champion, Geoff Duke, and owner of Duke Video] about seeing if Joey would be prepared to do a lap of the TT course with a proper film camera and a special mount to try to even out the shakes that had been obvious in previous attempts, including our own,' Wood continues. 'After speaking to Joey, along with Roger Etcell and Barry Symmons of Honda, it was agreed that, if we came up with a camera and mount that Joey and the Honda mechanics were happy with, Joey would come back to the island and film a lap for us during practice for the Manx GP (essentially an amateur version of the TT, held later in the year, where riders traditionally started out before moving up to the TT proper).'

Previous attempts to capture a full lap of the TT course at racing speeds, as Wood acknowledged, had been compromised by mounting a camera on a much slower road bike, or by using a lower-spec and poorly-fitted camera, which resulted in a very shaky picture. David Wood and Joey Dunlop were the first to get it right, and that allowed audiences to get closer to experiencing the thrill of racing at the TT than they had ever been before. It was nothing short of sensational.

Wood reveals how it was achieved: 'We took measurements and photos of the bike and set about making the mount. When we got to the Manx, the Honda boys fitted the mount to Joey's Honda V-Four. It cradled the fuel tank and had small rubber shock absorbers and the whole concoction was bolted onto the frame of the bike.' The camera itself was a £20,000 16mm Arriflex with a single wide-angle lens, which gave a rider's eye view – including the rev counter. The rev counter was important in proving the film hadn't been speeded up, as many viewers believed it must have been. 'We also removed the windscreen from the top of the fairing to give a clearer picture,' Wood says. 'Behind the camera, we fitted a mini tape recorder, microphone and battery, as back in those days film and sound were different entities. We were now ready to do a test lap and Joey had to half sit up behind the camera to see over it.'

With the heavy and ungainly camera in place, Joey set off on the first of what was supposed to be two laps, as he would only be able to film half a lap each time before the film ran out. The plan was to then join up the film footage in the editing stages so that it looked like one continuous lap. 'The camera magazine only ran for twelve minutes, so Joey would need to do two laps, with us changing the magazine after a lap and getting Joey to remember to switch it on about halfway round on his second lap. "No problem," said Joey. "Somewhere around Ballaugh I'll do just that." We had already fitted a small light switch next to the camera to make things a little easier for him. Practice was now in full swing, so we fitted the first film magazine and off went Joey. Now, Joey being Joey, he didn't know how to do a slower lap as he would need new lines and breaking points etc. So, what the boys out practising for the Manx thought about this bike with the rider sitting half up behind the camera, as he came flying past them, we'll only have to guess.'

There's no need to guess. One of those riders was future TT legend Steve Hislop, who was making his debut at the Manx. When interviewed by the present author for his autobiography *Hizzy*, the Scotsman explained, 'I remember getting passed by Joey Dunlop a few times in my first practice week at the Manx and he had a huge, big camera strapped to the tank. These days, the cameras are so small you don't even know they're there but in 1983 it was like having Steven bloody Spielberg sitting on the tank with a full camera crew in tow! Joey passed me so many times that I thought there was three of the little buggers – I didn't realise that he was continually stopping to adjust the camera.'

After returning from his first lap, Wood quizzed Joey on how it had gone. 'As always, he didn't make a fuss,' Wood says. "It was fine," he said. "Once I'd got used to it. Except that, when I sat up a bit at Ballacraine, I nearly got blown backwards off the bike." We thought that was a bit risky, even though Joey was quite laid-back about it, so the Honda boys came up with an idea and fixed a full-face visor on a bracket above the camera to give Joey some wind protection.'

The second lap was not without its problems either, not that Joey noticed. 'We changed the film magazine and off he went again, after being reminded to press the switch at Ballaugh. In came Joey after his second lap: "No problems – and I pressed the button," he said with a grin. Well, Joey may have thought there were no problems, but I knew there was – no lens. It had obviously unscrewed and come off, luckily not hitting Joey. "I thought a bird had come close at one point," said Joey, laughing. "Maybe that was it. Have you got another lens?" Well, of course, we had – and another camera, just in case. So, Joey says, "Right, you put some more film in, and the boys will put some more fuel in, and we'll go again." He was only supposed to do two laps, but it was typical of how helpful he was that he'd do another one for us.'

Joey's average lap speed over the three laps was around 113mph – with a heavy camera on the tank and with Joey having to sit almost upright all the way round. The outright lap record in 1983 was 116.19mph, set by fellow Irishman Norman Brown, without any such incumbrances. It was an impressive feat.

Despite feeling that filming was intrusive during the making of *The Road Racers*, Joey was fully committed during the filming of *V-Four Victory*, perhaps because it gave him the chance to complete more laps of his beloved TT course. He even agreed to be interviewed at length by journalist Chris Carter, as well as providing a commentary for the onboard lap. 'Joey couldn't have been more helpful,' Wood says. 'It wasn't easy to get him to talk about himself, as he was so modest and unassuming and could never appreciate just how good he was. But Chris did an excellent job in getting him to chat. Joey was nervous at first, though. We would do the first few questions and tell him we were just doing a sound-level check, but sometimes we would use those takes because they were some of the best ones. He was more relaxed that way. As soon as he was aware the cameras were on him for real, he would get more nervous. Once you got him chatting though, he was away.'

Like many other people who had to deal with Joey, David Wood had issues with his accent although, in his case, it was more about the speed at which Joey spoke. 'Yes, we did have problems with his accent,' he admits. 'We needed to tell him to slow down quite a bit, as he could get quite enthusiastic and would start talking so fast. He tried to slow down, but he had such enthusiasm once he got going that it was difficult for him. When he did the voiceover for the onboard lap, we had to do it time and time again because he was speaking so fast and making so many off-the-cuff comments. Narrating that lap of the TT circuit probably took us about three hours.'

Wood also filmed Joey on home turf at the 1983 Ulster Grand Prix where he won his second consecutive TT Formula One world championship. Despite the pressures on him – trying to clinch a world title in dreadfully wet conditions in front of his expectant home crowd – Wood says Joey remained fully cooperative and seemed no different than normal. 'He was just the same. If he was tense, then he hid it very well. He made himself available to us all the time at the Ulster. Sometimes you could see that he seemed lost in thought, but he was probably going round the circuit in his head. He had superstar status in Ireland, and he got the kind of reaction I had only seen with the likes of Mike Hailwood,

Giacomo Agostini and Barry Sheene. And not just in Ireland, but at the TT too.'

Rob McElnea went head-to-head with Joey at Dundrod in the battle for the F1 world championship that year and, as they headed into that final round, was only 2 points behind him. But to win the title he would have to beat Joey on his own home turf in the pouring rain. No easy task. McElnea remembers throwing in the towel early. 'It was absolutely pissing down. I got the holeshot [first off the line] but rolled off at the first corner and Joey came past me and took off at a suicidal pace. I was never really up for riding in the rain on the roads and every time I came past that corner for the rest of the race there was a crowd of Irish fans giving me the wanker sign!'

Dunlop won the race by 33 seconds from Mick Grant with McElnea further back in third place, his bid for the title over.

V-Four Victory remains the only film that documented Joey over a full season of the TT Formula One world championship (with the exception of the Assen round) and it shows him at the peak of his powers. The film and, in particular, the onboard lap, proved to be a sensation on its release and led to more than one viewer falling out of their seat. When leading biking newspaper *Motor Cycle News* showed the film as part of its cinema road show that travelled around the country, David Wood got to see the impact his film had on audiences.

'I went to a couple of shows to see the audience reaction and it was hilarious to see rows of people swaying from side to side as they lived the dream of being on the bike!' he says. 'At one particular show, a group of Hells Angels came in a bit late and a bit worse for wear and sat down in the back row, just down from the projection box. As usual, the lads were soon riding along with Joey and when they got to Ballacraine a twenty-something-stone guy on the end seat leaned to his right and overdid it, crashing down into the aisle, sending his popcorn and beer everywhere, much to the amusement of his mates. Joey would have liked that.'

o

By 1983, the famous Joey Dunlop look was complete. He already rode with his famous number 3 whenever possible and, thanks to a new deal with Arai Europe, his famous helmet design was now perfected. He had been wearing a yellow helmet with a black stripe since the early days, but they had been made by Boeri and, later, Kangol/Top Tek. When Arai Europe founder Ferry Brouwer started sponsoring Joey, he came up with the classic design that has since become one of the most famous racing helmets of all time. 'I happened to mention that the design that Joey had on his Top Tek helmet was rather dull – a yellow helmet with just a black line going from front to rear,' Brouwer explains. 'So, I suggested making a small pinstripe that could go round the helmet and then Davy Woods mentioned Joey's sponsor, Downtown Radio, so that was included too. When the first helmet was made, I went back over to see Joey again and he loved it.'

Never one to be concerned about aesthetics, Joey had stuck with the simple design because it might offer him a slight advantage on occasion – not because it looked good. 'I never asked him about the origins of the yellow helmet with the black stripe, but I think that in those days people didn't pay particular attention to what kind of design they had,' Brouwer says. 'The only thing Joey happened to mention was that, because there weren't many people wearing a yellow helmet, he would always stand out, and so his pit crew would always see him coming. I think that's the main reason for that famous yellow helmet.'

Joey would be loyal to both Honda and Arai for the remainder of his career and became firm friends with Brouwer, who says that his Arai was the first helmet that actually fitted Joey properly. 'The only thing he asked for that was different from a standard Arai was if we could make the helmet sit a little higher up his forehead, so that he could see forward more when he had his chin on the fuel tank. He said that, to achieve this in the past, he had stuffed his helmet full of cloths, but I pointed out that this was not contributing to safety! So, back in Japan, they accommodated for that and made Joey's helmets with a few extra millimetres at the top of the visor aperture.'

The growing trend at the time was for riders to wear dark visors to prevent glare from the sun, but Joey was not a fan of this adaptation at first. 'He didn't like dark or tinted visors – he always preferred clear ones,' Brouwer says. 'When I asked him why, he said, "Being a road racer, you have different kinds of Tarmac and sometimes there are oil spills and, with a tinted visor, you can't see the changes of Tarmac and the spills so well – it lessens the contrast."'

The 1983 season had been a total triumph for Joey and marked the start of his utterly unique arrangement with Honda that allowed him the freedom he needed to thrive. He would ride official bikes for Honda in the TTF1 world championship and at all the big road races, as well as contesting various UK races where the Japanese manufacturer felt it should be represented. But he was also given the previous year's factory 998cc machine and a 250cc machine and was allowed to enter whatever Irish races he liked, under his own steam and with sponsorship from Downtown Radio. Joey could be his own man again, just the way he liked it.

Unimpressed with the chassis on the previous year's bike that Honda had given him, Joey and Mervyn 'Curly' Scott decided to build their own. Curly had been helping Joey out for years and was an expert welder; so expert that he built a lightweight aluminium frame to house the 998cc engine that Honda had allowed Joey to take home to work on. Obsessive about weight, Dunlop even managed to source some titanium nuts and bolts for the bike through a friend of Ferry Brouwer in Russia who had worked on MiG jet fighters. This was Joey in his element once more, working on his own bikes, throwing them in the back of a van, and going racing on 'proper' Irish circuits.

The *V-Four Victory* film had captured Joey's triumphs at the 1983 TT and Ulster Grand Prix, and its title referred to the fact that it was Honda's new 850cc V-Four that had helped him to achieve those victories. He also had a two-stroke RS500 Grand Prix machine at his disposal for various British championship races and the Senior TT, as well as his 250cc bike, and the 998cc special that himself and Curly Scott had built and that he could race wherever he liked.

Joey gave the RS500 two-stroke triple and the RS850 four-stroke V-Four their debuts at the North West 200 in 1983 where he was hounded by Hector Neill's latest rider, Norman Brown. Another Northern Irishman, Brown would break Joey's outright lap record at the TT just a few weeks later and looked like being the man to take the fight to Joey, who was by now Ireland's top rider. Brown won the 350cc race (which Joey did not contest) and finished ahead of Joey in the first Superbike race, but Joey managed to win the 500cc event and the feature North West 200 Superbike race, with Brown in second place. But Brown's glory was short-lived – he was killed in the British Grand Prix just a few months later. Yet another promising career cut short by tragedy.

With Ron Haslam now riding for Honda in 500cc Grands Prix, Joey's new team-mate for the 1983 season was Lincolnshire's Roger Marshall, who soon found that being Joey's team-mate was as much of a curse as a blessing. 'There was loads of pressure to win the F1 championship for Honda because, whoever won the championship got next year's new bike, and the one who didn't win got last year's bike – and the new bike was always going to be better,' Marshall says. 'Unfortunately, I was always runner-up to Joey, so I never got Honda's new bike!'

Barry Symmons says the arrangement was even more specific than that. 'There was only ever one genuine factory bike in the team. The Japanese were more concerned about winning the TT than the TT Formula One championship – they always felt the TT and the Ulster Grand Prix were the biggest part of that championship. So, as far as Honda was concerned, whoever could win those two events would get the contract for the factory bike the following year, so Roger Marshall always ended up riding the previous year's bike.'

Marshall had been racing against Joey since the mid-seventies but still didn't know him very well. 'He didn't say a lot, so I couldn't really weigh him up at all,' he says. 'He was his own man, he had his own group with him, and he kept himself to himself. I obviously got to know him better when we became Honda team-mates in 1983. I travelled the world quite a lot with Joey and got to know him quite well after that. Barry Symmons sometimes asked me to share a room with Joey, because a lot of people couldn't understand him when he was booking into hotels and suchlike.'

The two would be team-mates for the next four years and, while Marshall usually had the upper hand on short circuits, he admits that Joey was in another league on the roads. 'On short circuits, it was usually all about me, Wayne Gardner and Ron Haslam in the early eighties, but if Joey got out of bed on the right side, he could win on short circuits as well. He was so talented, but I don't think he had his whole heart in short-circuit racing. But on the roads... I've followed Joey so many times on the roads and I used to learn a lot. Hairpin bends and slow corners, you'd think he was going to the shops, but on quick bits, on fast courses where you can make up lots of time through the quick bits, Joey was phenomenal; he was so smooth and so quick it was fantastic to see him. Incredible.'

Ian Simpson is another rider who believes Joey could have been a successful short-circuit racer if his heart had been in it. As a five-times British champion, but also a winner of three TT races and five North West 200 races, 'Simmo' knows what it takes to win in both disciplines, and he feels Joey's short-circuit abilities have been overlooked. 'It annoys me when people say they saw Joey at one short-circuit race and that he wasn't any good. He might have been having a bad day, or just didn't want to stick his neck out particularly that day. But to say he couldn't have cut it on short circuits is absolute rubbish. In my opinion, if Joey had put his mind to it when he was younger, and concentrated on short circuits, he would have been as good as anybody. I mean, when he was doing short circuits, he was racing against the likes of Wayne Gardner, Ron Haslam and Roger Marshall and those boys were some of the best in the world.'

Simpson believes there's another reason Joey preferred the roads, apart from feeling so comfortable in amongst trees, walls and houses. 'There's a lot less bullshit in road racing than there is in short-circuit racing, and I think that's partly what attracted Joey to it,' he says. 'He was so down to earth and anti-bullshit and was just such a genuine person, so he was never going to be comfortable around all the hair gel and sunglasses that you see in the short-circuit paddocks.'

Barry Symmons also testifies that Joey was not just a roads specialist. 'Towards the end of the UK Streetbike series, which Joey contested in 1981 and 1982, he was amazing, and that was all on short circuits,' he says. 'He was a far better short-circuit rider than people give him credit for.'

At the 1983 TT, while being filmed for *V-Four Victory*, Joey picked up another win, and this time it was his first in the Formula One race – a race which he would make his own by winning it six times in a row, from 1983 through to 1988. After two years as a factory rider for Honda, this was the first time Joey had won a TTF1 world championship round. It was a much-needed victory. He was so dominant on the new Honda RS850 that he won by 53 seconds and took a massive 8.2 seconds off Mick Grant's existing lap record in the class from a standing start. He could, however, only manage third place in the Senior Classic TT, thanks to the blinding speed of Suzuki's rising star Rob McElnea.

Sitting on the banking just after the 11th Milestone during that Senior race was a young Steve Hislop. He would go on to become one of the all-time greats of the TT, and his account of what he saw that day not only reveals the inspiration he took from Dunlop, but also captures the speed, danger and thrill of the TT, and paints a vivid picture of Joey Dunlop at work. 'I could hear the bikes setting off over the radio, but it was some time before I could actually hear them on the road for real. Eventually, I picked up the sound of Norman Brown's Suzuki RG500 engine screaming along the mile-long Cronk-y-Voddy straight coming towards us, then he blasted into view and shocked the life out of me. Having seen the normal road traffic going past for the last couple of hours, words cannot describe the difference in speed as Brown went past our spectator point. Fuck me, he came through the corner at the end of Cronk-y-Voddy, down towards the 11th Milestone, lifted the front of the bike over a rise in the road, braked hard and back-shifted two gears, before changing direction and blasting off towards Handley's. He was going so fast he almost blew me off the bloody banking.'

Brown's pace was, in fact, so fast that he would run out of fuel, but Joey wasn't going any slower as, Hislop recalled. 'Joey was hot on his heels on a Honda RS850, and he had it up on the back wheel too, and was pushing every bit as hard as Brown. I was like, "For fuck's sake!" I just couldn't believe that anything on earth could go that fast.'

Rob McElnea would also beat Joey in the second round of the TT Formula One championship at Assen in the Netherlands, a race that was held alongside the 500cc Grand Prix world championship round, meaning the crowd was massive. This was the first time the championship had taken in a round at a short circuit, and that played into the hands of the likes of McElnea who was a more committed short-circuit rider. 'Going to Assen for the first time and beating Joey Dunlop on the last lap in front of 300,000 people was one of the highlights of my entire career,' McElnea admits.

Joey might have been the reigning world champion, but he still wasn't interested in staying in five-star hotels. He had arrived at Assen in his Ford Capri and had been found sleeping under it, with only a blanket for comfort, before Hector Neill offered him a corner of his caravan to curl up in. Neill was attending the race because his rider, Norman Brown, was competing in the 500cc Grand Prix race. With a gang of his own countrymen to party with, Joey didn't miss the opportunity, and those in the paddock could hear accordions and spoons being played until the small hours on the night before the F1 race.

But as much as he loved his drinking and his late nights, Joey's racing never suffered. Barry Symmons remembers his professionalism. 'When we were going to Vila Real or somewhere else on the continent, Joey would take a few mates and they'd sleep in the van and go round and visit places of interest and make a trip out of it. I remember him reversing his van into a parking space at Hockenheim one year. The back doors were open and, when he stopped, an empty three-litre bottle of vodka rolled out, so it had obviously been a good trip! He was always there at the right time though – we had no complaints at all about his professionalism. Things were slightly different in those days though.'

He may have been part of the mighty Honda Britain team, but Don Morley remembers Joey very much doing his own thing as far as transport and accommodation went. 'He never travelled with Honda to foreign race meetings; he used to go over to the continent in a cattle truck with his mates,' he says. 'He hadn't even converted it, so there was no kitchen or bunks or anything – there was just a camping stove and some inflatable Li-los to sleep on. Joey and his gang would get drunk every night in the paddock. He had very little to do with the Honda team, as far as I could see. He had his own van and did his own thing.'

Although Rob McElnea had beaten Joey on the final lap of the F1 race at Assen after a fearsomely close battle, there were clearly no hard feelings on Joey's part. 'Immediately afterwards, Joey and I went back up to the top of the stand to watch the 500cc race and Joey brought a large bottle of vodka,' McElnea later recalled.[26]

McElnea's heart lay in 500cc Grands Prix rather than in F1, but he did enjoy his time in the series. 'I did it at a time when it was a really big thing. It was only three rounds then – the TT, Assen and the Ulster GP – but the factories took it seriously. It lost its way a little bit by going to some strange circuits. I thought it was the best thing since sliced bread while I was doing it, but afterwards it seemed to have lost a bit of kudos.'

McElnea may well have won the title in 1983, had it not been for the wet final round at Dundrod where Joey was untouchable, riding at his 'suicidal' pace. Joey had proved a point at Assen though: finishing second to an inspired McElnea proved he could cut the mustard on short circuits when he had to, which was just as well since the F1 championship would take in more of these kind of tracks as it expanded and grew throughout the mid-eighties.

Johnny Rea, for one, wasn't surprised at Joey's pace around Assen. 'He was a fantastic short circuit rider,' he says. 'Joey was brought up doing both road circuits and short circuits and so was I, but you definitely get more enjoyment out of winning a road race than you do a short-circuit race. I loved both, but Joey just seemed to prefer the roads.'

Rob McElnea would later become an outstanding team manager in the British Superbike Championship and clearly has an eye for spotting riding talent. So, it carried a lot of weight when he told journalist Jimmy Walker: 'Joey had a great talent – what a pity he didn't try to win the Grand Prix world championships. I think he would have gone close in that high grade.'

Joey Dunlop, on a par with eighties Grand Prix legends like Freddie Spencer, Eddie Lawson, Kevin Schwantz and Wayne Rainey? It's high praise indeed, but not so far-fetched as it might sound. Joey had raced regularly against Gardner, who went on to become 500cc world champion in 1987. Gardner had dabbled in pure road racing, but his focus had always been on short circuits. If Joey could beat him on occasion (as he did) on short circuits, what might he have achieved if he had focused on that style of riding rather than on the different discipline of road racing? It's a question that will never be answered, but McElnea's statement speaks volumes.

In 1983 Joey's V-Four handled better than the Suzukis, but at 850cc compared to the Suzuki's 997cc machines, it was down on power, so Honda would fly in a bigger 920cc version of their V-Four to ensure Joey won the Ulster Grand Prix and, with it, the world championship.

Dunlop rounded out the year with further victories at Mondello

Park and Aghadowey, although Johnny Rea did manage to beat him in one leg of the two-part John Player race there. Over the next decade or so, Rea would have close battles with Dunlop on both the roads and the 'shorts', and he was clearly impressed by what he saw. 'He [Dunlop] was very determined. *Very,* determined. But he was also so naturally talented it was unreal. He was a fantastic rider. He was so smooth that he didn't look quick, but if you tried to follow him, you'd get into bother! At the Ulster Grand Prix – up the back of the circuit through Budore and places like that – he would just come below you going 30mph faster than you were going. He would always give you plenty of room though. I would be using all of the road and he would still have a couple of feet spare everywhere. He was unreal to watch.'

And yet, despite Rea being such a threat out on track, Joey went out of his way to help the son of the man who had done so much for him. 'He had this knack of leaving people wanting more of him, you know?' Rea says. 'He was really funny like that. And if he could help you, he would help you. There was one time he helped me build my 750 in time to get to the Tandragee. He was racing at that meeting himself, but he worked with me on my bike until midnight and then he took me down to the Tandragee to show me round the course. He didn't get back to Ballymoney until about 3am and then had to get his own van packed up.'

Japanese race fans got their chance to see Dunlop in action at the Suzuka 8 Hours race in 1983. At that time, the 8 Hours was the most important single race in the motorcycling world or, at least, it was to the Japanese manufacturers, who viewed it as a unique opportunity to show their superiority in front of over 200,000 local fans, and in front of each other. With Honda owning the circuit, the 8 Hours was even more important to Joey's employers. Many of the top Grand Prix riders competed at the event in the

1980s, at the behest of their respective employers, so it was one of the most competitive fields Joey had ever raced against, but he wasn't given the proper tools to do the job. Barry Symmons had arranged for him and Roger Marshall to ride for Hirotoshi Honda (son of company founder Soichiro Honda) with the understanding that Honda would provide an exotic V-Four machine. But the bike turned out to be an old inline, four-cylinder that was dog-slow. 'We were both on top class bikes in England and in the TT Formula One world championship and they wanted us to ride for Soichiro Honda's son's team,' Marshall remembers. 'We thought we were going to be on a really trick bike, but it was dreadful. After the first test on it, Joey wanted to go home. All hell broke loose. Barry Symmons wasn't there but he was constantly on the phone, saying, "You've got to keep Joey there! You've got to keep him there!" Joey was very unhappy about riding that bike – it was so slow and was clearly just built to finish the race, but we were used to winning, and it was all I could do to keep Joey there. I put a lot of effort in and managed to qualify about twelfth, which was the best the bike could do – and that was just a one-off lap. When it came to stuff like that, Joey wasn't interested; he was there to win.'

Dunlop and Marshall could only manage lap times that were some 8 seconds off the pace of the leaders. As a final affront, the bike expired early in the race, but Ferry Brouwer remembers seeing Joey put in some stunning performances at Suzuka over the years, despite being shoddily treated by his Honda employers on more than one occasion. 'It was a big Honda event and there were so many Japanese mechanics swarming around Joey's bike and fiddling with things without Joey knowing about it,' Brouwer says.' So, he went out with the TT Formula One bike and, as he rolled up to the grid, he said, "Ah, Jesus, somebody's been fiddling with the rear suspension." I mean, he felt it immediately – the fact that they had very slightly increased the pre-load. They had also taken the Formula One engine out of the bike and put a standard road bike engine in. Barry Symmons was really angry.'

It didn't end there. 'Then, Joey had to compete in the Formula Three class, and Honda had given him an older model of bike than they had given to their two Japanese riders,' Brouwer continues. 'Their bikes had single-sided swingarms and all sorts, while Joey's bike just had old twin-shock suspension. I'll never forget that Joey just said, "Ach, it doesnae matter – I'll gi' them stick." He went absolutely berserk out on track and those two Japanese riders had no chance. One tried to stay with Joey and crashed, and Joey finished about 20 seconds ahead of the other one. Barry Symmons looked at the big Honda boss and said, "That serves you right for changing engines in Joey's F1 bike." When Joey had a point to prove, he could dig extra deep and really pull out a performance.'

Symmons was also impressed with Joey's pace around Suzuka. 'Some of his performances at the 8 Hour were impressive,' he says. 'He was up there with the best in the world and was holding his own.'

To round the season out, Joey took in another far-flung meeting at Macau on his Formula One bike, while Honda team-mates Ron Haslam and Roger Marshall rode their 500cc Grand Prix machines. Haslam, now a Grand Prix podium man, won both legs with Marshall and Dunlop taking a second and a third place apiece. It was as close as Joey would get to winning the event that he viewed more as of an end-of-season holiday than a serious race.

The 1983 season had been a lucrative one for Joey, not that he cared. Honda was paying him handsomely and he picked up £10,250 in prize money just for winning the Formula One TT. On top of all his other prize money, there was also money coming in from sponsors, but he never did push for better financial deals and sometimes didn't even bother accepting money from Honda at all.

Despite a general belief that Joey never actually had a contract with Honda, and instead sealed any deal with a simple handshake, Barry Symmons says that wasn't the case, in the early years at least. 'We had proper written contracts in those days and Joey was properly paid up until the Honda Britain race team folded in 1986. Whether it was all done with a handshake after that, and whether he got paid anything after that, I don't know, but I don't believe he was. But we certainly paid him and, from year two, we also supported his other racing activities with bikes and that sort of thing.'

Neil Tuxworth, who took over the running of the reformed Honda Britain team in 1990 and worked with Joey for the next ten years, testifies that Honda tried to pay Dunlop, but they weren't always successful. 'He very rarely signed a contract when I was team manager at Honda Britain,' he says. 'I think he signed a contract about twice. I would always post one out to him, but he very rarely signed them or sent them back. If I rang him about it he would say, "Of course I'll ride for Honda – I always do. I don't need to sign a piece of paper."'

Bob McMillan, who became general manager of Honda UK in 1987, knew that Joey didn't operate like any other rider and was happy to allow a more relaxed arrangement between Joey and Honda. 'I told Neil Tuxworth that I didn't need Joey to sign a contract,' he says. 'I just wanted him to be looked after, with all the bikes and all the parts he needed. But Neil is very correct in the way he works, so he insisted that everybody had to have a contract, so that everything was clearly laid out in black and white. That's the correct way to operate with every other rider, but I don't think Joey wanted to be tied to a contract and I don't think he needed one, either – he would do everything we asked of him. If we wanted him at the NEC bike show, he would be there, if we wanted him at the Alexandra Palace show, he would be there – he would even stand in the queue to buy his own tickets! He wouldn't even think to ring me up and say, "Bob, could you send me some tickets."'

The Honda Britain team fielded its riders in many different championships, from Grands Prix to British racing and the TT Formula One world championship, and Symmons says they were all paid roughly the same, no matter where they raced. 'In those days, our riders were paid very similar amounts, so I'm pleased to say that Joey did rather well out of it. But he got an awful lot of start money in Northern Ireland too, and a lot of prize money as well. After the trouble that Ron Haslam had with the tax man – he nearly lost everything – we convinced Joey to get a proper accountant.'

Armed with advice from his accountant, Joey decided to invest in his future. There were to be no flash cars or mansions with swimming pools though; instead, one of the most famous motorcycle racers in the world decided to buy his local pub. In 1984, Joey Dunlop, double world champion, started pulling pints and cleaning ashtrays.

CHAPTER 8

HIMSELF

'I REMEMBER BEER BOTTLES ROLLING ACROSS THE TRACK IN FRONT OF ME AT VILA REAL.'
Paul Iddon

Joey Dunlop always got along well with his team-mates. He kept himself to himself and was never confrontational, argumentative, needy, jealous or unsporting. In fact, it's practically impossible to find anyone that has a bad word to say about him. Roger Marshall is no exception, but in 1984 the two Honda Britain team-mates came to loggerheads in their battle to become F1 world champion. As Paul Fowler wrote in that year's edition of the bike-racing annual *Motocourse*: 'The tensions that bubbled beneath the surface in the Honda Britain camp erupted in a manner which hasn't been seen between rival team-mates in many a day.'[27]

Although he had come from a similarly poor background to Joey and, in his earlier racing years, had shared the same straggly long hair and unkempt appearance, Marshall had smartened himself up, cut his hair, and was more media-friendly than Dunlop ever would be. He was outgoing and had an easy charm, hence the speculation amongst some Irish race fans that Honda would rather see Marshall winning the F1 title as he was a more marketable commodity. These rumours were not lost on Joey, who may well have had similar suspicions. The catalyst for this intra-team rivalry would occur at the second round of the championship at Assen, but first there was the TT to take care of and, before that, the North West 200.

The North West brought its usual bag of mixed results for Joey. His bikes broke down in both the 250cc race and the feature North West 200 Superbike race, but he did at least dominate the opening MCN Masters Superbike race in wet conditions after both Mick Grant and Roger Marshall crashed out. With points being offered in the MCN-backed race (which formed part of a season-long championship mostly held on English short circuits), Joey's win meant he took the lead in the series though he would ultimately finish third behind Wayne Gardner and Rob McElnea, having opted not to contest every round.

He had been lucky to participate in the North West at all, after damaging his wrist and shoulder in a spill at Mondello Park the previous week. Once again, he turned to his 'charmer' – Joey's belief in Matt Gibson's methods had a powerful effect and he passed his pre-race medical at the North West.

The opening race of the Formula One world championship at the TT was packed with drama, not only for Joey but for most of his rivals. Having built up a fifty-second lead over Marshall, Joey then noticed clouds of blue smoke pouring from his 920cc V-Four, forcing him to stop at Braddan Bridge on the third lap, and then again at Union Mills just a few miles further along the track. 'I got off and parked her against the hedge,' he later explained. 'I thought the rear wheel had jammed, gave her a kick, then noticed that the exhaust pipe was jamming against the tyre.'[28]

In his frustrated state, Joey was uncharacteristically rude to two fans who tried to help him push-start his V-Four. Knowing that any outside assistance would see him disqualified from the race, he momentarily lost his temper in the heat of the moment and told them to 'fuck off'. He push-started the bike himself and rejoined the race some 24 seconds down on Marshall. The episode had cost him one minute and 14 seconds. With the red mist descended (a favoured expression amongst racers to describe riding angry), Joey shattered the lap record and circulated at almost 115.89mph, while Marshall's machine began to develop its own exhaust and fuelling problems. The Suzukis of Grant and McElnea both broke down, but the new F1 rules were already against them: the capacity limit had been dropped down to 750cc and, while Honda already had a year's worth of development on its V-Four (which, despite being bored out to 850 and then 920cc the previous year, was based on a 750cc motor), Suzuki was in new territory, and it showed.

With the Suzukis out, the race became a straight fight between Dunlop and Marshall. By now 'crabbit and angry' as he himself admitted, Joey rode like a man possessed and by Ramsey hairpin on the last lap – some 12 miles from home – he had cut Marshall's advantage down to 11 seconds. By the Bungalow, it was down to just five seconds and, from then on, Marshall didn't stand a chance. While Marshall's bike continued to slow due to the exhaust and fuelling problems, Joey just rode harder and harder, setting a new outright lap record on his way to beating his team-mate by 20 seconds at the chequered flag. It was round one to Dunlop.

Both the Junior and Senior TT races were disasters for Joey, however. His 250cc Honda broke down on the fifth of six laps, but it was a mistake of his own that finally ruled him out of the Senior.

Rob McElnea was one of very few riders who could beat Joey Dunlop in his prime at the TT. He only competed there for three years before moving over to 500cc Grands Prix, but he had won in his second year and was now blisteringly fast and knew his way around the course almost as well as Dunlop.

The Senior race was a titanic to-and-fro battle between Dunlop and McElnea, with the lead changing constantly. McElnea smashed the outright lap record on his second circuit with a speed of 118.23mph and took an eight-second lead but, by half distance, Joey led by 19 seconds. On lap five, Dunlop raised the bar even higher with a lap at 118.48mph. That astonishing lap gave him a 40-second lead and the race looked to be over when news came through that Joey had stopped at the Bungalow on the last lap, just a few miles from home. There were suggestions at the time that he had run out of fuel but, years later, Davy Wood said, 'The real problem was a broken oil seal along the gearbox. This caused the engine to seize, breaking the crankshaft. It was unfortunate, to say the least, for he had the race won.'

Wood, it seems, was trying to save face for his rider, as Joey himself later admitted his mistake, saying, 'I had one hell of a battle with Rob McElnea. We were both on 500s and I stopped on the last lap at the Bungalow when I ran out of petrol. I was concentrating so hard on the race that I came in to refuel on the wrong lap and got totally confused.'

McElnea still remembers that Senior clearly. 'That was a hard race – the 500 was a real handful round the TT. It was much harder work than the big four-stroke, 1000cc Suzuki – it was just so much more intense. Every gear shift was crucial and, once it started moving, you really had to hang on. There are two things I'll always remember about that race; one was that the sun was going down and my visor was covered in flies, but I still spotted Joey's bright yellow helmet by the side of the road and knew he was out. The other was the 32nd Milestone, which you probably get correct about twice in a lifetime, and on the last lap I got it absolutely inch perfect. It was a beautiful day and the roads were bone dry, but as I came out of the 32nd there was a wet patch right on the white line. It must have seeped up from underground and I slid right across the road – I'll never forget it. I've no idea how I got away with it.'

McElnea recovered from his monster slide and held on to win the race, but would never return to the TT. His decision to retire from the event was based on cold, hard logic. 'I loved doing the TT but the law of averages stack up if you keep doing it. I decided in January of 1984, without telling anyone else, that I wouldn't be doing the TT any more after that one. I told my team and my wife on the Friday night after winning the Classic that it would be my last TT.'

Opting to carve out a career on much safer Grands Prix circuits, the irony of what happened the next day was not lost on McElnea. 'We then flew to France for the Grand Prix and the next morning I broke my bloody leg at Paul Ricard!'

McElnea stuck to his decision and never did return to the TT. Joey Dunlop must have breathed a sigh of relief.

The next round of the TTF1 championship was held at Assen, and it was during the pit stops that things started to get nasty between Dunlop and Marshall. While Joey cut his engine during his refuelling stop – as the rules stated he must – Marshall apparently did not and, by breaking the rules (however intentionally), he gained an advantage and went on to win the race. To this day, Marshall denies any wrongdoing. 'They said I didn't stop the engine during the pit stop. The pit stops were so quick back then because we had dump cans [quick-filler systems] so you hardly had time to breathe – it was just "bang" and off you went again. I had a rapid stop and the team pushed me off but then it was claimed I didn't stop my engine, but I did: my engine was definitely stopped. That caused some aggro, though, and it left a bad taste. Joey never confronted me directly, it was his entourage who did that.'

As Barry Symmons remembers it, Marshall *did* fail to cut his engine, but Symmons himself now admits culpability for the oversight. 'I suppose I must take responsibility for that,' he says. 'I didn't remind Roger and his mechanics that they had to turn his engine off during his refuelling stop. It was my fault – which I didn't admit to them! There was a bit of a row about it because it was against the rules. I don't know quite what happened in the end because we weren't pulled up in front of the stewards. Someone eventually shouted, "Turn your engine off!" but the fuel stop was half over by then.'

Joey had led the race all the way up to the fuel stop but, while Marshall was in and out of the pits in seconds, Joey's stop took much longer. Marshall won the race by a full 13 seconds, most of which had been achieved by his ultra-fast pit stop. Dunlop, for one of the very few times in his life, was furious. He demanded that Symmons lodge a protest against Marshall for breaking the rules but, understandably, Symmons refused to protest a member of his own team. After all, what team, boss would? Protesting would also have revealed Symmons' own part in the cock-up. He remained silent.

There was, however, nothing to stop another rider protesting and someone did persuade fourth-place finisher Mile Pajic to do so. How could he have known Marshall didn't stop his engine unless someone in Joey's camp informed him? Who it might have been has never been revealed, but it didn't matter anyway – protests had to be lodged within an hour of the race ending and Pajic was too late. His protest was thrown out and the result stood: Dunlop and Marshall left the Netherlands equal on points.

Next up was the Vila Real street circuit in Portugal, about as different to Assen as a circuit could possibly be. 'Vila Real was very fast, but the surface was always covered in sand,' Mick Grant remembers. 'It was a road circuit and it was dangerous. I mean, people would have kittens nowadays if you suggested holding a race there, but at the time it was no big deal.'

Paul Iddon, who would soon start to challenge Joey for the F1 title, also remembers the chaotic nature of the circuit. 'I remember beer bottles rolling across the track in front of me at Vila Real. It wasn't done on purpose – the spectators just dropped them and they rolled onto the circuit. I remember following Andy McGladdery and his bike was spewing fuel over me because he'd over-filled it. At the same time a beer bottle rolled in front of me, and I also had so much sweat streaming down my face and congealing round my mouth that I could have chewed it off my lips.'

Even Roger Marshall admits Vila Real was a lethal place to race. 'You had to keep the bike upright as you crossed the tram lines and then whack it straight onto its side for the following corner. You also had to cross a bridge over the river – it was quite a scary place to go to, much worse than the TT or the Ulster GP circuits.'

For Joey Dunlop, the scarier the better. The roads were his arena and he should have had an advantage in Portugal, but the 100-degree heat proved to be his downfall in 1984. His lifestyle wasn't exactly that of a top athlete; Joey was happier relaxing with a vodka and a cigarette than he ever was going to the gym and, in Portugal against Marshall, his lack of fitness showed. Marshall was one of the fittest riders in the UK and regularly trained with Grimsby Town football club. The searing heat of Portugal was not an issue for him, and he finished the race a full minute ahead of his exhausted team-mate. Joey had to be lifted off his machine, stretchered away, and put on a drip to replace all the fluids he had lost. Barry Symmons even had to stand in for him on the podium.

The championship had swung back in Marshall's favour, but that didn't count for much since the next round would be at Dundrod. Joey would be back in his natural habitat, in a climate he was more accustomed to, and in front of his home fans. The race was as good as his before it had even started. Or so it appeared on paper. In reality, things turned out differently.

To the astonishment and dismay of Joey's fiercely loyal home fans, Marshall led for most of the race, and it seemed Dunlop had no answer. Until, that is, the pair approached the terrifyingly fast Windmill Corner. On the last lap of the race, and fast running out of options, Joey dived underneath Marshall in a move that Marshall described as 'lunatic'. Joey won the race by 2.6 seconds from his infuriated team-mate, who immediately confronted Barry Symmons and demanded he lodge a protest against Joey for dangerous riding. He had, according to Marshall, forced his way through, causing Marshall's bike to suffer what's known in the trade as a 'tank-slapper' (where the handlebars shake from side to side so violently, they threaten to throw the rider off). Some eyewitnesses claimed the move was clean and perfectly executed, and that Marshall had simply been taken by surprise as it wasn't a normal place to pass. Joey agreed. 'I went through, but we didn't touch,' he said in his defence. 'I just don't think Roger expected me to pass him there.'

Marshall was fuming. 'I took Budore corner the best I had ever taken it,' he says. 'It's a frightening right-hander but, if you get it right, it gives you great drive up towards Windmill and Wheeler's corner. So, I took Budore perfectly and thought, "Fantastic!" but then, as I tipped into Windmill, Joey came under me. Really, there was no room; I lifted my bike and skimmed the bank and, instead of driving out and getting down behind the screen, I had to change down the gearbox to get going again. To me it was a bad move, which wasn't like Joey. That was the last lap. I did nearly catch him again but, obviously, I came second and I was fuming. It was very rare that I lost it in racing, but I did that day. It all got a bit confrontational in the pits and Barry Symmons was trying to calm it all down. I was very irate, but I don't think Joey said much – which he never did anyway!'

Symmons, officially at least, said nothing. Instead, he took each rider aside separately and tried to calm them down. He couldn't protest a member of his own team, he had to explain for the second time in three races. There was to be no protest. The result would stand.

Some of Joey's fans, hearing of Marshall's outrage and still being angry about Symmons' handling of the Assen debacle, sabotaged the Honda Britain race truck and hurled abuse at both Marshall and Symmons. It was getting ugly. 'Joey had a lot of fanatical supporters,' Marshall says. 'I mean, I had a lot of Irish supporters too, because they liked to see me going over there and taking Joey on. Not every Irishman was a Joey fan! They appreciated you going over there to race. But some of Joey's fans got it into their heads that Honda wanted me to win the title that year, not Joey. I have no idea where that came from.'

The TT Formula One world championship had been expanded to five rounds in 1984, with the final race being held on the street circuit of Zolder in Belgium for the first time. Going into that final round, things simply could not have been any closer between Dunlop and Marshall: they had both scored two wins and two second places and both had exactly the same number of points – 54. The whole season, and the outcome of the world championship, would come down to one single race.

Marshall, who had always got along well with Joey, decided it was time to bury the hatchet over the Ulster Grand Prix incident. 'The last race was in Belgium that year and it was all over the papers

– all this supposed aggro between me and Joey. But when we got to Zolder, I went up to Joey and I shook his hand and said, "Look, let's get on with it – may the best man win" and then we got back on-track together.'

It rained all weekend, but that didn't bother the hundreds of Irish fans who, still convinced that Honda was backing Marshall for the title, turned up to ensure fair play. Symmons tried to reassure everyone that it was down to the best man on the day: 'The bikes are the same, we've done everything we can – a Honda's going to win, so really it shouldn't matter to me, but I know if anything goes wrong with Joey's bike there's going to be some angry Irishmen.'

For the first twelve laps of the race, Dunlop and Marshall duelled it out at the front of the pack, Marshall just seeming to have the edge. It really did look as if it was going down to the wire. But then it was Marshall's bike, not Dunlop's, that developed a problem, and started to slow. Joey took the lead as Marshall coasted into the pits to have his machine checked over. His mechanics couldn't see any obvious problem so sent him out again but, before Marshall had even managed to exit pit lane, the head gasket on his bike blew and his championship aspirations ended in a cloud of steam. It was over. Marshall made straight for his friend and former mechanic Roger Burnett's caravan and cried his eyes out while Joey, who had eventually finished second to Miles Pajic and was delighted to become world champion for the third consecutive year, wished he hadn't won it in such a manner. 'I'd rather have beaten Roger fair and square in a race than have mechanical failure decide things, but that's racing,' he said.[29]

The fierce rivalry between Dunlop and Marshall had kept race fans enthralled throughout the season and at the end of it all Joey was voted *Motor Cycle News* Man of the Year. A highly prestigious award at the time, it was made even more special since it was voted for by readers of the weekly newspaper: it was the people's vote. Those readers were free to vote for any motorcycling hero in the world that year, from 500cc Grand Prix champion Eddie Lawson to the retiring Barry Sheene, who had just completed his last season of racing. But they didn't, they chose Joey Dunlop. They chose Himself.

That awards night, at the Hippodrome in London, was significant for another reason – it was the first time that Joey would meet Bob McMillan. Then Honda's national sales manager, McMillan would soon become Honda UK's general manager and would prove to be one of Joey's greatest supporters. He would also become a close friend. The pair bonded that night over vodka and whisky.

'Barry Symmons asked me if I would look after Joey that night, so that was the first time, really, I got to know him,' says McMillan. 'He was the man that everybody revered, but he was just such an ordinary lad. We went to the pub next door and Joey started drinking vodka and I started drinking whisky and, before long, I realised I was in the company of a serious drinker! The MCN lads had to come and find us in the pub, because Joey was due on stage. The fans around him were so adoring but he was just an ordinary bloke. After the awards were over, Joey was driven up to Stranraer to get the ferry back home, but I was really ill, and, as I was walking back to my hotel, I had to nip down an alleyway to be sick. I enjoyed his company so much, though – we just seemed to gel.'

It was the beginning of a formidable partnership, and one that would produce some astonishing results. And more than a few hangovers.

○

Joey celebrated his third world title in his own pub. Now a motorcycling mecca renamed Joey's Bar, it was called The Square

Peg at the time Joey bought it, but he and Linda changed the name to The Railway Tavern as it formed part of Ballymoney train station. Cannily thinking ahead to retirement, and perhaps realising that he wasn't cut out for a team manager's job when he did hang up his leathers, the pub was an investment in the future for Joey and would provide another source of income for his growing family. The pub also had sentimental value – it was the same place where the Armoy Armada had essentially made their headquarters, and where Joey had spent many a happy night with Mervyn Robinson and Frank Kennedy. It was filled with memories.

Joey was also having a new house built on the Garryduff Road, just a few miles south-east of Ballymoney, and within easy reach of his pub. It wasn't flash, just a humble bungalow, and there would never be any sports cars parked in the driveway, but it was by far the most luxurious house Joey or any of his family had ever lived in. Naturally, he made sure it had a spacious garage, enabling him plenty of room to do what he loved best – work on his bikes. As a painfully shy country boy from a poor family, he hadn't done too badly for himself, all things considered. He had a still-growing family that he doted on, he had a new house being built to his specifications (the family would live in a caravan in the driveway while the house was being built), and he had his own pub as a source of income for the future, as well as his renewed contract with Honda (whether or not he signed it). Life was good.

Yet while he was now the acknowledged master of one of the most dangerous sports in the world, it wasn't the Isle of Man TT course or the hideously dangerous streets of Vila Rea that would leave him fighting for his life in just a few months' time: it was the Irish Sea. In 1985, the boat that Joey Dunlop was travelling to the Isle of Man TT in, sank.

CHAPTER 9

TORNAMONA

'JOEY HAD TO GET OVERBOARD WITH A PENKNIFE AND CUT US FREE. HE CERTAINLY SAVED ALL OUR LIVES.'

Andy Inglis

Killard Point, Strangford Lough, 54° 19' 00" North, 05° 31' 30" West

12.17am, Sunday, 26 May 1985

It was blacker than black: pitch dark out near the entry of Strangford Lough, the largest inlet in the British Isles. When the tide is low there it exposes dangerous rocks and reefs and, with strong tidal currents, it's a dangerous stretch of water to navigate.

There were twelve men aboard the sixty-five-foot *Tornamona* which, contrary to popular belief, was not a converted fishing boat but rather a converted Royal Navy target-towing vessel and mine sweeper that had been used in World War II.

The *Tornamona* weighed fifty tons and was launched in 1943 but was sold into private hands in 1966 and converted into a pleasure boat. By 1985, it was owned by one Archie Lappin. Ever since he had travelled to the TT aboard the boat and won the Jubilee race in 1977, a superstitious Joey Dunlop had regarded the *Tornamona* as something of a lucky charm and Lappin had taken him to the Isle of Man on it every year since. 'I always came over, near enough, on the fishing boat,' Joey said. 'We always did the Cookstown on the Saturday and then we had to be here [the Isle of Man] for Monday and there was no other way over.'

In the small hours of 26 May, the vessel was once again on its way from Portaferry to Peel in the Isle of Man, a journey that would usually take the *Tornamona* around six hours. As well as the twelve men and seven race bikes, there were also racing leathers, crash helmets, fuel tanks, and spare parts for the bikes aboard the vessel. The boat had left with the tide but then turned back to collect Brian Reid's bike, which had turned up late at the dockside. In the time it took to load Reid's machine the tide had turned, exposing the dangerous rocks and reefs at the entrance to Strangford Lough. Those rocks and reefs presented no problem at high tide, but they could be lethal when the water was lower.

'You're into the narrows there, you see,' says RNLI Helmsman Mark Browne, whose pager started beeping shortly after midnight. 'You're just this side of the bar mouth itself, so the tide's boiling there and there's a big ridge of rocks. Outside the bar, you've got about seven or eight fathoms of water, then you've got five, then you're back into seven or eight again. And there's rocks right up through that whole area and miniature whirlpools too, so it's a hazardous stretch of water. If you get wind and tide out there, it's rough.'

The darkness didn't help matters either. 'There's no lights on

St Patrick's Rock and when the tide starts to rise it covers it, so it would be very hard to see,' explains helmsman John Murray, whose pager also started to beep frantically that night.

Joey and Robert Dunlop were down in the depths of the boat, trying to get some sleep in their bunks. 'You were down in the hull of the boat, you know, quite low down, and there was really big thuds as the boat hits the water, but there was one a wee bit louder than the rest,' Robert later explained. 'I was sort of half sleeping, but Joey knew there was something wrong – I didn't realise anything was wrong, but Joey did. Obviously, that woke me up a bit cos I was half sleeping, and I seen Joey disappearing up through the wee hatch and then he puts his head down in through and says "Right, everybody out!"'[30]

The *Tornamora* had struck St Patrick's Rock and lost her rudder. Drifting in a rough sea with strong currents, she then struck Angus Rock and began to sink rapidly. The Belfast coastguard received a distress call at 12.17am and sent out a lifeboat crew from Portaferry. The rescue team reached the *Tornamora* thirty-seven minutes after receiving the first mayday call. A second call had been made twenty-one minutes after the original, with the skipper informing the coastguard that they were abandoning ship as water had drenched the vessel's batteries and they were about to lose communications.

'We were down in the bottom of the boat in these bunks trying to get some sleep,' Joey explained. 'It just started getting wild rough. It's always rough getting out through the bar mouth and the next thing there was this massive "bang!" and all the lights went out and everything just flew everywhere and, more or less, that was it. We knew we'd hit something. I actually thought, for a minute or two, it was another boat cos it was really dark by this time. But, once I got up to the top, I saw the bits of rock sticking up and I knew we were in big trouble.'[31]

Having run aground on Angus Rock, the *Tornamona* was now foundering badly in the angry, foaming white waters. Within five minutes of the collision, it sank some forty feet to the gravel bottom of the inky seabed. There was very little time for thinking or planning, and three of the men on board couldn't swim. Joey's long-term helper, Andy Inglis, was one of them. 'There was no lifebelts or nothin' so, Joey, he emptied the jerrycans and told us all to get a hold of a jerrycan. I had just turned over onto my face cos I couldn't swim so I thought I may as well get this over quick.'

Robert Dunlop, now an up-and-coming racer himself and known for having nerves of steel, started praying. 'I was afraid. I was afraid that night and I prayed. I did indeed. I was scared for my life. You know, I've had manys a scare on motorbikes, but never nothing like that.'[32]

Joey thought it was all over, too. 'I didn't think we would make it. It was really hard. Yer man [from the Portaferry Lifeboat] told us to keep out of the water cos of the rocks. The sea was just thumping against the rocks. Once we got away from the rocks, there was three of us couldn't swim. I was a bit worried then because it's hard on your friends. What do you do? Do you just jump in and leave them standing? Everything was going through your mind. Once we got the dinghies, it wasn't so bad.'

Even the seemingly fearless Joey Dunlop admitted to being scared. 'Aye, I was frightened alright,' he said. 'We'd almost geen up, so we had. Once we got off the rocks and got out a wee bit it was a bit calmer, so that kinna geen us a bit more spirit again. While it was on the rocks, we'd no chance. Yer man just told us to try and hing on to the boat to try and get off the rocks. "Try and get intae that water and you're beat," he says.'

For Joey, the scariest moment was when the boat was stuck on the rocks, being broken apart and threatening to dash the men to their deaths. 'We were just hingin' on an' the waves were comin' clean ower the tap o' us. We were just hingin' on to a wire rope and that was it. Just sitting, praying, hoping she was gonna come aff the rocks.'

Andy Inglis, who had resigned himself to drowning and was trying to get it over with quickly, remembers seeing salvation in the form of the Portaferry RNLI. 'A lifeguard came in a wee rubber dinghy thing. I can see the big man yet, with a ginger beard and the drips of water just dropping off him. So, he got us in, then we realised we were still tied to the boat – this rubber dinghy was still tied to the boat. So, Joey had to get overboard with a penknife and cut us free. He certainly saved all our lives. He kept a very calm head. He just walked about the same as he walked about the pits and was never one bit excited.'[33]

According to all reports, as scared as he was, Joey remained completely calm throughout the ordeal. 'Water started to come in and we went to look for life jackets but there were none,' he said. 'The captain, he was running about, shouting "Every man for himself." He'd a big suit on and he was alright. Some of the men couldn't swim so I started to empty some of the jerrycans out in the sea and that started a bit of a row as they said it might start a fire if there was a spark. But I was using the cans for them to float on. We were in the water and I remember seeing a dinghy lashed to the deck, so I swam down and tried to cut it loose.'[34]

Davy Wood was understandably impressed by his rider's bravery and coolness. 'Joey was again an unsung hero because several of the boys were not swimmers of any good degree and Joey tied petrol cans around them and lowered them gently into the water and told them to sit still and be calm and cool, and took command of the situation.'

When the Portaferry Lifeboat arrived at the scene, there were eight men in the *Tornamona*'s two life rafts and another four still onboard the vessel. 'It was quite scary,' says John Murray, who was one of the lifeboat crew. 'The *Tornamona* was a fairly big boat and she was sitting pretty low in the water, and she was going down by the back. I would say the water was near enough level with the deck of the boat. She had lost all power and the lights had gone out. They were probably a bit too close to the shore, trying to keep out of the main current. They obviously thought they would clear the rocks, but they didn't. She went down within three or four minutes of us getting the last men off.'

Another boat arrived on-scene to help. The *Cuan Shore* was privately owned by another RNLI Helmsman, Desi Rogers, and it would take Joey and the others back to Portaferry after the lifeboat crew had towed their life rafts over to it. 'Joey and several of the others were sitting in a life raft when we arrived but the crew and the man who owned the boat – Archie Lappin – were still on it,' says Murray. 'The boat was still floating at that point, it hadn't gone down, so they were doing their best to save the boat. I remember seeing Joey sitting in the raft unperturbed. There was no shouting or panic at all.'

No lives were lost in the sinking of the *Tornamona* but, according to the RNLI's Gabriel Rogers, it could so easily have been very different. 'If the conditions had been just a little worse, Northern Ireland could well have lost one of its world champions.'[35]

Joey was credited with playing a major part in saving the lives of his friends: he was a hero all over again and just as reluctant to accept the plaudits as he had always been. But in the face of extreme danger – and a kind of danger he most certainly wasn't accustomed to – he had shown his true mettle: he had remained calm, alerted everyone to the danger when the *Tornamora* first struck the rocks, had tied jerrycans to those who couldn't swim, and had jumped overboard with a knife to cut the life raft free from the sinking vessel. It was an outstanding act of bravery and calmness in the face of potential catastrophe, but Joey, as shocked as he appeared in the television interviews he gave the following day, shrugged it off with his usual modesty. He had other things he needed to be getting on with – like winning races at the TT in just a few days' time – and it was going to take more than a shipwreck to stop him.

o

Joey Dunlop's factory Hondas had already been taken to the Isle of Man by the Honda team, but the likes of Robert Dunlop and Brian Reid were not so lucky. Their bikes were amongst the seven which ended up on the seabed along with spare parts, riding gear, and tools with a total estimated value of £120,000. Despite being busy saving lives at the time, Joey later remembered the heartbreak of seeing the bikes sink. 'I think the worst bit was standing on the front of the boat, watching the bikes all go down below the water,' he said. 'You just felt like greetin'. You could see thousands and thousands of pounds' worth, and weeks and weeks of work, sinking below the water.'[36]

RNLI helmsman Mark Browne was paged when the *Tornamona* hit trouble but had been out of range and only got to the quayside as Joey and the others were being brought ashore. 'By the time I got there I could hardly get to the boathouse because of the crowds,' he says. 'The police were all over the place, too. The only reason I got through was because I was a helmsman.'

Browne immediately met with his friend, Archie Lappin, who owned the *Tornamona* and who had Joey with him. 'I met Joey just after he had been brought back ashore and he kept going on and on about the bikes. I told him to quit worrying about the bikes and someone said to me, "You do realise you're talking to the world champion, not some cowboy, don't you?" I didn't realise who Joey was because I wasn't into motorbikes. He wasn't shocked or traumatised by the ordeal – his only concern was for them bikes.'

The following morning, Browne – an experienced diver – was the first man down to try and salvage the motorcycles. 'I went for the smallest bike first because there was only three of us – and one had a dislocated shoulder – and we had to manhandle the bike up onto our wee boat,' he says. 'While I was down there, I put marker buoys on another couple of bikes. The bikes were tied to the gunnels of the boat, so I cut two or three of the lashings then got the first bike up and lashed it to the side of our boat. We just pulled it up with ropes, manually – we didn't have a hoist or anything like that. That's why I went for the 125!'

As conditions changed, the dive became more dangerous. 'I started to lift the second bike but the tide had started to change then and, when the bike was halfway up, the tide was running it through the rigging of the *Tornamona*. So, instead of getting a vertical lift, it was more like forty-five degrees. It was very disorienting, with the pull of the tide and the rigging and the mast getting in the way.'

On board the boat was John Murray, who had taken part in the rescue the night before. 'We only lifted one bike because the tide was running strong and the bikes were well lashed to the side of the boat, so Mark was having trouble getting them freed,' he remembers. 'We got the first one up and then the other boat arrived with more divers on it, so they brought the rest up.'

Salvaging the bikes was just the beginning of the work. 'We had to strip every nut and bolt off and we seeped them in diesel oil, then we washed them in petrol and started to reassemble the whole lot from scratch again,' Robert Dunlop explained.[37]

With TT practice already underway it was a mammoth task to try to get the bikes ready and most of them were never the same again, thanks to the corrosion they suffered in the salt water. Reid's 500cc Formula One Yamaha, for example, broke down on the second lap of the race. 'They were able to get the bikes working but the problem was that they had been under two atmospheres of pressure,' says Browne. 'So, if there was even a pinprick of a hole in the welding or wherever, the pressure would force the saltwater in. When we got the bikes back to the surface, they stripped them and cleaned them but what they couldn't see was *inside* the tubular frames of the bikes. What they should have done was drill a quarter-inch hole in every bit of the frame and flushed it out, but hindsight's a wonderful thing – nobody knew at the time.'

While most people would still be traumatised and would need time to recover from such an ordeal, Joey Dunlop flew to the Isle of Man the day after the sinking, to prepare for the upcoming TT. At that point in time, only one man in the long history of the event had managed to win three TT races in one week: Mike Hailwood. He had achieved the feat twice, winning the 125, 250 and Senior races in 1961, and the 250, Junior and Senior races in 1967. In 1985, just days after he had nearly drowned, Joey Dunlop would equal Hailwood's feat.

o

Shipwrecks aside, the 1985 season had started well for Dunlop. With a new, big-spending sponsor on board in the shape of Rothmans, and a new bike in the exotic Honda RVF750, Joey had everything he could have desired – and perhaps a little more. To launch the new-look Rothmans Honda Britain team, the sponsor had arranged for its riders (Joey, Roger Marshall and new boy Roger Burnett) to visit Austin Reed tailors in Savile Row to be fitted for smart navy-blue blazers. As uncomfortable as he looked in his new corporate gear, Joey meekly played along, feeling it was worth it in return for an RVF750 an RS500 two-stroke, a new RS250, and as many free fags as he could smoke. If he had to wear a blazer every now and then in return, so be it.

The RVF750 was a true factory special and only three were built by Honda in Japan – two for its FIM World Endurance race team and one for its roads specialist, Joey Dunlop. He truly was Honda's favoured son and his loyalty in turning down another offer from Suzuki ahead of the 1985 season was deeply appreciated. Speaking of the Honda bosses back in Japan, Barry Symmons says, 'I think they admired Joey for his individuality. Seeing someone who was an individual was a bit strange to the Japanese, who had a bit of a committee approach to things. So, to find somebody who knew what he wanted, knew where he was going, and how he was going to do it – and had actually *done* it – they admired him for that. And consequently, they listened when he said something.'

Joey made his debut on the RVF at the North West 200 and smoked everybody in the main Superbike race. His RS500, however, broke down, leaving Roger Marshall to win the 500cc race, but Joey also picked up a win in the 250cc class after beating Grand Prix riders Niall Mackenzie and Andy Watts.

Joey then took the RVF to another runaway win in the Formula One TT, just six days after he almost drowned. Today, TT races are often won by split seconds but, in 1985, at the peak of his powers, Joey Dunlop won the Formula One race by a staggering five minutes and 10 seconds from Tony Rutter, after both Roger Marshall and Mick Grant suffered mechanical issues and retired. With a new lap record for the class set at 116.43mph, Dunlop appeared to have had the perfect race; it was only afterwards that he revealed what he'd had to contend with. 'It was leaking brake fluid,' he said of his RVF. 'I thought it was oil at the start, but once I came in on the second lap it was brake fluid. Once I knew it was brake fluid, I was happy enough. But I couldn't keep my feet on the footrests through the tricky bits. My feet was flyin' off and probably people thought I was going too quick, but it wasn't really that.'

With the defence of his F1 world crown off to a perfect start, Joey then won on his new Honda RS250 after a close scrap with Brian Reid. The two old sparring partners from the Armoy Armada and Dromara Destroyers days were still closely matched on 250cc machines, and it looked like the race could have gone either way before Reid was forced to retire just two miles from the finish line, his bike out of fuel. He had taken a fourteen-second lead into the last lap, but all to no avail.

The sinking of the *Tornamona* almost affected the outcome of the race when Joey had to make an unscheduled pit stop due to a leaking fuel tank; the one he was using had been salvaged from the watery depths of the Irish Sea. It was Joey's first 250cc Junior TT win and it set him up for a crack at the treble: if he could win the Production B TT (for 251–750cc machines) or the Senior TT, he would become only the second man in the history of the event to win three in a week.

Joey was never keen on production bikes. Brought up on infinitely more adjustable thoroughbred race bikes, he never seemed able to find a set-up or feeling on production-based street bikes that would allow him to ride to the limit. And so it proved in the Production B race, which saw him riding his underpowered 400cc, three-cylinder, two-stroke Honda round to a disinterested twenty-second place. If he was going to do the triple, he would have to win the Senior TT.

After Mick Grant crashed out (and decided that would be his last TT), it fell to Roger Marshall to give chase to Joey, but he was once again outclassed and Joey beat him to the line by a comfortable 16 seconds to take his seventh TT win. The race was marred by the death of thirty-two-year-old Dover rider Rob Vine and Joey had been shaken as he passed the scene of that accident – and others. 'There was a hell of a lot of accidents around the course and it was detuning me a little bit,' he admitted.

But he'd done it. He had won three in a week and matched Hailwood's benchmark. And all this achieved within two weeks of fighting for his life in the Irish Sea. Davy Wood saw the potential for a new pre-TT tradition in the future: 'We ended up winning three races,' he said. 'I thought we should dump him in the water before every TT if this was gonna be the answer.'

It wasn't going to happen though. After the drama of 1985, Joey Dunlop would travel to the Isle of Man by more conventional means.

o

In 1985, the TT Formula One world championship had been extended again and would now take in six rounds. Crucially for Joey, two of these rounds were scheduled to take place on short circuits (Assen and Hockenheim). The series had originally been based solely on road courses and this shift towards safer, purpose-built short circuits could have threatened his dominance. He was going to have to prove his worth on both types of circuits now: if Joey Dunlop was merely a roads specialist, he would never win another F1 world title.

Fortunately, he wasn't, and his bid for a fourth title was also helped by the fact that he didn't have Roger Marshall snapping at his heels: Honda didn't have an F1 bike for Marshall in 1985, so Joey was the sole factory representative. In the end, no other rider was needed. Joey won all six rounds to end the season with a perfect score of 90 points to Mick Grant's 40. It really was no contest, even when Grant tried to level the playing field at the third round in Vila Real. 'Joey wasn't a very sociable person,' Grant says. 'I mean, I had plenty of drinks with him, but I never got to know him very well, and I think a lot of people who said they *did* know him well are maybe not telling the truth. He had his own tight-knit group of people around him and tended to stick with them. But we were racing in Vila Real in Portugal one year and it was my birthday. I was sat in a bar with my wife Carol and my mechanic Nigel Everett, having a celebratory drink. Joey passed by and asked what we were doing, so Nigel told him it was my birthday. Joey immediately went and bought some brandies – huge, big tumblers of the stuff – and they just kept coming. Nigel kept up with Joey, but I had to keep pouring mine into the plant pots when no one was looking. I eventually left them to it and thought, "Well, at least I don't have to worry about Joey in the race tomorrow," but the little bugger still went out and won it!'

According to Barry Symmons, the brandy-drinking didn't stop there. 'The night before the race at Vila Real, Mick Grant thought he would be clever and bought Joey a big bottle of brandy. I suspect he was hoping to give Joey a hangover for race day. Anyway, Joey polished half of it off, then decided he was going to do a lap of the track in my car – which I wasn't aware of at the time – with his mechanics, Chris Mayhew and Nick Goodison. Apparently, he was driving with one hand on the gear lever while his other hand held the bottle of brandy and the steering wheel. As soon as they stopped, poor old Chris Mayhew put his head out of the window and was violently sick. Joey didn't get a hangover, though, so Granty's master plan didn't work!'

Roger Marshall remembers the incident, but insists it happened a couple of days before the race, not the day before. 'I was sharing a room with Joey and we found some little bar in Vila Real. We fell out of there about two in the morning and Joey wanted to do a couple of laps of the track in his car. We were leathered, all of us. Chris Mayhew was in the back of the car while I was in the front with Joey. I remember Chris being sick as soon as he got out of the car and he lost his false teeth in the process. I managed to find them, in amongst all his sick, and handed them over.'

But the chaos didn't end there, as Marshall explains: 'I was sharing a twin room with Joey and at some time in the morning there was all this banging on the door. Outside of our small hotel there were two petrol pumps and Joey had abandoned the car on a plinth between the pumps, preventing anyone from getting petrol. There was a big queue of cars waiting. I couldn't wake Joey up, so I found the keys and went to move the car. We'd left all the doors of the car wide open, and Joey must have had a thousand fags in there and the glove box had about a grand in cash in it – that's how Joey operated. Anyway, I managed to get the car off the plinth and went back to bed. Barry Symmons turned up that day and he was furious. Joey never got up until the day after that – he was in bed for two whole days.'

Paul Iddon remembers Joey's crew using booze in an attempt to sabotage Iddon's own race efforts. Confident that their own man could easily race his way through a hangover, they would try to get Joey's lesser-drinking rivals drunk the night before a race. 'You could never say no to a drink with Joey's entourage,' he says. 'They'd try and get you blitzed before the race to throw everything against you. One time I was drinking with them but left at about 3am because I was absolutely paralytic. I got up with a thick head in the morning and Joey's gang were still sitting drinking crème de menthe because that was all that was left behind the bar! It was like a bomb had hit the place – all the curtains had been ripped down and the whole place was wrecked.'

Don Morley also remembers getting the Joey gang treatment.
'I was the official photographer for the Rothman's Honda Britain
squad, and we spent quite a lot of time in Joey's pub,' he says. 'He
would just keep pouring me drinks, to the point where I couldn't
even see through my camera lens, never mind take a picture! I could
never keep up with Joey and his crew when they hit the beers.'

Morley was astonished at Dunlop's ability to drink for hours
without showing any ill effects and cites one occasion at the North
West 200 as a classic example. 'I don't remember what year it was,
but I went back to my hotel after the racing and the bar was really
crowded and there was Joey, having just won the big race and still
wearing his racing leathers, sitting drinking with his pals. I had to
leave at 5am the next morning, so I asked for a wake-up call. The
night porter duly woke me up at 5am but he was clearly very drunk
and, when I came downstairs, I saw the reason why – Joey and
his pals were STILL sitting drinking at the bar and the porter had
obviously joined in. And yet Joey was stone cold sober. He seemed
to be able to get drunk, sober up again, and keep going.'

Modern motorcycle racers train as hard as Olympian athletes
but Joey came from a different era, when socialising and drinking
were as much part of a race weekend as the race itself. Mick Grant
says Joey did, however, change with the times – at least to a certain
extent. 'Maybe if he'd not drunk as much in his early days, he'd
have won more races!' he says laughing. 'But he did what he needed
to do to win. In the early days he could get away with drinking and
smoking but when things got a bit tougher for him as he got older,
he quit smoking in order to get fitter and be more competitive. So,
he did what he needed to do.'

Boozy nights or not, Dunlop was at the peak of his powers and
with Honda's exotic RVF750 proving to be a perfect weapon, the
combination was simply untouchable, and prompted respected

motorcycle journalist Nick Harris to write in *Motocourse* that Joey Dunlop was 'the greatest pure road racer of all time'.

It was hard to argue with Harris – and it seemed the Queen was convinced, too, because at the end of 1985, Joey Dunlop was summoned to Buckingham Palace to be awarded an MBE.

CHAPTER 10

THE KING AND THE QUEEN

'I HAD A GLASS OF CHAMPAGNE WITH THE QUEEN, SO IT WAS BRILLIANT. UNBELIEVABLE.'

Joey Dunlop

The Queen has been graciously pleased to give orders for the following promotions in, and appointments to, the Most Excellent Order of the British Empire.

To be Ordinary members of the Civil Division of the said Most Excellent Order:

William Joseph Dunlop. For services to Motor Cycle Racing.

– London Gazette, 31 December 1985

In December of 1985, the New Year Honours list included one William Joseph Dunlop. He was to be awarded the Most Excellent Order of the British Empire (MBE) on 6 March 1986. The honour is traditionally bestowed for 'an outstanding achievement or service to the community which has had a long-term, significant impact'. In Joey's case, it was for services to motorcycling, and the shy, unassuming little man from such humble beginnings in rural County Antrim could not have been more delighted.

Barry Symmons cites the day Joey was whisked off to Buckingham Palace as one of his fondest memories from all the years he spent working with him. 'I felt particularly proud on the day when Joey got his MBE because the Queen meant a great deal to him. He wasn't the person who was most concerned with sartorial elegance and we did wonder what he was going to turn up at the palace wearing, but he and Linda and the three kids all looked fantastic. He was only allocated four tickets, but he was going to make sure he took his whole family of five, come hell or high water. I arranged through a friend of mine, who worked for a company that owned a fleet of Daimlers, to provide a chauffeur-driven car and when Joey's kids got in, they said, "There's more room in the back of this than there is in our garden!" But that was one of my favourite moments – to see him going off to Buckingham Palace.'

Clean-shaven with a fresh haircut and dressed impeccably in a grey suit with grey-and-white-striped tie, slip-on leather shoes, and with a white handkerchief neatly tucked into his left breast pocket, Joey posed happily on a Honda VFR 750F street bike in front of the Palace before being presented with his MBE by Prince Charles.

He may not have got to meet the Queen on this occasion, but Joey would later get the chance at a reception at Buckingham Palace and felt greatly honoured. 'I went to a garden party one time, for all the world champions from Britain, and the Queen was there but we were kept behind bars and we didn't really get talking to her,' he said. 'But we were invited this time to a party in Buckingham Palace – not really a party, just a get-together – and the Queen came round and talked to us all, very, very nice, and I had a glass of champagne with her, so it was brilliant. Unbelievable.'[38]

He had come a long way from the small cottage with no running water and no electricity and yet he had never promoted himself, never courted publicity, never tried to become a superstar: he had simply been himself. But it was enough: the King of the Roads had now been recognised by the Queen.

The Queen was obviously a contentious figure during the Troubles in Northern Ireland, which played out during much of Joey's career but, as the *Belfast Telegraph* stated, Joey himself was 'fiercely anti-sectarian and apolitical' and was 'followed by Catholics and Protestants alike'.[39]

In fact, Joey was one of the few people who could actually bring communities together during the height of the Troubles, as former Irish Rugby union star Stephen Ferris pointed out: 'It didn't matter what side of the community you were from, if you were Catholic or Protestant, or whatever your beliefs were, everybody loved Joey Dunlop.'[40]

This universal love for Joey – even at a time when army helicopters were flying overhead at races and rifle-toting soldiers would check the courses for bombs the night before a race – meant that being associated with him was almost like having a special passport, as Ferry Brouwer of Arai Europe was astonished to discover. 'When I went to Northern Ireland, I always went to Davy Wood's house in Belfast and we would then drive up to Ballymoney, and I'll never forget on one occasion we were driving up at night and we were stopped at an army roadblock,' he says. 'We didn't have to show our passports or anything and we were quickly waved through. The soldier just said, "Give our regards to Joey." We drove on and thought, "How the hell does he know we're going to see Joey? We hadn't mentioned it once at the checkpoint.

'It wasn't until years later that one of Davy's friends – who was high up in the police – told us how that would have happened. He had been in the special forces and he asked us if we had seen the radio car at the roadblock. We *had* seen it, so he said, "Well, for about one mile in either direction from the roadblock there would have been highly sensitive directional microphones planted in the grass verges, listening into the conversation in your car." He also told us there would have been soldiers hidden in the verges with guns. We were amazed to discover this.'

Joey's church was Presbyterian – a reformed tradition within Protestantism – and Joey was on good terms with his minister, the Reverend John Kirkpatrick, even inviting him down to his pub on occasion, as his brother Jim recalls. 'I remember Joey invited the minister in one night. That was good craic. My da wasn't really religious but he knew the bible as well as anybody else and he argued or "debated" with the minister over some points. We were all sat in the wee back room and we drunk a litre of vodka with coke. The minister just drank coke, of course, but it was a great night.'

Whatever his innermost feelings, Joey kept his religious views to himself and never spoke publicly about the Troubles or the religious divide that was tearing the country apart. He was happy to race in Northern Ireland, Southern Ireland, or anywhere else for that matter. Joey's true religion was racing, and in 1986 he would prove to be as devoted as ever to his cause, though little did he know it would prove to be his last year as world champion.

o

As Joey Dunlop set out on his seventeenth season of racing, his acceptance was now universal. He had been voted Enkalon Rider of the Year in Ireland for a fifth time, he had been voted *Motor Cycle News* Man of the Year two years previously by readers of the world's biggest motorcycling publication, and he now even had royal approval in the shape of an MBE. And yet he remained the same humble, shy, grounded person he had always been.

His gong had led to increased interest from the media and Barry Symmons had, by now, found a way to get Joey more comfortable in front of television cameras. 'Joey didn't like doing television interviews and standing up on stage talking to people, but if you engineered it in such a way that he didn't have to sit and think about it beforehand, he was fine. If I'd said, "Right, there's a man coming at 1pm tomorrow to do a television interview," then, come one o'clock, Joey would be nowhere to be seen. But if I told the television company that Joey would be around at a certain time and if they just turned up and interviewed him, he'd be fine. So that's the way we learned to work it. I once got a TV crew to hide behind the pit building at Vila Real and I walked Joey along towards them and when the TV interviewer stuck a microphone under Joey's nose, he gave one of the best interviews I'd ever seen him do. He rattled on for about twenty minutes! He did get better at giving interviews though, and once he got better, he didn't mind so much.'

It was testament to the loyalty and love that Joey inspired in those around him that he was never asked to do anything he was uncomfortable doing – at least, once those people realised what made him uncomfortable. Ferry Brouwer very quickly learned not to make demands of his rider. 'I didn't even bother to ask Joey to do any PR events for Arai,' he says. 'Don't ask somebody to do something that you know they don't like. So, I let him be and we just used photographs of him as promotional material. For example, I would *never* have considered inviting Joey out for a luxurious dinner because I knew he would not feel comfortable with that. He was happier eating peas or beans straight out of the can, so I would join in with him and eat the same – and that's when you got the best conversations out of Joey. If he had to, he could look smart in a suit and be well-shaven and have his hair all cut and washed, but that was not Joey. Davy Wood understood that and that's why he was able to do so much for Joey – he would explain to people what to expect from Joey, but also what not to expect.'

Graham Sanderson had the unenviable task of being Honda Britain's press man for many years when Joey was riding for the team. Yet while getting Joey to speak about himself was never an easy job, Sanderson also just accepted Joey for who he was. 'I can't remember Joey ever *not* doing something that I wanted him to do PR-wise,' he says. 'In the Rothmans Honda days he was forced to wear a blazer, slacks and a tie, but that pressure came from Rothmans and Barry Symmons. I found Joey to be fine to work with.'

Ferry Brouwer believes Joey's habit of keeping himself to himself and never publicly stating his intentions, had the unexpected side effect of psyching other riders out before a race. 'Because of his personality – not mixing with people etc., etc. – Joey had already psyched-out most of his rivals before they raced!' he says. 'He didn't give anything away and he was always just Joey, sitting in the grass or working on his bikes and never behaving like a superstar. And I think that psyched people out because they were always wondering what Joey was going to do. And the more time they spent focusing on Joey, the less time they had to focus on their own preparations. The easier it is for a rider to win a race, the better it is for them, so if you can start a race having already psyched-out your rivals, you have already achieved an advantage. He didn't do it on purpose –

he wasn't *trying* to psyche people out; it was just a side effect of the way he was, and he probably realised that.'

More relaxed and confident in front of crowds and television cameras, Joey's team-mate Roger Marshall often found himself shouldering the responsibility for PR work. 'I did a lot of the Honda PR events on my own because Joey didn't want anything to do with that, he just wasn't interested,' Marshall says. 'It's not that he didn't like people, he was just shy. Honda didn't try to force him to do PR events. Our contracts with Honda were massive and we were both supposed to do all that stuff, but Honda never forced him because they knew how Joey worked and they liked him. As long as he rode their bikes, they were happy. They knew what a fanbase he had around the world, and what he did at the TT meant everything to Honda, so he was treated in a different way to the likes of me, Wayne Gardner, Ron Haslam or Roger Burnett. Joey was just a one-off person.'

The news reporters, television cameras and PR gigs were no more than a distraction for Joey, however, as he prepared for another season of racing. For the first time ever, the opening round of the TT Formula One world championship was not being held on the Isle of Man, but rather at Misano in Italy. Now comprising eight rounds, the championship was at a tipping point as it now had, for the first time, as many rounds on short circuits as it had on public roads courses. Joey would have to master Misano, Hockenheim, Assen and Jerez, as well as the more familiar TT course, Dundrod, Vila Real, and Imatra in Finland (a circuit which included a railway line that had to be crossed) if he wanted to retain his title.

This increase in the use of short circuits started to attract a different breed of rider to F1, including some very famous ones. In the opening round at Misano (and again at Assen, later in the year) Joey would have to race against the 1981 500cc Grand

Prix world champion, Marco Lucchinelli. The Italian may have been slightly past his prime but he was still a big name and Joey acquitted himself well; after changing tyres in the wet conditions at Misano, he pulled back Lucchinelli's twenty-second lead and was just about to pass him when his RVF750 spluttered and ran out of fuel. He wasn't the only one to suffer this fate. At 160 miles, the race was so long that only Lucchinelli and Sweden's Anders Anderson made it to the finish line. It was a farcical situation, but since Joey knew Lucchinelli would not be contesting the roads circuits like the TT and Dundrod, it didn't matter as much as it otherwise might have done.

Hockenheim in Germany was next, and this time Joey really proved his worth on short circuits. After fluffing the start because he was adjusting his knee sliders when the flag dropped, he was as far down the field as twentieth on the opening lap, but by lap three he was in the lead. Suzuki's Paul Iddon temporarily inherited the lead after Joey had to stop to refuel while he himself didn't need to, but Joey would reclaim it and then build an eight-second advantage that he held to the flag.

Iddon, riding Suzuki's awesome new GSX-R750, which had been launched the previous year, was now a serious contender for the championship and would have many close battles with Dunlop. He explains why the series suited Joey down to the ground. 'It was a lot more laid-back and a lot more fun than world championship paddocks today – you didn't have all the corporate hospitality and stuff. You were still professional when you had to be, but our feet were much more firmly on the ground.'

After Germany Joey headed back home for the North West 200, but things didn't exactly go to plan there. On the fourth lap of the opening 250cc race he touched a white line, which had become slippery after a rain shower, and crashed out at Juniper Hill chicane.

He damaged his knee in the fall and had to receive stitches, then sat out most of the meeting to save his strength for the feature North West 200 Superbike race that traditionally brought the curtain down on the event. In a finale that sent the home fans wild with joy, Joey went out and beat his old rival Roger Marshall to take the win. The pair had, after their running spat in 1984, become good friends again, and with Roger having won the opening Superbike race in Joey's absence, they left the meeting with equal spoils.

Only then would Joey get to race in a round of the world championship on a 'proper' roads course. The TT now formed the third round of the series and, after being delayed by two days due to atrocious weather, the Formula One race would bring Joey yet another TT win, this time ahead of Geoff Johnson and Andy McGladdery – neither of whom were a realistic threat in the F1 championship. His closest challenger in the title chase was Anders Anderson who only managed to finish twelfth at the TT in what was his debut at the event.

One man who was seriously unhappy with the 1986 Formula One TT was Roger Marshall, who still believes his efforts to win the race were sabotaged. 'In 1986, I got Joey's old bike – the 1985 RVF – and when I first rode it at the North West 200 I couldn't believe how good it was. I won the North West on it and I remember thinking how good that bike was going to be at the TT and that I would definitely win the Formula One race on it, but I barely managed to complete a lap on that bike, either in practice or the race. It never ran right. That bike had never missed a beat the year before when Joey rode it. To this day, I'm convinced there was something done to that bike to stop me from winning the TT which, in my opinion, was a very dangerous thing to do. I can't really elaborate because I don't want to get confrontational with Honda, but something wasn't right that year on the Isle of Man.'

Marshall's ex-Joey Dunlop factory RVF suffered a misfire through-out the race before eventually expiring and forcing him to retire.

The rest of the week was a disappointment for Dunlop too, with just a fourth place in the Production Class C race and another fourth in the Senior, after losing two minutes in the pits fixing a broken steering damper bolt. With Joey struggling, Marshall should really have made the most of the opportunity to finally win a TT, but he didn't. Instead, he had to suffer the indignation of seeing his former mechanic, Roger Burnett, win the Senior TT in what was only his fourth attempt. Marshall had been trying since 1978.

The 1986 TT will sadly be remembered for all the wrong reasons. Four riders were to lose their lives over the fortnight, including promising young Irish rider Gene McDonnell. His death was one of the most horrific ever witnessed on a course that had seen more than its fair share of horrors. When Brian Reid crashed out of the Junior 250 race he sustained a broken collarbone and wrist and had to await the medical helicopter. When the helicopter landed in a field near Ballaugh Bridge, it startled a horse. The horse jumped out of the field and onto the TT course, right into the path of hard-charging McDonnell. Both rider and horse were killed instantly. Incredibly, the race continued.

In the Formula Two TT, Joey's younger brother Robert also came close to losing his life. He crashed at the 13th milestone and shattered his jawbone, broke some ribs, punctured a lung and broke an ankle and shoulder blade. His condition was described as critical. 'Robert drifted in and out of consciousness and we thought we had lost him,' his wife Louise said. 'All the family were there, hoping against hope that he would pull through.'[41]

While his brother fought for his life in intensive care, Joey withdrew from the Production B race to be by his bedside. It was only when Robert regained consciousness and the doctors pronounced him stable that Joey went back to work but, even then, he seemed distracted and made a rare mistake, crashing out of the Junior race at Sulby Bridge. For Joey to crash at the TT was almost unthinkable and most people put it down to the distraction of him worrying about his brother, but in fact he crashed because fuel had leaked onto his rear tyre. He remounted and continued, but a damaged exhaust ended his race.

It had been a disappointing TT for Joey, to say the least. 'I feel it's the worst week ever I had at the TT,' he said at week's end. 'But ach, not too bad, you know. I had that good a year last year I had to have a bad year shortly, and this was it. I've won the Formula One, right enough, so that was a good thing.'[42]

His win in the F1 TT put him back in the lead of the championship ahead of Sweden's Anders Anderson, who had led the series before his lowly finish at the TT. For the next round at Assen, Joey would face some formidable new competition from two exceptional riders. The first was Neil Robinson. Just twenty-four years old, with movie-star good looks, a mop of blonde hair, and an affable, charming character, 'Smutty' also spoke well and was a natural in front of television cameras. He was also a devastatingly fast rider on both road circuits and short circuits and had won the British 250cc championship in 1983 at the age of just twenty-one. Robinson had it all. As unthinkable as it might have seemed, here was a Northern Irish rider who might one day rival Joey for the fans' affections. Suzuki foresaw this and signed Robinson up to ride its Skoal Bandit-liveried GSX-R750 alongside Paul Iddon.

Although he was no relation to Joey's late brother-in-law Mervyn Robinson, Smutty Robinson was close friends with both Joey and Robert Dunlop and often travelled to races with them, his hometown of Ballymena being just eighteen miles up the road from Ballymoney. His older brother Donny Robinson had been a successful 250cc Grand Prix rider but retired from the world scene in 1985 (sadly, he would make a comeback at the North West 200 in 1999 but was killed during practice). Joey was happy to show Robinson round courses he didn't know and passed on whatever advice he could to his young friend. Smutty was most definitely in camp Dunlop.

Joey would also face another mighty challenger at Assen in 1986 – Kevin Schwantz. Being groomed by Suzuki as a future 500cc Grand Prix rider, Schwantz was entering any and every race he could in Europe in order to gain experience. He would eventually win twenty-five Grands Prix, took the world title in 1993, and is now considered one of the all-time greats of GP racing. In 1986, he was just two years away from winning his first 500cc GP, yet Joey Dunlop beat him fair and square at Assen, a circuit that Schwantz loved. It was further proof of Joey's abilities on short circuits.

Joey might have beaten Schwantz, but he'd had no answer for Neil Robinson early in the race. His fellow Irishman had led comfortably before his chain jumped the sprocket and jammed his back wheel. The result went Joey's way but Smutty had shown what he was capable of and he was clearly going to be a threat in the future.

Not that Joey allowed that to spoil their friendship. Delighted with his now healthy lead in the championship, Dunlop and his gang felt it was time to celebrate and Neil Robinson was invited along to join them. 'The night after the race, Joey and about five or six others had been drinking and decided to take the Rothmans Honda car for a lap of the circuit,' Paul Iddon explains. 'Joey rolled the car and it ended up on its roof in a ditch. His race trophy went flying around the car in the melee and my team-mate, Neil Robinson, spent a night in hospital, Joey broke some ribs, and Neil's mechanic broke his jaw in the crash. He had to drink through a straw for months after that and lost loads of weight. Somewhere in Spain he had rice soup which kept locking his jaw up, which we all thought was quite funny.'

In most retellings of this story, it's one of Joey's mechanics driving the car, not Joey himself. But Don Morley says there's a very good reason for that. 'They had all come back from Groningen, where they had been on a pub crawl, and Joey decided he wanted to do a lap of the track but ended up putting the car upside down in a ditch. It was Joey who was driving, but one of the mechanics was persuaded to take the rap for it because it didn't look too good.'

The next round of the series was at another short circuit, this time at Jerez in Spain, and Joey's post-race antics at Assen would play a part in the outcome of the race. With his five broken ribs still not healed, Joey struggled to breathe in the 37-degree heat and also suffered constant pain as his ribs got battered by his fuel tank. In the end he could only manage a hard-earned fifth place while Robinson – who had got off more lightly in the car crash – came home third behind winner Paul Iddon and second-placed man Graeme McGregor. It was enough for Joey to retain a lead in the championship, but not a comfortable enough one. Vila Real was next.

With his ribs healed and his motivation running high, Dunlop fought a tremendous battle with Iddon round the 4.3-mile Guia street circuit, eventually winning by 3 seconds and extending his championship lead to 17 points with only the Imatra and Dundrod races remaining.

The Imatra circuit had always been inherently dangerous, with railway lines running across the track and the proximity of so many trees at the edge of the circuit. Scottish world Sidecar champion Jock Taylor had been killed there in 1982 and the circuit had been shortened in the name of safety afterwards. There was almost further carnage at the start of the 1986 Formula One round when four bikes, all jockeying for position in the early stages of the race, collided and went down. Joey somehow managed to avoid the wreckage but, once again, he could do nothing about runaway leader Neil Robinson, until Smutty suffered yet another stroke of bad luck when a puncture forced him to drop to third place, handing Joey the win and second place to Paul Iddon.

It was enough to secure Joey's fifth consecutive TT Formula One world championship title, meaning he had won half of all F1 championships ever staged. It should also have meant that Joey, with the pressure off, could have gone to Dundrod and put on a masterclass in front of his home fans by destroying the opposition. But that's not how things turned out. For there was another man there who could call on an army of home support and he would stun everyone by beating the King of the Roads on his own home circuit, and in the wet too. Neil Robinson truly came of age at the 1986 Ulster Grand Prix.

Smutty had led so many of the TTF1 races that season only to be blighted by bad luck. His chain may have jumped the sprockets at Assen and he suffered a puncture in Imatra, but he had no such issues at Dundrod and simply ran away with the race, providing one of the biggest shocks in road racing in years. Robinson had finally arrived. Three weeks later, he was dead.

o

Neil Robinson had won the F1 race at the Ulster by over a minute. Joey had been caught up in Paul Iddon's crash early in the race and had lost too much time fighting back through the pack, but even an on-form Joey would have struggled to beat Robinson on that day. It was only his second visit to Dundrod and he had ridden superbly, yet he was quick to deflect the praise that came his way.

'Don't be calling me the new king of the road,' he said. 'That title still belongs to Joey Dunlop.'[43]

Racing at the Oliver's Mount parkland circuit in Scarborough for the first time, shortly after the Ulster, Robinson crashed on the sixth lap of practice as he climbed up the steep Quarry Hill section away from Mere Hairpin. He suffered a broken leg and serious head injuries and was rushed to Hull Royal Infirmary, forty-five miles away, with a motorcycle escort. He died of his injuries later that evening. He was twenty-four years old. Joey Dunlop had lost yet another close friend and Northern Ireland had lost its greatest racing prospect.

For all that road racing had given to Joey Dunlop, it had taken away much more. The 1986 season had been another tragic one in many ways. It was also the last time Joey would win a world championship, but then, what did a world championship matter if you didn't have a bike to ride in it? At the end of the year the Honda Britain team folded, and Joey Dunlop found himself unemployed.

CHAPTER 11

FERRARI

'JOEY WAS A HARD LITTLE BASTARD WHEN HE NEEDED TO BE, NO DOUBT ABOUT IT.'
Mick Grant

The Honda Britain team was the biggest bike race team in the UK, and also in the TT Formula One world championship, so it came as something of a shock when the announcement was made that it was folding. 'Honda Britain stopped racing at the end of 1986,' Barry Symmons says. 'Bike sales had plummeted, and the money just wasn't there.'

Honda had decided to focus on supporting more 'dealer teams' (where standard or race-kitted bikes would be supplied at a favourable price but the running costs would be down to individual teams, often run by motorcycle dealers) rather than having one full factory effort and this, to a large extent, left the likes of Joey, Roger Marshall and Roger Burnett out in the cold.

Joey had raced with Honda Britain for six years and brought

them five Formula One world championships, six TT wins, and a multitude of race wins elsewhere. What was he to do? If he signed for one of the other factory teams, he may not be able to come to the same loose arrangement he had enjoyed with Honda; an arrangement that had allowed him the freedom to work on his own bikes and do his own thing. It also took Joey time to trust people – it would be like starting out all again.

While Davy Wood approached Suzuki to assess their level of interest in signing his rider, Joey's heart really lay with Honda, and it was Wood who then helped to convince Honda bosses in Japan that they should continue to support Joey in his bid to defend his F1 title. So, with sponsorship from Rothmans and team clothing by Hugo Boss, a new outfit was set up to defend it. It consisted of Peter McNab (a frame specialist and fabricator who had worked with Honda extensively) as team manager, Nick Goodison as chief mechanic, and Tony 'Slick' Bass as second mechanic. Bass would later become famous for helping Carl Fogarty to take four World Superbike titles but working with Joey was his first professional gig as a race mechanic. It would prove to be a life-changing experience. 'I was a teetotaller until I worked for Joey,' he says. 'I was eighteen and the most I'd ever had was a shandy. Joey said, "I can't teach you how to fix a motorbike, but I can teach you how to drink" and he lined up three vodka and cokes on the bar!'

While Joey did receive a bike for the 1987 season, it was a far cry from the exotic, hand-built factory RVFs he had been used to in recent years. It was based on Honda's VFR750 production bike, which had been released the previous year and would become known as one of the finest all-round motorcycles ever built. But it was built for the street, not the racetrack, and Joey never liked production-based machinery. 'He had been brought up on proper race bikes,' Bass says. 'When he started racing, you couldn't do it on production bikes – you had to go out and buy a proper race bike. Even I wasn't a great fan of production bikes at that time, but racing was changing and becoming more production bike-oriented, so you just had to accept it. Production bikes were getting better, but they were still like bullets with no direction.'

It might have been production-based, but the bike Joey was given was still a special version. 'It was a VFR X6 750,' Bass says. 'It was a full factory bike that, I think, had been raced in America the previous year. It was a half "sit-up-and-beg" American-style Superbike, but we put drop-handlebars and stuff on it to make it look more like a normal European-style racer. It was really trick though. It might have been based on a production VFR750 but very few parts were interchangeable with a standard bike. Joey didn't like the bike at first, but he grew to love it. It was a quick bike and it handled really well, so it was just a case of making some changes until he felt more comfortable and got used to it.'

Nick Goodison had worked with Joey for several years and had his trust, while Bass was just setting out on what would be a highly successful career as a race engineer. 'Joey trusted Nick completely because he'd worked with him before,' Bass says. 'He would talk to Nick more than me about the bike, and then Nick would talk to me about what we were going to do. Joey didn't say much to me, but if you got a wink out of him for doing a good job, that was reward enough to keep you working like a Trojan for weeks. It meant so much, precisely *because* Joey didn't say much.'

The 1987 season started well with a hat-trick of wins at the North West 200, including a debut win for his new VFR in the opening Superbike race. Joey used a standard version of the bike to win the 750cc Production race (a rare win for him on production machinery) but chose his RS500 two-stroke machine for the feature race of the day. He could have used either the RS500 two-stroke or his VFR four-stroke (such were the rules at the time) but opted for the 500 at the last minute, simply because the weather was changing and that bike was already fitted with slick tyres, whereas the VFR was on intermediates. In damp and tricky conditions, he beat Alan Irwin and Phil Mellor to take his third win of the day. It was Joey's first – and only – triple victory at the North West, and it was a great confidence booster for both himself and his new team. Despite being thirty-seven years old, he was clearly still the man to beat on the roads.

With the TT Formula One world championship no longer focusing solely on roads courses it continued to attract a different kind of rider, and one of them was Virginio Ferrari. Of all the men who might have dethroned Joey as Formula One world champion, no one thought it would be the swarthy Italian. Ferrari had been a great 500cc Grand Prix rider, racing against, and often beating, the likes of Barry Sheene and Kenny Roberts. He had last won a 500cc Grand Prix at Assen in 1979 and had finished second to Roberts in the championship that year. More recently, he had been racing in 250cc Grands Prix and finished fourteenth in the world championship in 1986. But in 1997, after signing to ride for Bimota, he decided to enter the opening F1 world round at Misano in his native Italy.

Significantly, for both Ferrari and Dunlop, only two of the eight F1 rounds in 1987 were to be staged on roads circuits – the TT and the Ulster Grand Prix. Joey might have been allocated inferior machinery in 1987, but his biggest problem was that the F1 championship itself was evolving: it had once played to his strengths, it was now working against him.

Ferrari was joined in the Bimota team by Davide Tardozzi, now better known as Ducati's team boss in MotoGP. Another big name to join the fray in 1987 was America's Fred Merkel who, like Joey, was Honda-mounted. Roger Marshall had signed for Suzuki to join Paul Iddon and, all of a sudden, Joey had a real fight on his hands.

Iddon drew first blood at Misano as Ferrari crashed out and Tardozzi suffered a mechanical failure. Marshall was also side-lined with machine issues, meaning Joey finished second. It was a solid enough start, but the second round was held at yet another new circuit for the championship – Hungaroring in Hungary – and it did not go so well for him. Riding hurt from a rare crash in practice, Joey was then pushed around on-track by an aggressive Tardozzi and could only bring his VFR home in eighth place. Ferrari, meanwhile, won the race to take a two-point lead in the championship.

Despite his ultra-smooth riding style and humble manner, Joey Dunlop could be just as aggressive as Tardozzi – or anyone else – out on track, as Mick Grant testifies. 'He was an aggressive rider when he had to be. I remember catching him about three laps from the end of the race at Assen in 1985. I'd been taking chunks out of him, so I thought I would just sit behind him and take him on the last lap. Big mistake! Every time I tried to get past him, he cut my nose off, and he even had me on the grass at one point. Joey was a hard little bastard when he needed to be, no doubt about it. He definitely wanted it bad, and he was a very different person when the visor came down.'

Smoothness, rather than aggression, would be key at the next round in the Isle of Man, where Joey knew Virginio Ferrari would not be competing. This was his chance to take back the lead in the championship. Joey blitzed the opposition in the F1 race to take the win by almost a full minute from popular Yorkshireman Phil Mellor, despite making a mistake. 'The exhaust came off,' he said after the race. 'It was my own fault – I missed a gear, and she blew the exhaust off.'

In such dominant form, Joey even had time to observe the antics of his gang of helpers who were holding out signalling boards for him at the Gooseneck to let him know his position in the race. 'They had arranged to drink a bottle of vodka for every lap that Joey was leading,' Slick Bass remembers. 'He led the six-lapper from start to finish and, apparently, you could see Joey's shoulders going up and down with laughter as he rounded the Gooseneck, because he knew about the deal. His signalling boards were upside down and the wrong way round towards the end of the race. How those boys got back from there after six bottles of vodka I'll never know!'

Joey still had the use of his three-cylinder 500cc two-stroke Honda, although he now ran it – and his RS250 machine – with the backing of Shell Gemini Oil and prepared both machines himself. While Rothmans no longer wished to sponsor a domestic race team in the UK, they did continue to sponsor Joey's TTF1 championship effort, so the now familiar blue and white livery remained on the (rather pedestrian-looking) VFR. It may have had a factory race kit containing some special parts, but it was still a drop down from the full works efforts of previous years. The VFR was, and looked like, a production machine, and they aren't designed to go racing. Joey wanted a thoroughbred. 'The VFR felt very slow compared to proper race bikes,' Ron Haslam testified. 'It wasn't even meant to be a sports bike.'

Riding a completely standard version of the VFR750 in the Production TT race, Joey seemed to prove this point by only managing an eighteenth-place finish.

Joey would put his Shell Gemini RS500 to better use in a hideously wet Senior TT; it was so wet and dangerous, in fact, that many other riders pulled out of the race. Even the vastly experienced Dunlop admitted it was frightening. 'It was raceable on the first lap but after that, dreadful… Dangerous,' he said. 'On the first lap, I aquaplaned all the way down Bray Hill, then I had a big moment on new tar at the Black Hut. The bike went four times from lock-to-lock, trying to spit me over the top. I thought I was down, but stayed on. On the last lap, I caught a dozen back-markers in the mist. You couldn't see Creg-ny-Baa until you were on it. All the people who stayed on to watch deserved a medal.'[44]

When a soaked Joey was asked by a television reporter, 'What does a victory here, under conditions like this, in the Senior TT mean?' he replied, 'It means I won't do it again; I know that. It never should have been run – it was desperate.'

Joey had at least bookended his TT race week with wins before heading to Assen with a 13-point lead over Ferrari and Iddon in the F1 championship. And yet, after winning all six rounds of the series in 1985, and taking five wins from eight rounds in 1986, his TT win would be his only F1 victory in 1987. With the championship moving towards short circuits, and without a full factory bike from Honda, the odds were now stacked against Joey.

Fred Merkel carried a slogan on the back of his crash helmet that read, IF YOU WANT BLOOD, YOU'VE GOT IT, and Joey was certainly baying for Merkel's blood after the American punted him off at the final chicane at Assen. A frustrated Joey could do nothing but flick Merkel the V-sign from the gravel trap as he watched Ferrari take the win and the championship lead, by two points.

It shouldn't have mattered too much. After all, Joey's home round at Dundrod was next, and Ferrari was no road racer. At least, he hadn't had any intention of racing on the roads, but with a world title in the offing, the Italian flew to Belfast with a view to competing. It didn't last long. He couldn't believe his eyes when he completed a lap of Dundrod for the first time. It was a dangerous enough course at the best of times, but in the pouring rain it must have looked truly lethal to a man more accustomed to riding on Grand Prix circuits. He took part in the first practice session and posted a time that put him thirty-fifth fastest but, by the time the second session began, Ferrari was on his way home. 'I quit,' he said. 'This course is too dangerous. I quit. It's crazy. A crazy track. A crazy place. A crazy race. I like to win the championship, but I like my life to go on as well. I go home.'[45]

One practice session at a wet Ulster was enough to convince Ferrari that road racing was a suicidal occupation, and a world title was not worth dying for.

While Irish fans laughed at the Italian's retreat, they weren't laughing for long. 'We lost Klaus Klein at Dundrod,' Paul Iddon says. 'That race should never have been started. I actually pleaded with the clerk of the course not to start the race because it was so wet. Going down the Flying Kilo on the warm-up lap my bike was going lock-to-lock, aquaplaning at 180mph. I got off my bike when we got back to the grid and said, "You cannot start this race – someone's going to get killed," but the clerk of the course said he had a duty to his sponsors, and that was that. I was following Klaus Klein and had only just gone past him when the accident happened. He was the closest friend I lost in an F1 world championship race.'

Klein was thirty-three years old at the time and had been a solid competitor with two fourth-placed finishes at the TT in previous years. Joey had been right behind him when he crashed. 'When I saw him fall, I just closed my eyes and braked, but nothing happened,' he said. 'I don't know how I missed him.' The meeting was abandoned after the fatal crash and Virginio Ferrari must have felt entirely justified in his decision to withdraw from the event.

The cancellation of the Ulster meant the Italian carried his slender two-point championship lead into the Japanese round at Sugo, where fast local riders and Australian wild cards (who often raced in Japan) were expected to dominate. The race was won by rising Grand Prix star Kevin Magee from Australia, with local rider Yukiya Oshima in second place. Rounding out the rostrum was another young Australian who would go on to win five consecutive 500cc Grand Prix world championships – Mick Doohan. Joey could only bring the VFR home in a disappointing twelfth place, but it was still better than Ferrari managed – he clipped Joey's rear wheel and crashed out of the race.

With neither rider scoring any points in Japan, Dunlop and Ferrari resumed their battle at Hockenheim in Germany, where the Italian took his third win of the year while Joey struggled to a hard-fought fourth place. Neither rider seemed able to take command of the championship, which had been a topsy-turvy affair with cancellations greatly affecting the points standings. Not only had Dundrod been abandoned after the tragic death of Klaus Klein, but Imatra had also been cancelled following the death of a six-year-old spectator the previous year, and Vila Real was dropped from the calendar as an indirect result of a Portuguese general election. That meant that only one round of the championship, which had started out as a roads-only series ten years before, was held on a public roads course – the TT.

The title would be decided at yet another short circuit, Donington Park in England, where, with Ferrari taking a seven-point lead into the race, he could afford to finish behind Joey and still win the title. Joey, in fact, out-performed Ferrari on a circuit which should have been much more suited to the Italian, but it wasn't enough; even though Joey came home third while his rival could only finish seventh, it was enough for Ferrari to claim the title by a meagre 3 points.

If Joey hadn't been knocked off by Merkel at Assen, if tragedy hadn't struck at the Ulster, or if he had just managed to finish higher than twelfth in Japan, then the title could have been his for a sixth consecutive year. 'If he had just gained a few more points in Japan then things could have been different, and he could have won the championship,' Bass says. 'But he didn't take the hot weather too well. I remember when he came into the pits in Japan, we had prepared a bucket of iced water with a towel in it. We didn't tell him about this and, when we poured it down his back, he shot off like a little rodent that had its tail trodden on! When it was that hot – with the heat from the engine and the ambient temperature in Japan in the summer – he said he couldn't wake up properly and felt half asleep on the bike. But his eyes were on stalks when he went back out after the iced water, and he went quite quick for a while until the heat got to him again.'

Ferrari had endured his share of bad luck during the season too, so there was no point in dwelling on what might have been. Joey had lost his title – and he wouldn't get it back.

CHAPTER 12

FOGGY

'HE WAS NO SPRING CHICKEN, THEN, FOR SURE, AND HE WASN'T THE FASTEST GUY IN THE WORLD ON SHORT CIRCUITS.'
Carl Fogarty

The World Superbike championship was first held in 1988 and has since become the premier series for production-based, four-stroke motorcycles. When it started, the TT Formula One world championship was still in full swing, meaning there was a crossover period when some riders competed in both championships. The biggest difference was that WSB operated solely on purpose-built short circuits, whereas the TTF1 series still took in several pure roads events. But otherwise, the two championships were incredibly similar. Something had to give.

'I think there are two reasons why WSB went from strength to strength while F1 disappeared,' says Mick Grant. 'First of all, the organisers can't make any money from road circuits because they can't charge people to watch. And in racing, money is the be-all and end-all. The second reason is that some of the top riders would not race on public roads. In my career I had to race on roads as well as circuits, otherwise the factories didn't want you. By the 1980s, you could almost make a choice which way you wanted to go, and the main names chose short-circuit racing. But I think the main reason is that they couldn't make any money out of it. The North West 200 is one of the best-attended spectator events in Europe. Imagine if you could charge 150,000 people £30 a head – I'd still be racing!'

There had at one point been plans to run both series, though with radically different-looking bikes, according to F1 star Paul Iddon. 'The original plan was to have both F1 and World Superbike championships, but with WSB running big American-style, sit-up-and-beg bikes. But I think the manufacturers got involved and wanted a series for race replica bikes like the Honda RC30. They also didn't want any world championship round to be at the TT, so the writing was on the wall for F1.'

According to Barry Symmons, it was the sheer danger of the F1 championship that proved to be its undoing. 'I think one of the reasons why F1 died was because Paolo Flammini did a much better job promoting the World Superbike championship. He realised that people wanted to see big four-strokes going round, and that it wasn't the best PR to have riders racing around stone walls and sometimes crashing into them. He also realised that a lot more people would be interested in racing at places like Misano and Mugello than at the Isle of Man. The tighter tuning regulations in WSB also meant that teams could buy road bikes and go racing at a fairly low cost.'

The first-ever World Superbike race was held at Donington Park on Sunday, 3 April 1988, and Joey Dunlop not only raced in it, he also finished on the podium. For that one meeting only, there was an unusual points-scoring system in place: despite there being two legs, results were combined to give just one podium and

Above: Joey's thousand-yard stare proved he had his 'race face' on and was up for the fight. © David Wallace

Below left: Taken during filming of *The Road Racers*, director David Wallace's picture shows a young Joey in his natural environment. © David Wallace

Below right: Joey with his brother-in-law Mervyn Robinson – the man who ignited his interest in racing. © David Wallace

Right: About as far from the glamour of a MotoGP paddock as it's possible to get. On the grid at Carrowdore, 1977.
© David Wallace

Below: Leading Rob McElnea in the TT Formula 1 world championship race at Assen in 1983.
© Don Morley

Now a factory Honda rider, Joey reluctantly poses on his brutish RCB in 1982.
© Don Morley

What it takes: even back in 1981 top level motorcycle racers had a lot of back up. Joey is pictured with fellow factory Honda riders Ron Haslam (*left*) and Alex George. *© Don Morley*

Above: When he won hist first TT in 1977 Joey didn't know how to open a bottle of champagne. By 1985 he was an expert. He's flanked here by Mick Grant (*left*) and Mark Salle at the Dutch F1 round, 1985. *© Don Morley*

Below left: Looking like a seventies rock star, Joey cradles the yellow-and-black Arai helmet that would become so famous. *© Don Morley*

Below right: The best pictures of Joey Dunlop were always candid ones and Don Morley was an expert in capturing them. *© Don Morley*

Above: Joey consults his mechanics at the North West 200 in 1985 as they attend his exotic Honda RVF750. *© Don Morley*

Below left: Team boss Barry Symmons congratulates his rider after Joey took yet another Formula 1 win at the TT in 1986. *© Don Morley*

Below right: Joey never gave two hoots about his appearance. He might have been a superstar, but he certainly never acted like one. *© Don Morley*

Spraying the bubbly after taking the first of six consecutive Formula 1 wins at the Isle of Man TT. Mick Grant is on Joey's right while Rob McElnea is to his left.

© Getty Images / Bob Thomas

There's no circuit like the TT circuit and Joey was its master on any size of bike. Here he rounds Guthrie's on his little Honda RS125. © Getty Images / Ian Walton

An iconic corner and an iconic rider. Joey negotiates Creg-ny-Baa during the 1993 TT on his Castrol Honda RC45. © *Don Morley*

Left: His greatest race. After a twelve-year wait, Joey reclaimed the TT Formula 1 crown in 2000 on Honda's SP-1.

© Don Morley

Right: 7 July, 2000. More than 50,000 mourners flood the Garryduff Road, County Antrim, to say goodbye to one of Northern Ireland's most beloved sons.

© PA Images

Left: 'Irish eyes are smiling': Joey's whole face lit up when he smiled.

© Getty Images / Bob Thomas

that podium consisted of 1981 500cc Grand Prix world champion Marco Lucchinelli, eventual WSB champion Fred Merkel, and Joey Dunlop. So much for the roads-only specialist. Here was Dunlop at almost forty years old, racing on a short circuit, and battling former and future Grand Prix and World Superbike champions.

It was an impressive performance and it left Joey at something of a crossroads as to which championship to pursue. When asked how the opening rounds of the new World Superbike series had gone for him, he replied, 'Och, not so bad – it's very tight. It's a lot different to Formula One, I'll tell you that.'

Despite opting not to fly to Japan for the opening round of the F1 championship, Joey still intended to enter most of the other rounds. 'Aye, I'm doing most of them,' he confirmed. 'I might miss a couple at the end of the year, but I'll do the first three or four, I think, and see how things is goin.' I'll know then whether to go on in Superbike or whether to go Formula One.'

Since none of the F1 regulars attended the Japanese round, Joey's overall points tally didn't suffer and, after winning the second round at the TT, his mind seemed to be made up: Joey's heart still lay in the TT Formula One world championship. He would only contest the first three rounds of WSB (and was lying fourth in the championship at that point) before concentrating on regaining his F1 title.

Although Carl Fogarty would later become a four-time World Superbike champion and a true legend of the series, in 1988 he was gunning for the F1 title, meaning Joey Dunlop faced a formidable new challenger, both on the short circuits and the roads. Foggy was equally at home on both and, at just twenty-three years old, he was almost young enough to be Joey's son. In fact, Joey had frequently raced against Carl's father George Fogarty (who had been second when Joey took his first TT win in 1977).

The unique team arrangement Honda had devised for Joey in 1987 did not continue into 1988. 'It was supposed to be a three-year deal, but it fell apart after one year,' Slick Bass says. 'I don't know if that was a money thing or what, but it cost so much for Honda to go Grand Prix racing and one of the teams had to go – although the entire cost of our team going F1 racing wouldn't even have covered the tyre bill for Honda's GP team.'

Honda didn't have any interest in fielding a full factory team in the World Superbike championship because the rules were so restrictive that research and development potential was severely limited. 'Honda always contested GPs and the F1 championship, but didn't bother much with WSB because it had little interest in developing a road bike once it was on the road,' Symmons says. 'To their way of thinking, developing a current road bike on a racetrack would mean there was something wrong with the road bike in the first place!'

But for the 1988 season Honda's secret weapon *was* a road bike, and it was a game-changer: it was the RC30. Because Superbike race machines had to be based on road-going models, Honda decided to make a road-going model that was essentially a race bike with lights on. Hand-built and exquisite in every detail, the RC30 became the new benchmark in racing over the next few years and, in 1988, Joey Dunlop was given one by Honda. The only problem was, Carl Fogarty had one too.

With no proper team to field Joey in, Honda came to a new arrangement with its most favoured son. It would provide bikes, parts and spares while all the running costs would be covered by sponsors. 'Honda Britain had collapsed because we lost the Rothmans money and I had to let Barry Symmons go,' says Bob McMillan, who was general manager of Honda UK at the time. 'We muddled along after that, really. We got the RC30 to Joey in 1988 – we knew we had the best bike on the planet then so we didn't really need an official team, we just made sure we got some riders on those bikes. There was never any doubt that Joey was going to be one of them. I wasn't managing him or anything – we supplied the bikes and Joey just sort of looked after himself from that point onwards, while Davy Wood did the organising.'

It was a set-up that must have suited Joey down to the ground. He was free to work on his own bikes and enter whatever races he pleased. He was also able to go about his racing in the way he had always preferred – out of the back of a van, with minimum creature comforts. 'Joey and Honda came to a very loose arrangement in that they provided the bikes but left him to do his own thing, and I think that's when he was at his happiest,' says Don Morley. 'When he was with Honda Britain and Rothmans Honda, I think he felt slightly awkward. I went with him to collect his world championship medal from the FIM one year, when he was dressed up in a blazer and badge, and he was so uncomfortable. That just wasn't Joey, and he couldn't wait to get out of the place. He always used to stay somewhere else instead of in the hotel with the team. He never seemed very happy about other people working on his bikes either. I think he felt much happier once Honda just gave him the bikes and left him to his own devices.'

Despite the apparent suitability of the arrangement, rumours circulated that Joey was seriously disappointed by Honda's lack of support and, most particularly, their failure to give him a factory bike. Instead, he was handed a standard RC30 and a race kit that included some special parts (which were also available to anyone else who could afford them). There were even whispers that he would be looking elsewhere for a ride the following year if Honda didn't increase its support.

Honda did at least provide a mechanic in the form of Nick

Goodison, who Joey had worked with for several years. Goodison would move into the Dunlop household – which would be the centre of operations – with the rest of the team being made up of Joey's old gang of trusted helpers. It was essentially a privateer set-up, but with official Honda motorcycles and backing: a unique arrangement in racing and something of a culture shock for Goodison, who was more accustomed to working in full factory teams. 'There'd be kittens all over the workshop and kids playing with racing pistons in the rain,' he would later recall of the chaotic set-up at Joey's house.

If there was a downside to this happy family team, it was the amount of time Joey spent working on his bikes, rather than concentrating on racing, and Goodison feels this affected his performances in 1988, more than the fact that Joey's Superbike wasn't any different to what any other racer with a bit of backing could buy.

Joey's mind certainly seemed to be elsewhere at the North West 200 that year. Another Irishman, Steven Cull, riding Joey's old Honda RS500 triple, had a healthy lead going into the last lap of the feature race but slipped off at York Corner, handing the lead to Joey. The race had been gifted to him, but when Dunlop looked over his shoulder with just over a mile to go, he was shocked to see a remounted Cull right on his exhaust pipe, and even more shocked when Cull out-braked him into the final chicane and took the win. 'I fell asleep on the last lap, I think,' Joey said. 'I didn't expect him to come back and my bike was… I was holding back. It was geein' me a lot o' trouble, and I knew it was the last lap, and I knew that me and Steven was away ahead, and I says to myself, "Just take it easy." But I come out of Portrush and Steven was sitting on my back wheel. I couldn't believe it. But, ach, that's racing like. I coulda kicked masel' afterwards, but it was his day and he won it.'

With his new RC30 cutting out in the first Superbike race, the only win for Joey at the 1988 North West was in the 750cc Production class. It was a rare win for him on a production bike but a good indicator that the RC30 was going to be a weapon of some note, even in an untuned state. Dunlop was, however, only gifted the win when runaway leader Steve Hislop (also on an RC30) crashed out.

But a win was a win, and this proved to be a significant one. It was Joey's thirteenth victory at the North West, and that made him the most successful rider in the event's long history. It would also be his last at the meeting that had claimed the lives of two of the Armoy Armada. Joey would never win another North West.

o

While Joey kept his options open by racing in the first three rounds of the new World Superbike championship in England, Hungary and Germany it was the second round of the TT Formula One world championship on the Isle of Man that proved to be a watershed. By winning the TT Formula One race on his new RC30, Dunlop took the lead in the F1 series and decided to pursue that championship instead of WSB.

It was another spectacular week for Dunlop at the TT as he equalled Mike Hailwood's feat of winning three in a week for a second time. As well as the F1 race, he also won the Junior and Senior races, taking his overall win tally to thirteen – just one short of Hailwood's all-time record of fourteen wins. One more and he would equal the greatest of all time. But when asked after the Senior TT if he was aiming to equal or beat Hailwood's record, Joey typically played the situation down. 'I don't know – that really took a lot out of me. I'm getting too old for this carry-on.'

As ever, Joey celebrated the end of another successful TT week by drinking more than his fair share of vodka and coke. This would not have constituted a problem, had he not discovered in the middle of the night that he had run out of cigarettes. Jumping in his car to drive to an all-night garage, Joey was stopped by a policeman for having a faulty rear light. He was breathalysed, found to be over the drink driving limit, fined £200 and banned from driving on the Isle of Man for eighteen months. It hardly mattered; he didn't live on the Isle of Man.

According to Carl Fogarty, age may have played a part in Joey's decision not to continue in WSB. 'Maybe he was just a bit too old by the time the World Superbike championship started up, I don't know,' he says. 'He was no spring chicken then, for sure, and he wasn't the fastest guy in the world on short circuits. He went well – I remember watching him in the early eighties at Donington, racing against the likes of Wayne Gardner and Roger Marshall, and he could hold his own with them, but once it got to the late eighties, he wasn't really able to run up front at the short circuits anymore.'

Fogarty says WSB was a far tougher series than F1, right from the outset. 'There was quite a difference between those championships, even in the first year of WSB. I won F1 races pretty comfortably in 1988, 1989, and 1990, to be honest, but when I raced in WSB I was battling really, really hard just to get in the top seven or eight. It was a different level altogether. For me, short-circuit racing is a lot tougher than racing on the roads. I mean, winning the TT is hard because of the nature of the circuit and the nature of the challenge, but you're out on your own, racing against the clock.

When you're on short circuits at world level, you're battling really, really hard against twenty or thirty other guys going into that first corner. It's just really different. But winning the TT is more satisfying. My Senior TT win stands right up there alongside my best WSB wins, if not more so. It's something I'm still proud of to this day.'

There were eight rounds in the 1988 TTF1 world championship and, after five of them, Joey led Carl Fogarty by 12 points. He had beaten him at Assen, had scored points in Portugal when Fogarty didn't, and then beat him again in Finland. Next up was Dundrod, where a home win was almost a foregone conclusion. Joey seemed to have one hand back on the trophy he had lost the previous year.

But things didn't work out that way. Even with all his vast experience, Joey was involved in the same tyre-choice lottery as everyone else ahead of the Ulster race: some parts of the circuit were dry, some soaking wet. Joey changed tyres twice on the grid, eventually opting for a slick rear. It would prove to be a costly mistake. Realising it was impossible to race on the wettest sections of the course with a slick, Joey pitted and changed tyres, rejoining the race in fifteenth place before bravely fighting back to seventh. But it wasn't enough to stop a runaway Fogarty, who had made the correct tyre choice and won the race by 17 seconds – his first world championship race win.

'I won the Ulster Grand Prix that year which shocked everybody, including myself,' Fogarty admits. 'I think I qualified in about twenty-first place, but came right up through the field and won, and then I had a chance of winning the world championship. That's where it all started for me, really. I was coming back from two years of injuries, having broken my leg badly in 1986 and then again in 1987. In 1988 I wasn't even meant to be racing, to be honest, but when I got on the Honda RC30 I realised I was comfortable for the first time in nearly two years after the leg injuries.'

With that unexpected win, Fogarty was now just 5.5 points behind Dunlop in the title chase (only half points were awarded in Portugal, as darkness descended before the delayed and re-started race could run its full distance) with just two rounds to go – Pergusa in Sicily and Donington Park in England. But Dunlop's title bid was effectively over before racing began in Sicily: he crashed during practice, heavily injuring his arm and badly damaging his bike.

'After he had crashed in practice, my boys really looked after Joey because he was pretty much on his own – he only had his friend Derek McIntyre with him,' Fogarty says. 'So, two of my lads went to hospital with him and the others fixed his bike up for him to get it ready for race day.'

After sitting out final qualifying to rest his arm, Joey bravely tried to race but was struck by further bad luck when a valve spring broke on his RC30, leaving him to watch helplessly as Fogarty took the win and a 14.5-point lead in the championship. 'I got away first and was dicing for the lead with this local lad, then something happened to him and I won the race by a country mile,' Fogarty recalls. 'That result pretty much clinched me the world championship, because all I had to do then was go to Donington and finish in the top ten. I was pretty sure Joey wouldn't win against all those short-circuit boys, like Niall Mackenzie and Roger Burnett.'

With just one round to go and only 20 points for a win, Joey was going to have his work cut out in the final round. Adding to his points disadvantage, he was still carrying his arm injury when he arrived at Donington – a circuit that was always going to suit Fogarty better. On top of that, because it wasn't being staged on a dangerous road circuit, the race attracted entries from a host of short-circuit specialists who would make it even harder for Joey to score big points.

One of those specialists, Niall Mackenzie, won the race, while Foggy rode a careful race to fifth place. With Joey only managing eleventh spot his championship was over, and Carl Fogarty took his first world title with apparent ease. 'I ended up winning the TTF1 championship when I wasn't even riding that hard, if I'm honest. I was too frightened of falling off because I couldn't afford to damage my leg again. So, it was quite bizarre that I ended up winning that championship.'

Joey Dunlop was never a sore loser and that night he headed up to Blackburn to celebrate with Fogarty and his crew. 'Because my boys had looked after him in Sicily, Joey and his gang came back to Blackburn with us that night to help me celebrate. We had a great night in my local pub, The Barge. The next day, I heard a story that Joey's van was seen in a ditch on the road to Stranraer to catch the ferry. To this day I don't know if they crashed it or had just parked up in such a way that it looked like it was in a ditch.'

It had been disappointing for Joey to lose the TTF1 championship for a second time in as many years, but he had run Foggy close and he had completed a treble at the TT, so the season couldn't be viewed as a complete disaster. The 1989 season, on the other hand, could. Joey Dunlop was about to undergo the biggest crisis of his career to date.

CHAPTER 13

THE RETURN OF
THE KING

**"PEOPLE SAID TO ME AFTERWARDS, I WOULD HAVE BEATEN HIM IF I
HADN'T HAD TO REFUEL, BUT I DON'T HONESTLY BELIEVE I WOULD.'**
Robert Dunlop

Following his Good Friday crash at Brands Hatch in 1989, Joey
Dunlop faced a crossroads in his career. Carrying the worst injuries
he had ever sustained, and approaching forty years of age, most
people felt he should retire. But Joey chose to race on. Two months
after badly breaking his leg and wrist, he turned up at the Isle of
Man TT on crutches, fully intent on racing. His determination
impressed everyone, including TT commentator, Peter Kneale. 'I
will never forget it,' he said before his untimely death in 2002.
'Here was this man who was clearly a TT legend, hobbling to the
grandstand on crutches to see if he would be passed fit to race.'

He wasn't. The TT's chief medical officer refused Joey permission
to race on the grounds that his wrist had not healed sufficiently to
allow him to control a motorcycle at racing speeds. For the one

179

and only time in his career, Joey Dunlop was forced to sit out the TT, and he hated every minute of it. The only time the fans got to see him out on track was when Bob McMillan took him for a parade lap on the back of a Honda CBR1000 after the Senior TT. 'When I knew for certain that Joey wouldn't be allowed to ride that year, I asked him if he would sit on the back of me to let the fans see him, because they had all come to see him and would want to let him know that he was missed,' McMillan says. 'That lap was the most amazing thing I've ever done on a bike in my life. The fans were standing out on the course everywhere, in their tens of thousands, waving, clapping, cheering, waving programmes, taking photographs, and all the while Joey's hanging on with his good arm and waving with his broken one. There were just so many people cheering and yelling for him, I could feel the hairs on the back of my neck standing up. And coming back to the grandstand, they had all the number threes lit up and flashing on the scoreboard and the cheers were deafening.'

While everyone else might have enjoyed the lap, Joey certainly did not, as McMillan now admits. 'I've never said this publicly but, when he got off the bike and back on his crutches, he didn't say, "Thanks for that, Bob". He said, "Fucking never again!"'

With Joey on the sidelines during race week, Steve Hislop headed up Honda's TT effort and became only the third rider after Mike Hailwood and Joey Dunlop to pull off a TT treble. He also became the first man to lap the mountain course at an average speed of 120mph. The goalposts had moved: if Joey Dunlop was going to win a Superbike race at the TT again, he would have to up his pace.

It would be another six weeks before Joey was fit enough to return to any kind of racing and, when he did, it was on a machine completely unfamiliar to him – a Honda RS125. Even in his earliest racing days, the smallest bike Joey had ever ridden was 200cc, so this was new territory, but his injuries were such that he simply couldn't manhandle a big Superbike with any degree of confidence. A 125cc machine was much lighter, much less powerful, and much easier to change direction on; in short, it was perfect for the condition he was in. Local businessman Andy McMenemy would sponsor Joey's outings on the 125 from this point onwards and would become an integral part of the Dunlop gang. It was an association that would later prove to have massive consequences, though no one could foresee it at the time.

As the smallest racing class, the 125cc race at any meeting did not hold the same prestige as the Superbike class, which stole all the limelight, media attention, big-money sponsors and television coverage. Joey was going back to a much more grass-roots type of racing but, fortunately for him, the TT organisers had reintroduced a 125cc Ultra-Lightweight TT in 1989 for the first time since 1974. It meant that Joey would still have a chance to add to his haul of TT wins.

Ian Simpson says the smaller bikes were safer for Joey to ride with his injuries, though not necessarily easier. 'I wouldn't say it was much easier to ride the smaller bikes, because you're so cramped on a 125 or a 250cc machine, especially around the Isle of Man, because the races are so long. So, it's definitely not easy, but it is less physically demanding in terms of the strength needed to muscle a Superbike around. Superbikes in Joey's time were so much more unstable than they are now – they would have tank-slappers everywhere and you'd be hanging on for dear life. He would have felt safer and a lot less likely to crash on a 125 or a 250 because they just went where you pointed them without tying themselves in knots. But your knees and your neck get proper sore on those little bikes, so I would say they were safer, rather than easier.'

As chance would have it, one of the hottest prospects in 125cc racing at the time of Joey's comeback was his own brother, Robert Dunlop. Robert was the youngest of the three Dunlop brothers and his career had begun around the time that Jim Dunlop's had ended. Struggling to find financial backing, and perhaps lacking the sheer determination of big brother Joey, Jim Dunlop had retired from racing in 1982. 'I had no money,' he says. 'I thought if I stopped racing that somebody would come and offer me a bike, but it never happened. I had two bikes, but I couldn't afford to run them. In those days it wasn't easy going – running a bike every weekend when there wasn't much sponsorship about – and, in the end, I just had no money. But then, if I hadn't stopped racing I might not be here. You know, there were three of us all racing from the one family at the one time, and the law of averages said that one of us was going to get hurt at some stage or other.'

Robert Dunlop had turned professional just before Jim Dunlop retired and was now starting to make a name for himself. He had won the Manx Grand Prix Newcomers Junior Race in 1983 and the 350cc race at the North West 200 in 1986, and would go on to win fourteen races at the same meeting – one more than Joey, and a record tally that stood for more than twenty years. In 1989, as Joey sat on the sidelines, Robert won his first TT when he took victory in the Ultra-Lightweight race. The tiny 125cc machines were perfectly suited to Robert's diminutive size, and he was so adept on them that he not only won road races, he also won the 125cc British championship in 1991.

Robert appeared to have the same iron will and commitment to racing that his eldest brother had, and yet they appeared to be very different characters. More clean-cut, more articulate and more willing to play up to the media, Robert seemed to be much more outgoing than Joey, but there were reasons for that, as Jim Dunlop explains. 'Robert always had to go begging a lot for sponsorship and was always having to chat to people to try and get a pound or two, so he sort of had to be more outgoing. Joey got in with Honda early on and didn't really have to do that. There was boys round Joey at that time that got him the ride with Suzuki in 1980 then, after that, Honda signed him. Once Joey got in with Honda, he never had to go looking or talking to people for sponsorship. Robert had to do whatever he could to get some backing, so he had to shout that bit louder than Joey.'

Barry Symmons had been Joey's team boss at Honda from 1981 until 1986 and would then become Robert's team boss at JPS Norton in 1990, so he worked closely with both men. 'They were both very fine riders but were at opposite ends of the scale personality-wise,' he says. 'Robert was very much the outgoing character, whereas Joey was the shy one.'

'I think they had a lot of respect for each other but there was a rivalry there,' adds Neil Tuxworth, who became team boss of the newly restored Honda Britain team in late 1989. 'Robert was a more professional rider than Joey and gave off a more professional image, and I think Joey found that a bit hard to deal with, but they had a lot of respect for each other and thought a lot of each other. Some people said they didn't get on very well, but I disagree with that – there was just that bit of personal conflict between them because it *was* a battle, and they were two entirely different people altogether; there's no question about that.'

Bob McMillan says Joey had absolute trust in Robert, and also respected him greatly, even though the pair didn't spend huge amounts of time together. 'I think they were very close, but you never really saw them together that often, so you never saw that closeness,' he says. 'They had massive respect for each other, but I don't think you would say they were in each other's pockets. I remember seeing Robert changing the gearing on Joey's RC45 at the Ulster Grand Prix in 1999, though, and Joey would only trust Robert to do that. So, that's a big level of trust, right there.'

Whatever the differences in their characters, the brothers were now perfectly matched out on track, Joey's injuries negating the advantage he had in terms of experience compared to Robert.

Joey made his racing comeback at Fore in July, four months after his accident, but a solitary eighth place in the 125cc race was all he could manage. He had made the decision to restrict his early outings to a 125cc machine but was still clearly uncomfortable on the bike and lacking in confidence after sustaining such serious injuries. 'He was a long time on the mend and lost his drive, got a bit demoralised, and got into a rut,' Robert said of his brother.[46]

After his comeback race at Fore, Joey took a fifth place in the Munster 100, again on the 125cc machine, one week later. But when he then tried to ride his big RC30 Superbike at the Ulster Grand Prix, it became clear just how badly affected he had been by the Brands Hatch crash. Struggling to twentieth place in a race that he was so accustomed to winning was all the proof anyone needed: his days on a big bike were surely over.

There would be no wins for Joey in his much-shortened 1989 season; his best result would be third place on the 125 at the Mid Antrim. His final outing of the worst season of his career would be in the Sunflower Trophy race at Kirkistown but, even then, some seven months after his crash, he could only hustle his Superbike to thirteenth place.

Apart from the final round at the Ulster, where he struggled not to be lapped, Joey had not contested the TT Formula One world championship in 1989 and could only watch helplessly as Carl Fogarty romped to a second world title.

Bowed but not broken, he went into the off-season licking his wounds, working on his fitness, and planning his route back to the top of the sport he lived for. Somehow, some way, he was going to find the will to win again and the strength to be able to do it. But if he wanted to be back on top, then the man he had to beat was his own brother. The battle between the Dunlops was about to begin.

o

Robert Dunlop wasn't just a 125cc specialist. Despite his small stature, he had also been delivering results in the Superbike class and, for the 1990 season, had been signed up by the all-British JPS Norton team, managed by Barry Symmons. Although he was now in a rival camp, Symmons' loyalty to Joey was not so easily extinguished. 'We had a long association and you don't forget that overnight,' he says. 'When I was at the TT with Robert Dunlop and the Norton, Joey was having a problem with his Honda and he came to see me to ask if we could help with his front forks. So, Chris Mayhew and I, along with Joey's manager, Davy Wood, arranged to meet Joey in a private garage away from prying eyes, to help him set up his suspension.'

It was a measure of the deep affection and loyalty that Joey Dunlop inspired in people, and that affection was only increased because of the obstacles that he now faced. Sponsorship was now hard to come by, and the former full factory Honda rider was now riding a plain white RC30 with only a few sponsors' stickers on the fairing. Robert, meanwhile, looked resplendent in the iconic black-and-gold livery of the JPS Norton team, and it was he who stole all the limelight at the North West 200 in 1990 by pulling off a treble, winning not only the 125cc race but also both Superbike races, while Joey had to be content with two fourth-place finishes for his day's work. Advantage Robert.

It was a similar story at the TT, where Robert once again won the Ultra-Lightweight race and took an impressive third place in the TT Formula One race, in which Joey struggled to eighth. It was the best finish he could muster in what was a disastrous TT. He had been battling for the podium in the Ultra-Lightweight race before his Honda RS125 broke down and forced him to retire. He then suffered a similar fate in the Junior race and could only limp home in sixteenth place in the final race of the week, the Senior TT.

The TT Formula One world championship had been downgraded for the 1990 season, losing its world championship status and becoming the FIM TT Formula Cup. By season's end the series (which had been reduced to just five rounds) would be abandoned altogether and the blossoming World Superbike championship would become the sole production-based world championship for Superbikes.

Joey contested the final season, nonetheless, and managed to put up a credible fight against Carl Fogarty. Having sat out the Japanese round at Sugo as usual, Joey's eighth place at the TT was followed up with a third place at Vila Real in Portugal and fifth at Kouvola in Finland. The last-ever round of the championship was to be held at Dundrod, and with Fogarty already having been crowned champion for a third time, he opted to sit it out. That left Joey and Robert Dunlop to fight it out for second place in the championship. Going into the Ulster GP there were just two points between them, with Joey enjoying the advantage because he had competed in three rounds of the series compared to Robert's two. The home fans were in for a treat.

With Fogarty not in attendance and Steve Hislop sidelined with mechanical issues, the race became a straight fight between the two Dunlop brothers and their respective Honda and Norton mounts. Robert initially took charge at the front and, after looking over his shoulder during the first lap and seeing that his big brother was way behind him, he relaxed into a fast, but safe, pace. It wasn't fast enough. 'After a couple of laps, I had a look back again and I could see he was getting closer,' Robert recalled in 2003. 'I thought, "Bloody hell – Joey! Right, better kick on a bit here!" I remember having a look at Lethamstown, and then again before Ireland's, and the gap was pretty much the same. By then I had started to ride harder and was pretty much going as fast as I could go.'[47]

It still wasn't fast enough. 'By the time we got up through Budore to the Windmill, he had passed me,' Robert continued. 'I was trying up though there; it's a fast section and my bike was fast, but he still managed it.' Like so many competitors before him, Robert was stunned at Joey's pace. 'I couldn't understand how he pulled so much ground on me in that section – I think about that yet. There's perfection – and road racing is hard to perfect – but Joey had that down to a fine art; he just pulled so much ground on me from Ireland's to Wheeler's.'[48]

Digging deeper than he ever had before, and with the tens of thousands of spectators at fever pitch, Robert managed to re-pass his brother going into the hairpin and held the lead until he had to make a pit stop to refuel. Joey then played his ace card: with his slower Honda being less thirsty than the super-fast Norton, he had calculated that he could just about finish the race on one tank of fuel. Having dealt with Robert – and being miles in front of third-placed man Dave Leach – Joey slackened his pace to ensure he made it to the finish line. When he did, he was 17 seconds ahead of Robert and, for the one and only time in his career, the most undemonstrative man in motorcycle racing punched the air in delight. He had just won his first major international race since 1988, had won his first race on a Superbike since his Brands Hatch crash, had beaten his little brother who was the star on the rise, and had set a new lap record to boot. The King of the Roads was back on his throne.

'I always admired Joey for that one,' Robert said. 'People said to me afterwards I would have beaten him if I hadn't had to refuel, but I don't honestly believe I would.'[49]

Nobody had seen such spectacular racing between two brothers on the roads before, and two such popular ones at that. Joey Dunlop, still injured, with barely any sponsors on his bike, and with his scruffy, mismatched leathers, had won the last-ever race in what had been the TT Formula One world championship (even though it was now downgraded to 'Cup' status). Having made the championship his own in the 1980s, it was a most fitting end to an era that had begun with the likes of Phil Read and Mike Hailwood back in the late seventies. Joey was ecstatic. He had proved his doubters wrong, and he had proved to himself that he still had what it took. It had taken seventeen months of hard work and grim determination, it had been a painful and sometimes humiliating road back, but he had cemented his legend.

Joey Dunlop faced the new decade a rejuvenated man. It would be his fourth decade of racing and he was still winning. This was new territory, but there was one thing he still wanted to do above anything else: he wanted to win a fourteenth TT race to equal the late, great Mike Hailwood. The only thing standing in his way was his own brother.

CHAPTER 14

YER MAN

**'JOEY RETIRED FROM THE RACE WITH DOUBLE VISION,
BUT THE REASON HE HAD DOUBLE VISION WAS BECAUSE
HE'D BEEN OUT ON THE PISS ALL NIGHT!'**
Nick Jefferies

Following the demise of the TT Formula One world championship, Joey Dunlop's main focus during every racing season for the rest of his career was the Isle of Man TT. His whole year would be built around two weeks in June and, having stopped racing on short circuits in England, he became a pure roads specialist. He would still race at short circuits in Ireland such as Kirkistown, Mondello Park and Aghadowey, but he became more and more focused on the natural roads circuits where he had always felt most comfortable. It became something of a standing joke that Joey would be much faster on short circuits if they had walls and trees around them. 'One time at Assen, when Joey wasn't going particularly well, his mates painted trees and hedges on the inside of his bike's fairing, so it looked to Joey like he was in a road race!' Don Morley recalls. 'I remember them saying, "Ach, yer man likes walls and trees roon' aboot him. He'll be faster now!"'

It might have been a joke, but there was a certain element of truth in it. Short-circuit racing at international level was just too frantic for a man who liked nothing better than being out on his own, racing the TT circuit at his own pace. 'The TT's different because you're riding on your own and I was always good at that,' Joey told Jackie Fullerton in a 1997 documentary for BBC Northern Ireland. 'If I could get out on my own, I could go as quick as any other rider that's there – without any trouble I can go as quick. It's when you're in among the short circuits and you're diving in and pushing people oot... In my later career, I'd back up and say, "No, that's silly," but I used to be able to do it – I'd do the same thing. At the TT you're not doing that, you're on your own. And if I get on my own and gets going, I can still go as quick as anyone.'[50]

The TT mountain course is not for the faint-hearted. It has claimed the lives of some 260 riders since the first race was held in 1907. 'It's the most dangerous track in the world,' Mick Grant testifies, while Roger Marshall's summary is even more chilling: 'One mistake and it's the last mistake you'll ever make in your life.'

There is no room for error. Because of this harsh reality, motorcycle racers – and particularly real road racers – are often thought to have no fear, but this is not true. Fear is what keeps them alert, fear is what protects them, fear is necessary; they just have to learn how to contain it. 'Oh, you have fear, you have,' Joey said of the TT. 'But see once you get to Bray Hill? It's gone. Everybody's the same. But once that flag drops, you're in a completely different world – you're on your own.'

Graham Sanderson remembers seeing the look of intense concentration on Joey's face before the flag dropped. 'I wouldn't say he was nervous before a race, but you could tell he was focused. I mean, he wasn't exactly shaking, but he looked to be on the verge of it – like the next movement would have been a quivering lip. He thought so intensely about what was going to happen and was really, really focused before a race.'

While he admitted to being afraid before a race, Joey also rationalised that fear to make it more acceptable. 'I know the TT's dangerous, but so is every racetrack. There's been people killed at every racetrack in the world – or most of them. There's been people killed at some of the safest tracks. You don't have to have roads or trees to get people killed. But what keeps me going at the TT – I work with my own bikes and I really enjoy the TT, and I don't take any chances. I have scared myself, I have ran onto the grass, I've had near shaves and all that but, at the same time, if I'm really struggling I know to ease off. I know if I'm beat, I'm beat. And I think, if people would do that at the TT, it wouldn't be as bad.'[51]

As sensible as he was capable of being at the TT, Joey was also very pragmatic about the risks. Paul 'Moz' Owen, a leading privateer at the TT for many years, remembers Joey's no-nonsense advice on how to take the ferociously fast and blind Ballagarey Corner (nicknamed Ballascarey by the competitors). 'I told him I was changing down to fifth gear and rolling off the throttle to steady the bike up, but he said, "No, no, leave it in sixth gear and just drive through smoothly." Then he asked me how fast I was taking the corner and I told him about 130mph, so he said, "Well, what happens if you hit the wall at that speed?" and I said I would obviously get very badly hurt. He said, "Exactly, so you might as well leave it in sixth then"!'

In for a penny, in for a pound. By 1991, Joey had fifteen years' experience at the TT and had made almost every mistake a rider could. This ensured he wouldn't make the same mistakes again, but it also meant he was wise enough to back off and settle for a lower placing if things weren't going right. By now, his experience counted for more than youth around the TT course, and it would ensure his TT career lasted much longer than it really should have done.

The only problem facing Joey as he travelled to the Isle of Man for the 1991 TT was that the fans might turn against him if he took one more win and equalled Mike Hailwood's record. Such was the love for Hailwood, there were those who wished to see his record remain intact, and Joey was painfully aware of this. 'For a couple of years, I was under a lot of pressure,' he admitted. 'Some people wanted me to beat it, but most people didn't want me to beat it. At times I thought I could beat it but, if I do beat it, people will go against me.'

For the 1991 TT, Honda shipped in two extremely exotic, full-factory RVF machines – modern versions of the ones Joey rode and helped to develop back in the eighties. In 1990 the Honda Britain team had reformed and was now aiming to spoil Yamaha's big plans to mark thirty years of TT racing. But the special bikes were brought over from Japan not for Joey Dunlop but for the TT's new hot shots, Steve Hislop and Carl Fogarty. With Fogarty having to miss the Senior TT at the end of the week due to World Superbike commitments, Joey was to be given the RVF for that one race, but it must have felt like a slight to have to ride his old RC30 in the Formula One race: he was clearly no longer Honda's favourite son, although Bob McMillan insists he accepted this without complaint. 'Joey didn't get one of those bikes because he wasn't the top big bike rider at that time,' he says. 'But he accepted that and didn't have a problem with it. And he did get to ride one in the Senior.'

Hislop destroyed the outright lap record with a circuit at 123.48mph in the F1 race, taking the win from Fogarty in the process. Joey's much more standard RC30 lasted just one lap before he was forced to retire. When he was given the RVF for the Senior, he posted his fastest TT lap to date with an average speed of 121.51mph. It was almost 2mph slower than Hislop but still impressive, especially as he admitted he still wasn't fit enough to maintain a winning pace over six laps of the long and gruelling course. Hislop, in a warming tribute to his hero-turned-teammate, caught Joey at Ramsey on the last lap of the Senior but, rather than blasting past him, rode alongside him for the final twelve miles, giving fans and photographers an unexpected treat. It was a mark of respect from one master to another.

Joey's best chance of a race win had been in the 125cc Ultra-Lightweight TT but his bid for a fourteenth victory was scuppered by his brother Robert. The pair had put on a truly inspiring spectacle at the North West 200 just two weeks earlier as they battled side by side, Joey on the Honda and Robert on the JPS Norton. With long straights to rest on, Joey could manage his Superbike more easily at the North West than at other circuits, and when he and Robert took the Ballysally roundabout side by side (giving rise to one of the most famous pictures ever taken of the brothers) he looked like he could win the race. But with just one mile to go, the chain broke on his RC30 and Robert took the spoils, some 37 seconds ahead of his team-mate Trevor Nation. Such had been the pace of the Dunlops.

There had never been two brothers so evenly matched, and battling at the front in road racing and, siblings or not, no quarter was asked or given. Five-times North West winner Ian Simpson had a grandstand seat for some of Joey and Robert's epic battles and could see just how hard the brothers raced against each other. 'You can race really hard against another rider but still give them respect,' he says. 'Me and Jim Moodie were the best of pals, but we had many proper hard races against each other – *proper* hard. It makes it more fun, racing against someone you're great pals with, so I imagine that went for Joey and Robert as brothers, too. There was nobody I liked beating more than Jim Moodie but, at the same time, there was nobody I wanted to win more than him if I couldn't win.'

Jim Dunlop says the rivalry was never anything but friendly. 'It didn't bother them who won the race or who came second in a situation like that,' he says. 'They both enjoyed it and whoever won, won – there was no real rivalry.'

In the main North West 200 race, it was Robert's turn to break down, leaving Nation to win his first Superbike race on the 8.9-mile 'Triangle' course. Joey was second again but was closing Nation down towards the end of the race. He was clearly getting back to some sort of form.

Robert had also taken the win from Joey in the 125cc race at the North West, so there was no doubt who was going to be the main opposition to Joey in the Ultra-Lightweight TT. And so it turned out. Joey had not won a TT for four years now, but after he had built up a twenty-five-second lead over his brother, after two laps of the four-lap race, his legions of fans dared to dream. The dream was short-lived. A slow fuel-stop at the end of the second lap allowed Robert to take the lead, and after he set a new record lap of 106.71mph, the race was his. There were some Joey fans who felt Robert should have allowed his brother to win, so that he could equal Hailwood's record, and Robert was well aware of this. 'It won't have helped my popularity to have stopped Joey equalling the record,' he admitted, 'but we're a competitive family and I'd rather have beat him into second place than beat him for fifth spot.'

The problem for TT racers is that they have to wait a full year before having a chance to win more races, and Joey didn't have time to waste. By the time he lined up on the Glencrutchery Road start line again in 1992, he was forty years old and had been racing for twenty-four years. His age didn't show in the Formula One race, however, and Joey took an impressive third spot behind Honda team-mate Phillip McCallen and Steve Hislop on the Norton.

While Joey had been slowly working his way back from injury, Phillip McCallen had established himself as the new Irish kid on the block. Intensely aggressive and wild-riding, McCallen's style on a bike was the polar-opposite of Joey's but it worked every bit as well, and he proved it by taking that first TT win in the 1992 Formula One race. He would rack up another ten victories by the time the decade was out and would undoubtedly have won more had he not been forced out of racing after breaking his back. Happily, he made a full recovery.

Despite being the Irishman most likely to steal Joey Dunlop's thunder, the two were always good friends. 'Joey was my hero really,' McCallen says. 'I remember the first time I beat him I thought, "Jesus Christ, I'm some rider now – I beat Joey Dunlop!" It was only afterwards, when people told me Joey was having a bad day, that I got knocked down a peg or two.'

Despite having never liked production machines, Joey added a Honda CBR600 Supersport bike to his stable for the first time in 1991 and made a lifelong friend in the process. John Harris owned a bike dealership in Crowborough, East Sussex and, together with his brother Steve, also ran a small race team in the British Supersport championship. A die-hard road racing fan, Harris's hero was Joey Dunlop, so he was struck dumb when Neil Tuxworth called one day to ask a favour. 'Our race bike had been supplied by Honda at a reasonable price on condition that, if Honda wanted it for any other events, they could borrow it,' Harris explains. 'Neil Tuxworth rang me one day and asked if it would be okay for Joey to ride my 600 at the TT. At first I thought it was a wind-up because Joey was such a hero of mine.'

Neil Tuxworth takes up the story. 'I found out from Linda that Joey was looking for a 600 to ride, so I rang John and told him I had found a rider for him and that it was Joey Dunlop. The line went silent for a while and I said, "Are you still there, John?" He said, "You're taking the piss, aren't you?" I really had to convince him that I wasn't joking. He was speechless – absolutely lost for words. After that, him and Joey really hit it off and became fantastic friends because John is another very down-to-earth guy.'

Harris was over the moon when he realised it wasn't a joke. 'It was real and so I said, "Yes, please!" That was April of 1991. I hadn't even met Joey at that point, and I didn't meet him until about an hour before the start of the Supersport 600 TT that year. We had a quick chat and I asked him if the bike was okay and he said, "Oh, it's right enough" and off he went. He had never been a big fan of production bikes but thought he would give it a try. He didn't know how he was going to get on after his Brands Hatch injuries and this was a way of trying himself out. He ended up sixth in the TT, so he made a good account of himself and we were over the moon. In September of that year, I flew over to the Skerries and offered him our 600 to ride on the roads the following year and he accepted.' It was a partnership that would last for the remainder of Joey's career.

But Joey's main focus of TT week was the Ultra-Lightweight 125cc race. He had practically starved himself in the weeks leading up to the 1992 event in order to improve the power-to-weight ratio when he was on the tiny little machine. His brother was smaller in stature and Joey couldn't afford to give Robert that kind of advantage. The size and weight of a rider is crucial in achieving the optimum power-to-weight ratio, and Nick Jefferies believes that

Joey's stature – even though he was not as slight as Robert – gave him an advantage over taller and heavier riders like himself. 'While Joey was very fast and smooth and he knew *exactly* where he was going on the TT course, he was small too, like Phillip McCallen and Carl Fogarty,' he says. 'They were all about ten and a half stone and five foot, six inches, which was a massive advantage, in my opinion. Joey and me did some testing together at Jurby Airfield on the Isle of Man in 1991 and we had his Honda RC30 and the full factory RVF. We would ride alongside each other in second gear and then, when we got to a white line on the tarmac, we would crack the throttles full open. When Joey was on the RVF and I was on his RC30 he would just piss off into the distance, about forty yards ahead of me. When we swapped bikes, so I was on the RVF and Joey was on the RC30, he stayed dead level with me and that was purely down to his light weight, so it was a huge advantage.'

Joey's rapid weight loss appeared to have affected his ride in the Senior TT at the end of the week when he retired from the race due to suffering double vision. When asked how he felt after pulling in, he replied, 'Knackered – and I only did two laps. 'I couldn't see where I was going. Robert and Phillip came past me and I didn't know if it was one rider or two riders so, I said, "Forget about that, that's it."'

According to Jefferies, however, there was a simple explanation for Joey's early exit. 'Joey retired from the race with double vision, but the reason he had double vision was because he'd been out on the piss all night!'

But while hustling the big Superbike around the TT course was too much for the emaciated (or hungover) Dunlop, the 125 was much more manageable, although practice week had not gone well. Of the four laps he started on the bike, Joey didn't complete one of them without a problem and his best lap was 3mph slower than

Robert's best. While Robert topped the leader board with a lap at 104.26mph, Joey was languishing down in eighth place, over half a minute behind his brother.

The night before the race Joey worked late, as usual, to ensure his machine was perfectly prepared, and it was fortunate that he did because otherwise he wouldn't have found the broken part that would have ended his race 'We worked on the bike until 1.30 in the morning and found one of the engine mountings had broken,' he explained. 'We couldn't get a replacement at that time of the day so we used one that Robert had thrown out.'

In a race that was only ever going to be between the two Dunlop brothers, Joey would be using a cast-off part from Robert's bike to try to beat him. In the Dunlop household, blood was always thicker than water.

That wasn't so obvious once the flag dropped, however. Joey had gone four years without a TT win, and he was motivated in the extreme to end that drought. With a bad practice week behind him, he hit the ground running in the race and got round the first lap some 3.6 seconds quicker than Robert. On lap two Robert upped his pace and both he and Joey broke the lap record. Some timing points around the course were reporting a dead heat – the brothers could not be split on time.

By the end of the second lap, as he came in for fuel, Joey's lead was a mere 0.2 seconds, but a super-slick pit stop played in his favour and a new lap record of 108.69mph (a full 23 seconds faster than Robert's existing record of 106.71mph) was enough to put him back in command. Just. There was still less than a second between the brothers for most of the last lap.

Once Robert had crossed the line, all he could do was wait for Joey to do the same before knowing who had won. The TT is a race against the clock, with riders being sent away in pairs at ten-second intervals for safety reasons. Only when the riders cross the finish line can their race times be calculated, and a winner declared. As the famous yellow helmet appeared over the crest of the Glencrutchery Road the crowd was howling its approval, every race programme was being waved furiously, willing and urging Joey to the line. Robert was a hugely popular rider in his own right, but the spectators knew what this meant; they knew they were witnessing history being made.

As Joey flashed under the chequered flag the timekeepers confirmed it: he had won the race by 8.4 seconds. And he had won it from a 125cc specialist, the reigning 125cc British champion, and the man who had won the last three Ultra-Lightweight TTs: he had beaten Robert at his own game. He now had more TT wins than any man alive and was equal with Hailwood in the all-time wins list. 'Maybe he'll pack up now and give us all a chance,' Robert said after the race, only half joking.

Joey seemed more relieved than elated. The fourteenth win had become something of a psychological barrier for him and he had finally broken it down. He was also sensitive about the memory of the late Mike Hailwood. 'I was just glad to get it over, to tell you the truth,' he said some years later. 'And I was glad the way the people took it because I didn't want the people to go against me... I've been talking to people and they told me, they says, "We definitely never wanted you to ever beat Mike Hailwood's record, but now you did, we're glad it's all over" – the same as I was.'

If he still harboured any doubts about how he would be received by race fans after equalling Hailwood, they were dispelled instantly at the TT prize-giving presentations at the Villa Marina in Douglas. When respected motorcycle journalist John Brown introduced Joey to the stage, he couldn't say another word for five whole minutes as the 3000-strong capacity audience, packing every available standing space, gave Joey a deafening standing ovation. Only the blasts of air horns could cut through the cheers, applause and yells that greeted the shyest man in motorcycle racing and Joey could only stand there grinning sheepishly as he waited for the rapture to subside. It was more like a rock concert than a motorcycle event, except the man at the centre of it was as far removed from a rock star as it was possible to be.

TT fans are extremely knowledgeable about their chosen sport; they *knew* what Joey had been through to get to where he was at that very moment; they *knew* they were witnessing history; they *knew* they were in the presence of one of the greatest road racers of all time, and they felt proud to share in Joey's moment of triumph. As Bob McMillan said at the time, 'This is the greatest night I have ever seen here. We have never witnessed anything like it and probably never will again.'[52]

Since returning from his Brands Hatch injuries in 1989, the TT had become the focal point of Joey's racing season. Everything he did was geared towards it, so to be winning again, even if only in the smallest capacity class, was as important as any other victory in his career to date.

But throughout the 1990s, Joey would have another focus, and it would have nothing to do with motorcycle racing. He tried as hard as he could to keep it quiet, and only those involved and those very close to Joey knew that he was doing it, but during the winters when there was no racing, Joey Dunlop took on a series of one-man mercy missions, putting his own life in danger to help ease the suffering of orphans in some of the most inhospitable countries in Europe. The true character of Joey Dunlop was about to be revealed.

CHAPTER 15

MERCY

**'IF THERE WAS EVER A POINT THAT WE WERE FEELING DOWN,
IT WAS THE PERIOD BEFORE JOEY DUNLOP ARRIVED.'**
Siobhan Carter

Like most good stories, this one began with a man walking into a bar. 'A man come into the bar one day with a wee package and he was going to post it to his daughter who was over in Albania, or one of those countries,' Linda Dunlop explained of the origins of her husband's mercy missions. 'He got talking to Joey about it and, when he explained a few things – she was a nurse out there – Joey decided this would be something worthwhile doing.'[53]

That 'something' was delivering aid to an orphanage in the remote village of Ungureni in Romania, where conditions were truly brutal. Under the twenty-five-year communist reign of Nicolae Ceau,sescu, Romanians had been forced to have more children (contraception and abortions were outlawed and couples without children were heavily taxed) in the belief that a larger workforce would bring prosperity. The policy led to the abandonment of around 100,000 children who, due to learning difficulties or physical disabilities, were deemed 'incurable' and hidden away from public sight in one of twenty-nine state orphanages. The conditions in these orphanages were barbaric, the children so undernourished it was practically impossible to tell what ages they were. In some cases, there would be one spoon for each dormitory, meaning the children had to fight for it to eat. The strongest prevailed, while the weaker children were forced to scavenge scraps from the urine-soaked floors. Many starving infants were neglected, and even older children went naked. When Ceau,sescu died in 1989, the Western world became aware of the horrors he had left behind and word eventually reached five-times world champion Joey Dunlop.

Siobhan Carter (at that time Siobhan Lagan) was a nurse from Portglenone, some fifteen miles south of Ballymoney, who was working at one such orphanage in Ungureni and had called home to beg her father and some family friends to gather together any aid they could and post it out for the children. 'The food supply for the children, it was just like a gruel,' Carter recalled in 2000. 'Things like chicken heads were being boiled and there was a dry bread given, and that was really the rations for them.'[54]

When it was explained to Joey that it was costing £40 to post out just one small box of aid to Romania, he decided to take action. It would have been easy for Joey to lend his famous name to an appeal to raise funds and leave others to sort out the details, but what he did was altogether more extraordinary. He visited shops, chemists, schools, friends, local businesses – any place, or anyone, that might be able to help – and filled his race van and trailer to the brim with food, medical supplies, clothes, toys, and anything else that might make life a little more comfortable for the children who were living in those far-flung orphanages in such appalling conditions. 'People brought stuff from everywhere and Joey gathered up stuff from everywhere,' mechanic Sammy Graham recalled. 'He piled the van up till you couldn't put another sock in the van – it was full.'

Joey had always been a family man and, by now, had five children that he doted on. When he was made aware of the plight of less fortunate children in Eastern Europe, and the hardships they were having to endure, he took direct action and tried to do something about it. Even more telling, he kept his efforts quiet, refusing to give any interviews even to the local newspaper that had caught wind of the scheme. When Joey Dunlop gave to charity, he didn't need the world to hear about it – it wasn't about him. When a reporter from a local newspaper gave him a camera to take on his mercy mission and told Joey he would write a story upon his return if he could take a few pictures of the orphans, Joey politely accepted the camera. When he got home, he handed the camera back without having taken a single picture. 'I don't want any publicity if you don't mind,' he told the reporter. Polite but firm, the message was clear: 'I'm not doing this as a publicity stunt.'

Ungureni is over 2,000 miles from Ballymoney but Joey insisted on driving the whole way himself in his overloaded van with its overloaded trailer. The Reverend John Kirkpatrick of Garryduff Church, who helped Joey plan the trips and arranged all the documents he would need to pass through various countries, estimated he was hauling around seven tons of aid. Each round trip was around 4,000 miles and Joey went not once, but five times in total, to Romania, Albania, Bosnia and Yugoslavia – 20,000 miles, driving alone through some of the most dangerous countries in Eastern Europe, and sleeping in his van by the roadside in temperatures that dropped as low as minus-30 degrees. He always made the trips in winter, before the racing season started.

'It took me three weeks – it's a long run, like,' he eventually said of his first trip in 1992. 'I had a good load of stuff and I just took my time. I didn't want the van blowing up and a lot of trouble... And all the things that people had given me – if you break down over there, they'll just steal everything. You can't afford to break down.'[55]

Barry Symmons was one of the few men Joey spoke to about his trips. 'He told me that one time it was so cold the diesel in his van froze. He couldn't get his primus stove to light either because it had frozen too, so he had to chip away at a tin of frozen beans with a screwdriver, trying to get some solid lumps out for his breakfast.'

Personal comfort was a luxury Joey didn't seem to care for and, besides, sleeping in the van was the best way to prevent his goods from being stolen (when he travelled to Eastern Europe on his own to race in the late 1990s, he would place a plank over his bikes and sleep on it so that any would-be thieves would have to wake him to get to the bikes).

Hector Neill remembers happening across Joey in a layby at the start of one of his mercy missions. 'I was driving through England one night with my son, Phillip, and we saw Joey parked in a layby in an old van. We stopped our motorhome as it was time to park up anyway and there was Joey, sound asleep in the driver's seat with his head over the steering wheel. I rapped on the window and offered him a spare bed in our motorhome, but he was like, "Ach, no, I'm fine – I'll be heading away early, anyway," and he just slept at the wheel of his old van.'

In the 1990s, countries like Romania and Albania were highly dangerous places to travel through, but Joey insisted on travelling alone. 'I'd have loved somebody to have gone out with him but he just liked his own company, and if somebody would have been chatting the whole way over to him, that would just have done his head in,' Linda Dunlop explained. 'So, he decided to just go his own pace, and he didn't want somebody to meet him halfways, because he wanted to make sure that it [the aid] got there himself, which he did.'[56]

By the time Joey reached the orphanage at Ungureni on his first trip, he was suffering from mild hypothermia. It was so cold that even the fluid in his cigarette lighter would regularly freeze. Because of the extreme cold, he would drive during the night and sleep during the day when it was slightly warmer – and also slightly safer – than parking up overnight. Siobhan Carter remembers seeing him arrive that first time. 'He looked as if he'd a bit of shellshock and was hypothermic,' she said. 'At this point, temperatures were minus-thirty.'

Even at the orphanage, it wasn't safe to simply unload the aid in the main building, for fear it would be stolen. Instead, Joey handed it to nurses through the windows of the small bungalows they lived in so it could be more securely stashed. 'I had to hide it from the local police and all,' Joey said. 'And the nurses, they kept it in their bedrooms. They had flats – wee bungalows – round about the orphanage, and they put it in their bungalows.'

Carter was humbled by Joey's incredible actions. 'Joey's visit raised morale greatly with the staff and children,' she later recalled. 'For me, seeing someone from near my hometown in Northern Ireland, arriving with supplies which he had personally struggled to deliver to his destination, without translators, and sleeping alone in minus conditions in his van, touched me greatly.'[57]

The sight of a frozen and exhausted Joey Dunlop pulling up in his overloaded and filthy Mercedes 711 D van was a sign of hope for all at the orphanage, and it proved a real turning point in the struggles of the establishment. 'If there was ever a point, when I think back, that we were feeling down, it was the period before Joey Dunlop arrived,' Carter said. 'And when we opened that van and I saw, you know, little boxes – I mean every box had a message – everyone could benefit from what was in that. So, that van was a goldmine.'[58]

For a family man as fond of children as Joey was, the sights that greeted him at the orphanage would have torn at his heart. He never did speak about what he saw but, for those close to him, he didn't need to. After the 2000-mile drive back to England he stopped at John Harris's house to collect a bike and Harris knew by the look in Joey's eyes, and the even quieter-than-normal tone of his voice, that he had been deeply affected by the experience. 'He was pretty tired after driving all that way and I could tell by his voice and the expression on his face that the things he'd seen hadn't been pleasant and it hadn't been easy for him,' Harris explains. 'My wife was very impressed with what he had done. She said, "John, that man is a real Christian." She loved him for what he did.'

'It wasn't an easy place to visit,' Siobhan Carter admitted. 'Probably one of the most difficult places – certainly if you're a father or anyone who's in touch with children, to see children like that. You know, that whole field of humanitarian work brings different people and I think that people do it for different reasons, but I think he was one of the most genuine.'[59]

Carter believed Joey had 'received a calling to help others following his visit' and so he set about arranging another trip and would eventually complete five epic missions around some of the most deprived and dangerous countries in Europe over the next ten years. Each trip took several weeks and every time he stopped to sleep in a layby, Joey was at risk of being robbed, kidnapped or developing severe hypothermia. He was also at risk from corrupt police and border guards and was arrested at gunpoint in Albania for not having the correct documents to travel through the country. While he might have appeared fearless as a motorcycle racer, Joey admitted to being 'a bit scared' when the gun was pulled on him. 'Although I live in Northern Ireland, I'm out in the country and mostly away from the Troubles, so seeing a gun is still a shock.'[60]

His van and trailer were impounded, and Joey was held in a cell (or a cage, as Neil Tuxworth understands it) for several hours. The situation looked grim but, for once, Joey had reason to be thankful for his fame. 'They were looking at the van and they saw the sticker on the front of the van – motorbikes – and by good luck the chief bloke was really into 500cc Grands Prix and Formula 1 cars and he asked me about it. I had a *Motor Cycle News* and there was a photo of me in the *Motor Cycle News* and I showed him this name "Dunlop" and got me passport out and showed him the "Dunlop" and all, and after that… a big pass; free as long as I wanted. It was hard to believe – they just gave me this pass and he signed it. I was stopped a lot of times afterwards and as soon as I showed them this pass: "Oh, sorry, Mr Dunlop. Sorry, Mr Dunlop." And that was it.'[61]

Typically, on the few occasions he did speak about them, Joey played down the difficulties of making such mammoth trips. But in 2003 a group of Irish motorcyclists calling themselves the Lost Riders paid tribute to Joey by replicating one of his trips to Eastern Europe and delivering more much-needed aid. Their epic adventure was featured in the BBC Northern Ireland documentary *The Last Lap: In the Footsteps of Joey.* While Joey travelled alone, the Lost Riders were fifteen-strong and made the trip in a convoy of four vans and five motorcycles. Yet even with such strength in numbers they found the trip was the stuff of nightmares. One of their bikes was stolen in Poland while they slept, there were eight-hour waits at borders and endless problems with documentation, red tape and getting lost – not to mention the trauma of seeing the condition the children were in.

Joey had to deal with all of this completely on his own and John Harris, who made the trip with the Lost Riders, knows better than most how hard that must have been. 'When we went on that trip in 2003, we had each other to help us deal with what we saw, but Joey had 2,000 miles driving back alone and had to deal with it all by himself,' he says. 'That couldn't have been easy at all. That trip really helped me to appreciate what Joey had been through. When we got to those border posts, the amount of time it took us to get through them, and the sheer length of the journey... And, obviously, Joey was on his own and having to cook for himself so, yes, I got a better idea of just what he had to go through to deliver those goods. He went up even more in my estimations after I made that trip. He didn't speak about those trips in any great detail though, and I didn't ask him because I knew how he was.'

'The whole charity thing was just something Joey felt he needed to do,' says Barry Symmons. 'The Irish are very generous people, especially as far as kids go. Using his name, he managed to fill his van up with all sorts of things the kids needed and off he set. He loved driving on the continent, so there was a bit of pleasure in that, but it was mostly just about being a good Christian. We hadn't really seen that side of Joey before his mercy missions but now that I've lived in Northern Ireland for thirty-odd years, I can understand it more, as quite a lot of that sort of thing goes on over here. There's more of a community spirit.'

Bob McMillan believes those mercy missions revealed more of Joey's true character than anything else he did. 'Those trips proved just what a complete one-off Joey Dunlop was,' he says. 'How many riders in the MotoGP paddock – or any paddock – would do that? He was so compassionate and so caring and not many people realised that about Joey. He wasn't looking for publicity or for praise, he just did it because he thought it was right.'

Joey had quietly been involved in charity work in Northern Ireland for years. He took part in fundraising events for local schools, he visited sick children in hospitals, he donated one of his iconic race helmets to be auctioned off by the RNLI at Portaferry after being rescued from the sinking *Tornamona*, but he never sought publicity for his generous actions and all his charitable work might have gone completely under the radar had Buckingham Palace not become aware of his mercy missions to Eastern Europe.

Ten years after being awarded the MBE for services to motorcycling, Joey was recalled to the palace to be awarded the OBE for his humanitarian deeds. It made him the only motorcyclist ever to be awarded both an MBE and an OBE, and it clearly touched Joey deeply. 'This means more to me than winning any motorbike race,' he said after receiving his second honour. In fact, he would go further, and describe his second trip to Buckingham Palace as the proudest moment of his life.

'That meant a great deal to him,' John Harris says. 'It was very well deserved. OBEs are given out quite freely now but, back then, you really had done something very special if you were awarded one, and Joey certainly did. It meant more to him than any race victory – Joey loved his queen and country.'

Bob McMillan, as ever, was by Joey's side to make sure everything ran smoothly. 'Joey was mega proud of that,' he says. 'And so were his family: not only Linda and the kids, but his mum and dad, and his sisters and brothers. We booked him into a hotel in Kensington and had a meal with him the night before. The next day I arranged to get him a limousine with a driver to take him to the palace, but also to have at his disposal for all of that day and the next day. I told him to just ask the driver for a tour of anywhere in London he had ever wanted to go. Joey and his family loved it, but he didn't feel all impressed with himself because he had a limo at his disposal

– he just felt it was something we didn't need to do for him, even though he appreciated it.'

Joey Dunlop was a man of few words and very few people ever got close enough to him to know him well. But then, by taking on such epic mercy missions, there was no need for Joey speak in order to reveal his innermost feelings. It was in these heroic and selfless trips that people finally saw into the very heart of the real Joey Dunlop – and it was a far nobler heart than even his greatest admirers had given him credit for.

CHAPTER 16

LOCAL HERO

'THE CROWD WAS GOING CRAZY – AND I RECKON EVERY MARSHAL ON THE TT COURSE MUST HAVE WAVED AT ME.'
Joey Dunlop

If Joey Dunlop thought the pressure would be lifted off him once he had equalled Mike Hailwood's record of wins at the TT, he was wrong. Because, as soon as he had equalled it, the next thing everyone wanted to know was, could he beat it?

Aside from his picking up his fourteenth TT win, the 1992 season had been quite a lean year in terms of results, Joey's only other victories coming in the 125cc race at the Ulster Grand Prix and in both the 125cc and 750cc races at the Southern 100.

But something changed in 1993. Four years on from the crash that almost ended his career, Joey found a new lease of life and started winning more regularly again. Early season, there was a double win at the Cookstown, a treble at the Tandragee, and a podium on the Superbike at the North West 200, before it was time to head across the Irish Sea once more to the Isle of Man to face the music. But this time he was fitter, this time he was coming off a roll of wins, this time he looked much more like his old self. And Robert Dunlop knew it.

Perhaps feeling the pressure in practice, Robert crashed at Waterworks, right in front of his big brother. Fortunately, he escaped with minor injuries and still finished practice week in second place on the 125cc leader board, ahead of Joey in sixth.

Race week didn't start well, with Joey describing the Formula One as 'the worst TT ride I've ever had' after something broke in his bike's rear suspension. The breakage meant Joey could only limp home in an uncharacteristic fourteenth place. The RC30 might have been long in the tooth by this point – it was the bike's sixth year of racing – but Joey did at least look like he was part of a factory team again, resplendent in Castrol Honda Britain colours and, as Joey's results improved, he was once again racing under the official Honda umbrella as a third rider in addition to Phillip McCallen and Nick Jefferies.

Joey started the Ultra-Lightweight race in determined mood, taking 8 seconds out of his brother on the first lap despite suffering clutch problems. With the clutch lever coming right back to the handlebar with no effect, Joey rode single-handedly along the straights while adjusting the lever with his left hand.

Despite Robert Dunlop regaining 6 seconds thanks to a faster pit stop, Joey's only real problem for the remainder of the race were the well-meaning spectators who were going crazy around the course and distracting him. 'The reception I got on the last lap was incredible,' he said. 'Way greater than last year when I equalled the record. But there were some fans *on* the track waving to me on the last lap which put me off a bit. Take Rhencullen: I always line up on one of the telegraph poles, but I couldn't see the bottom of the pole for people waving. The crowd was going crazy – and I reckon every marshal on the TT course must have waved at me.'

If race fans had gone crazy when Joey scored his fourteenth TT win, they went ballistic when he took his fifteenth. Both Joey and Robert smashed the lap record on the final lap, proving that Robert was still trying everything he knew. But it wasn't enough, and Joey finally crossed the finish line some 5 seconds ahead of his brother to become the most successful Isle of Man TT racer of all time – a title he still holds, some twenty-eight years later. Naturally, the first man he acknowledged after removing his helmet was Hailwood himself. 'If he'd been here, I know he would have been the first man to congratulate me,' he said. 'He was that kind of bloke. I admired him.'

The remainder of TT week was beset by technical issues and Joey was forced to retire in both the Supersport 600 and Senior races, although he did manage a podium finish in the 250cc Junior TT.

But elsewhere, the wins kept coming: victory on the Superbike at the Skerries, four straight wins at Fore, another at the Temple 100, and one more at the Mid Antrim. There were double victories at Dundalk and Carrowdore, a 125cc win at Killalane, and even a short circuit win on the 250 at Aghadowey. He was clearly on fire again. In fact, so dominant was Dunlop in the Irish national meetings in 1993, he won the hotly contested Regal 600 championship on John Harris's Honda CBR600, against fields of much younger and more aggressive riders who were far more used to racing production-based machines. He would also win the 250cc Irish road racing championship that year.

In September, Joey's achievements were once again formally recognised when he was awarded the Freedom of Ballymoney by the town's mayor. Being given the freedom of a town is now a symbolic gesture and a matter of civic pride, rather than conferring any actual powers or privileges on a person, but it is an honour nonetheless and Joey was naturally delighted to take part in the formal reception and the dinner and dance held in his honour. He was a local hero like no other, and the people of Ballymoney could not have been prouder of him.

o

What made Joey Dunlop such a great TT rider? How did he come to win the world's most dangerous race more times than any other man in history? 'It's difficult to put a finger on what made him such a good TT rider,' Mick Grant says. 'I suppose his upbringing on the Irish roads was a big advantage. Although he wasn't slow on short circuits, I always said that if you'd put some wallpaper with trees and stone walls on it, round tracks like Donington Park, he'd probably have been faster! When I was running race teams and was looking for staff, I never looked for riders or mechanics with the most experience, I always looked for the ones that wanted it most. And the one thing that Joey had in abundance was "want". You can have a clever rider, a rider who may be incredibly gifted with lots of natural riding ability, but if you don't want it bad enough, then you're just going to be pissing into the wind.'

Joey clearly wanted it, as Roger Marshall testifies. 'Joey was one of the hardest men – one of the hardest riders ever on the roads when he wanted to win, but he was fair too. The only time we ever had a word against each other was that particular day at the Ulster [when Marshall complained of a hard move by Joey on the final lap].'

With the TT mountain course being so long, to be successful on it takes time, patience and a willingness to learn. According to Barry Symmons, Joey possessed these attributes, too. 'He was always interested to learn. A lot of riders of Joey's stature, if they go somewhere and don't do very well, it winds them up and then they try too hard and start falling off. Joey was never like that – he would always approach things with the belief that these things were new to him, and he would take his time to learn. To learn a course as long as the TT course takes a bit of time – or it did in the days before onboard laps and TT computer games were available to help.'

Good machine preparation and bike set-up is crucial in a race as long, bumpy and demanding as the TT, and this was another area where Joey excelled: his engineering skills and his ability to set a bike up to be smooth and reliable were key to his success. 'Ah, he was nobody's fool, was Joey,' says Johnny Rea. 'He might not have had that many qualifications, but he was a clever fella and a fantastic engineer.'

Neil Tuxworth confirms that Joey was far smarter than people generally thought. 'Joey wasn't stupid,' he says. 'A lot of people don't give him credit for that. He was a clever guy when it came to engines and tuning and setting bikes up. People used to think Joey was stupid, but he definitely wasn't.'

Joey's deep mechanical understanding meant he could always get the most out of any given machine. 'He never had a bad-handling bike,' says Slick Bass. 'When you saw him racing, his bikes always worked, so he obviously knew what he wanted and he had a very good mechanical brain. He could strip a bike down, strip a clutch down, or strip a whole engine down; he could strip his forks, his rear shock… He had a great knowledge of these things and knew exactly what he wanted.

'He liked his bikes to feel stable,' Bass continues. 'He never liked them moving around too much. He was also careful to make sure his set-up worked on worn tyres too. There was no point in having a bike that worked on fresh tyres but not on worn ones, especially at long races like the TT. He was very clever with that stuff.'

David Wood, director of *V-Four Victory*, remembers seeing Joey fastidiously checking all his bikes over, even when he didn't need to. 'He'd have all these top Japanese mechanics from Honda working for him, but he was still the last one to give the bike a final check over – every time.'

It was this ceaseless attention to detail that paid dividends so many times for Joey, particularly at the TT where such a high percentage of the machines suffer mechanical failures due to the demanding nature of the course.

Joey's vast experience of different conditions on the TT course also gave him an edge over younger rivals like Ian Simpson. 'I was always impressed by how quick Joey was – especially when you wouldn't really expect it. In dangerous, really slippery conditions, you'd think it would be the daft young riders who would be quick and sticking their necks out, but that's where Joey impressed me a lot. In horrible, treacherous, tricky conditions he was incredibly fast and smooth and had such a feel for what was going on.'

In 1994, Simpson would win the British Superbike championship, but in June of that year he still got a lesson from the old master on how to ride a 250cc machine round the TT course. 'He passed me at the start of the last lap, so I followed him for a full lap and that's when I learned how to ride a 250,' Simpson says. 'I learned more on that one lap than everything I'd learned previously. I posted the second fastest lap of the race, just by following Joey – I speeded up by miles! I learned how to be more flowing and to just keep the throttle open instead of giving it big handfuls of throttle and handfuls of brakes. That's how you ride a Superbike – it's quite erratic really – but to ride a 250, you need to be the opposite of erratic; you need to be fast and flowing and you need to use all the road and keep your speed up.'

Johnny Rea remembers being given a similar riding lesson in the 1990 Junior TT. 'Me and Joey were together on the road for about three laps, passing each other everywhere. He was so tidy, and you knew you could trust him. If you tried to make a pass, he would let you through – he wouldn't try to block you or do anything daft.'

Simpson admits that having superior machinery makes a huge difference at the TT, and Joey did have an advantage during the 1980s when he was the star of the Honda Britain team and given full factory machinery. After his big crash at Brands Hatch, however, he was usually supplied with the same machinery as every other Honda rider. 'The Honda RC45 I raced at the TT in 1998 was a proper factory machine, but every other year I just got bikes with a race kit,' Simpson says. 'The factory one was so much better it was unbelievable. It was quite depressing, knowing that I'd have to ride a much lesser bike after that. Most of the time in the 1990s Joey would just have been given the same sort of kitted bike that the rest of us got. It wasn't until 2000 that Honda gave him a proper factory bike again.'

Whether on a full factory bike or not, Joey's smoothness belied his blinding speed, as Graham Sanderson testifies. 'I remember watching him so many times going down Bray Hill, and at different parts around the TT course, and never looking like the quickest rider, and yet he held lap records and won races because he was just so effortlessly smooth,' he says. 'He was the kind of man who made ordinary people think "I could do that." They couldn't, of course, but he made it look so effortless that they thought they could.'

Ferry Brouwer noted another weapon in Joey's arsenal that stood him in good stead as he raced on into his forties. 'I wasn't surprised that he continued to win TT races because he was still very, very devoted to his racing,' he says. 'He mentioned, on occasion, that he still got very nervous before a race and several other riders have told me that, when you stop being nervous before a race, then it becomes dangerous. As long as you're nervous, it means you're switched on 100 per cent. The moment you lose that, you're in danger.'

To race fans around the world, it may have looked like Joey had conquered the uniquely daunting Isle of Man TT course, but the man himself knew differently. Speaking in a rare BBC television interview in 1997, he said, 'I'm not trying to beat the course now because you'll never beat the course, put it that way. The course will always be there, will always be the same – it doesn't matter how much you learn it, you're still going to get into trouble at times; you're still looking to go at 100 per cent, you're still going to get into trouble with the weathers… There's so many things on the course that you can't beat the course – the course will always beat you.'[62]

By simply competing in the TT for as long as he did, Joey was able to learn from the many mistakes he made over the years and he made sure they didn't happen a second time. 'I learned things years and years ago about breaking chains and running out of fuel – you've never won the race until the chequered flag comes down,' he said. 'I always remember that, and I always keep that in my mind, especially at the TT because it's so long.'

He may not have conquered it in his own mind, but Joey Dunlop came closer to mastering the TT mountain course than any man has ever done. Yet he knew the course was always capable of throwing up new challenges, new problems and new risks. And in 1994, he was given a shocking reminder of just how dangerous the most famous ribbon of Tarmac in the world could be.

CHAPTER 17

ROBERT

**'IT WAS THESE HALLUCINATIONS THAT I WAS GETTING –
TRYING TO FIGHT OFF PEOPLE WITH RAZOR BLADES.'**
Robert Dunlop

Having slammed into a stone wall at around 130mph, Robert Dunlop lay unconscious on the TT course, his life hanging by a thread as other racers tried to avoid his prone body and the wreckage that was strewn all over the road. Mechanical failure is what TT racers fear the most as there is often no warning at all before a catastrophic failure occurs. Dunlop had just landed safely, having leapt over the humpbacked Ballaugh Bridge, one of the many unique quirks of the TT course. Milliseconds later, the rear Marvic wheel on his Honda RC45 (a lightweight, aftermarket racing wheel which had been fitted in place of Honda's original wheel) completely collapsed, resulting in him being thrown into a low stone wall and suffering life-threatening injuries.

Robert's long-time friend and mentor, Liam Beckett, rushed to

Noble's Hospital along with Robert's father Wullie and his brothers Joey and Jim, each one of them in a state of shock. Robert lay helpless on a bed in the trauma room, his face obscured by an oxygen mask, while teams of surgeons fussed around him. 'I will never forget the pool of blood lying below Robert,' Beckett wrote in his 2016 book *Liam Beckett: Full Throttle.* 'And what shocked me, in particular, was how thick it was: almost like red mercury. It's an image I'll never be able to erase from my mind for the rest of my days.'[63]

Robert was in serious trouble and when Beckett, Joey and Jim were permitted into the trauma room to see him, Beckett was convinced it was to say their final goodbyes. The nerves in Robert's right arm and leg had been completely severed and both limbs – which were also badly broken – were fast turning black, a sure sign of gangrene setting in. A double amputation was the most likely outcome. But, because of the TT races, the surgeons at Noble's Hospital were expert in dealing with serious traumas and after a six-and-a-half-hour operation, Robert was moved to a high dependency unit where two other TT racers were lying, one with severe head injuries and the other, Rob Mitchell, on a life-support machine. As an organ donor, Mitchell was being kept alive until a suitable heart transplant recipient could be found. One of Ireland's top riders, Mark Farmer, had already lost his life during practice week. It was a black year for the TT.

The next forty-eight hours were touch-and-go as Dunlop fought for his life. Beckett never left his side. Night and day he watched over his rider and friend, moistening Robert's lips with ice cubes to keep him hydrated, waiting all the while for him to regain consciousness. When Robert did start to come round, his struggle was not with pain – it was with the hellish hallucinations caused by the amount of morphine that was being administered to him. 'They kept me on morphine, which is a horrible drug – a *horrible* drug,' Robert later explained. 'I had hallucinations and it was terrible. I was moving about the bed quite a lot and they [the nurses and Liam Beckett] more than likely thought it was pain, but it was these hallucinations that I was getting – trying to fight off people with razor blades. It was horrible; really horrible.'[64]

Robert's wife Louise had been in the south of Ireland looking at horses when she was notified that her husband had crashed at the TT. She was asked to return home. Unaware of the extent of Robert's injuries, she was stopped by the Garda for speeding but, as soon as the officer saw the name 'Robert Dunlop' on the side of the car, he allowed her to carry on immediately. Only then did Louise realise how serious the situation must be.

After several days of mental and physical torture, Robert Dunlop pulled through and his family were told his injuries were no longer life-threatening. They were also told that Robert's career was over. He would be lucky to ever have any use of his right arm and leg and certainly would never be able to race a motorcycle again. Robert wasn't so sure.

Eight years and more than twelve operations later, Dunlop accepted an out-of-court settlement of £700,000 in compensation for the accident, since it had clearly not been his fault and it had ruined his future career prospects. Amateur video footage of the accident showed his wheel collapsing and Robert duly sued Italian manufacturer Marvic, their UK distributor Racing Lines, and Medd Honda team boss Stuart Medd. The lightweight racing wheels they had supplied might have been strong enough to handle smooth short circuits, but they hadn't been able to cope with the rigours of the TT. The delay in his being awarded compensation meant Robert had to sell his ten-bedroom farmhouse and move into accommodation costing just £85 a week, his ability to earn money completely ruined by the crash.

Joey also had a couple of close calls during that ill-fated Formula One TT. 'I was just out of Barregarrow when I saw a van on the left-hand side of the road,' he said. Fortunately, he managed to swerve past the van, which had been left there by a Highways Department worker who 'forgot' there was a race on. One lap later, as Joey sped past the Highlander pub at 180mph, he faced another obstacle. 'A dog was running about on the track,' he said, before casually adding, 'But the marshals gave me a good warning, just as they had for the truck.' He would finish the race in third place, behind his much younger Honda team-mates, Steve Hislop and Phillip McCallen.

With Robert fighting for his life in hospital, it was a difficult decision for Joey to take part in the Ultra-Lightweight TT but, with some signs that his little brother was out of immediate danger, he decided to go ahead and, in doing so, racked up a sixteenth TT win. 'Robert and me are very close,' Joey said, 'and it was tough to race on knowing he was ill.' Without Robert to push him, Joey won the 125cc race by 71 seconds from Dennis McCullough – nephew of Ray McCullough, who Joey had raced so hard against in the 1970s. Joey dedicated his win to his brother and said, 'I just wish Robert had been out there racing with me.'

It had been six years since Joey had won a TT on anything bigger than a 125cc machine, but he pulled off an unexpected victory in the 250cc Junior race after leader Phillip McCallen ran out of fuel – for the second year in succession – just five miles from home. Joey had been some 16 seconds behind McCallen and had settled for second place, since he had lost his right footrest and had to rest his foot against the hot exhaust instead. McCallen's demise handed Joey his seventeenth TT win.

A seventh on John Harris's CBR600 in the Supersport race, and a third place in the Senior on his new Honda RC45, rounded out a hugely traumatic week for Joey; the extreme highs and extreme lows of the TT had seen him experience almost every emotion possible in the space of just a few days. His brother would, at least, live, but Robert would never truly recover from the injuries he sustained at the 1994 TT.

○

At the start of the 1994 season, Honda had given Joey one of its new RC45 machines that had replaced the ageing RC30. Another exquisite and exotic V-Four, the RC45 was nevertheless a vicious bike to ride in its early days and Joey, like most other Honda riders, struggled to set the machine up to handle properly. Speaking about the first few laps of practice at what would be his last TT, Joey's Castrol Honda team-mate Steve Hislop said, 'If I ever needed convincing that the TT was too dangerous, riding the RC45 round there was proof enough – it was absolutely lethal at the beginning of practice week. On my first lap, I clipped a kerb at 150mph on Bray Hill, then smacked my leg off a wall at Ginger Hall and ripped my leathers and my knee open. The bike had a mind of its own and just went wherever the hell it wanted. It was so out of control that, for the first time in my life, I considered withdrawing my entry and going home, and so did Joey Dunlop. He came into the garage on the first night of practice, threw the bike into his van and said, "That fucking thing's not going to kill me."'

Castrol Honda's third rider, Phillip McCallen, felt the same way, according to Hislop. 'Phillip was terrified of his bike as well, and that's saying something, because he was always out of shape at the TT. I can honestly say I had more frights in those two weeks than I'd had in the last eight years of competing at the TT.'

Ian Simpson, who would go on to win two TT races on an RC45 in 1998, agrees with the late Hislop's analysis. 'It was incredibly unstable to begin with. You had to hit every bump absolutely square-on, with the wheels perfectly in-line, or it would tie itself in knots. A lot of it was to do with the tyres – I've since ridden an RC45 on modern tyres and it was a hundred times better.'

Robert Dunlop had enjoyed early success on the bike, taking a Superbike double at the North West 200, while Joey finished third in the main feature race. With his deep understanding of bike set-up, Joey soon got the RC45 sorted for use on other circuits and took his first win on it at the Tandragee, but the TT has always been a very different proposition and setting up a motorcycle to handle at sustained high speeds over varied road surfaces has never been easy.

Upon returning from the Isle of Man, Joey won on the RC45 again at the Skerries and Mid Antrim (where he also won the 125cc and 250cc races) before lining up against Phillip McCallen at the Ulster Grand Prix at Dundrod. After dealing with a van and a stray dog on the course at the TT, Joey faced yet more unexpected drama in the opening Superbike race at the Ulster. The race was red flagged after just three laps when car thieves drove a stolen vehicle onto the circuit at the hairpin. The Royal Ulster Constabulary (RUC) soon dealt with the thieves, but it was just one more example of the hazards of racing on public roads, even if they were officially closed by law to the public.

The drama wasn't over, however. McCallen blasted off into an early lead in the restarted race while Joey endured a frightening slide on oil dropped by another machine. When he was forced to take to a slip road, unable to stop in time for the approaching corner, he lost 7 seconds to McCallen and his race looked to be over as Jason Griffiths took his turn in battling for the lead. No one could afford to give the dominant McCallen that kind of advantage at Dundrod and hope to claw it back. No one except Joey Dunlop, that is.

With 45,000 fans getting behind him and urging him on, Joey dug as deep as he ever had and clawed his way back up to McCallen's rear wheel, finally catching and passing him to lead by the start of the last lap. McCallen forced his way through halfway round the lap, but as both men howled into sight at the hairpin, Joey was back in the lead. Nick Jefferies says the contrast between the two rivals' riding styles could not have been greater, despite their similar overall speeds. 'Joey was line perfect round Dundrod. He must have despaired at Phillip McCallen because he never had a line in his head. Phillip's lines were unbelievable – he had no idea! But he carried so much corner speed that he somehow managed to do it, and he was light and always had good tackle too. But that's the great thing about sport – Joey and Phillip were polar-opposites in terms of style, but they could both get results.'

Such was McCallen's pace, he set a new outright lap record of 125.03mph during the race, but it still wasn't enough to shake off Joey. The two men exited the hairpin on the final lap practically side by side, meaning everything came down to whoever could take the Flow Bog section the fastest. So close were the two battling, McCallen's front wheel touched Joey's leg, almost resulting in both riders crashing out. Undeterred, Joey stood his ground and forced the young, aggressive McCallen aside, taking the race win by two-tenths of a second. In his forty-second year, Joey Dunlop had taken his forty-second win around the Dundrod circuit.

'He put a hole in my leathers, and it was brave and tight,' he said after the race. 'There was no room where he was trying to pass me. I think he got a shock seeing me go by instead of Jason [Griffiths]. He only had between the hairpin and Quarries to get me and I made sure he wasn't going to. He tried the impossible. I think it was the only time I've ever had any bother with Phillip, and I've had some really good races with him.'[65]

It had been a nail-biting race, and as good a confrontation as anyone could remember around Dundrod. Joey was clearly back to his magnificent best and proved he was still capable of handing it to the new generation of ultra-aggressive road racers, most of whom were young enough to be his sons.

There was to be another outing on the TT course for Joey Dunlop in the late summer of 1994, when he took part in the Manx Grand Prix for the second time. Essentially an amateur version of the TT proper, where young riders can learn the course before progressing to the TT, the Manx also hosts classic races and Joey had agreed to ride a 250cc Aermacchi for Manx enthusiast Terry Teece in 1993. The problem was, Joey rode the 1960s vintage bike *too* hard and destroyed it after a single lap. 'Joey was just too fast for the bike and was virtually riding it flat against the stop all the way around the course,' Teece said. Joey rode for Teece again in the 1994 Manx and this time finished second, despite suffering further mechanical issues, this time caused by him braking too hard. So much for easing into the gentlemanly sport of classic bike racing – Joey Dunlop was still riding like an aggressive youngster and was simply too fast for old machinery. It would be his last Manx outing.

o

Joey somehow managed to conquer his fear of flying in the winter of 1994 and put up with a long-haul flight to New Zealand, no doubt aided by a few vodka and cokes. North West 200 race organiser Billy Nutt had arranged for a team of riders to travel out to New Zealand to take on the locals and Joey was naturally the star attraction. Kiwi race promoter John Shand remembers the sensation he caused by visiting. 'Well, down in New Zealand Joey's a legend,' he said. 'He came to New Zealand in 1994 and raced in the national series… At all the race meetings in New Zealand, we had the biggest crowds we'd ever had for twenty years, and most of those people had just came out to see Joey Dunlop. He was mobbed everywhere he went.'[66]

The trip would also allow Joey to spend November and December in the sunshine of the southern hemisphere, relaxing, visiting sites of interest, and generally preparing for the 1995 racing season in a more pleasant climate.

There was a lot of drinking to be done too. Joey quickly discovered that in New Zealand there were 'more Irish bars than in Ireland' and the team of riders made the most of them. There were regular late-night parties and only one rule – if anyone fell asleep before the party was over, one of their eyebrows would be removed with hair removal cream. Of the sixteen riders and helpers who made up the UK and Irish crew, Joey was one of the few to return from New Zealand with both eyebrows intact.

When he wasn't racing his Honda RS125 against a wide variety of other bikes (to make up numbers, grids were comprised of 125cc, 250cc, 400cc, 500cc and 600cc machines of varying configurations) or drinking with the rest of his team, Joey would take every opportunity to explore this new country, borrowing a van and a sleeping bag and heading off alone for days on end, the way he loved to live.

The trip seemed to revive him because Joey began 1995 with a new attitude. He approached the season a fitter man after doing a bit of weight training and general exercise and would finally quit smoking later in the year. If he was going to continue to fight against much younger rivals like Phillip McCallen, he knew he was going to have to be in better shape. His success in quitting cigarettes even inspired the great Barry Sheene to do the same: 'If Joey can quit the bloody things, so can I.' The two most famous smokers in bike racing were smokers no more, and Joey was proud of finally being able to kick the habit.

Modern motorcycle racers train every bit as hard as Olympian athletes, yet the hard-drinking, heavy-smoking Joey Dunlop had never been associated with any kind of training and was still able to beat his younger, far more athletic rivals. But it seemed nature had given him a helping hand on this front. As his manager Davy Wood said, 'Joey has that inbred ability – I think it's his determination, his will. Joey's eating habits, sleeping habits, drinking habits, socialising habits, wouldn't probably be written up in the fitness manual of some of these other young chaps, and yet he can transcend all of that. He's not running for two or three hours in the morning or eating special health foods and so on.'

In 1997, Joey visited Queen's University Belfast to have his fitness levels assessed. He was forty-five at the time and, while the resting pulse rate for the average man of his age is 70–75bpm, Joey's was 62bpm. After a battery of tests, it was concluded he had the fitness of a thirty-five-year-old, and that this was a purely natural phenomenon. Speaking of Joey's performances at the TT, Queen's University Sports Science specialist Harry Brennan said, 'The event itself would be very physically demanding and would call for quite a high endurance capacity in terms of stamina which, Joey would show from his results, would be a natural phenomenon more than a training phenomenon, as we know he doesn't do that much physical training.'

To further help with his fitness, the five-times world champion even took to helping brother Jim with his steel-erecting business and he would make use of bodybuilding mechanic Sammy Graham's home gym. When Joey set his mind to something – even something that was not particularly appealing to him – he generally succeeded, and it was a fitter, healthier Dunlop who came out fighting at the start of the 1995 season.

Since the demise of the TT Formula One world championship

in 1990, there had been no roads-based championship for Dunlop to contest, so when Billy Nutt tried to launch a new series taking in some little-known tracks in Europe, Joey was keen to be involved. In 1995 he would make his racing debut at the Mettet road circuit in Belgium and would also travel to a circuit in Eastern Europe that few fans back home had heard of. It was called the Pirita-Kose-Kloostrimetsa circuit, and it was situated in Tallinn, Estonia.

The races were all very low key and Nutt's series never really took off in any meaningful way, but Joey enjoyed taking in the odd race meeting and would turn each long drive out to the far-flung circuits into a mini touring holiday, taking in historic sites like Colditz prison and Treblinka concentration camp. After winning the 125cc, 250cc and Superbike races at Tallinn on his first visit, Joey would become a regular at the tree-lined circuit where he was treated like a demi-god. Local fans could not believe that the great road racing hero they had watched on television and read about in magazines was actually competing in their own back yard, so far from home and even further from any kind of glitz or glamour. But that's precisely why Joey loved racing there. With riders operating out of the backs of vans, and with no hospitality trailers or pomp of any kind, it was exactly what Irish road racing had been like back in the 1970s. Joey could race, enjoy a few beers round a campfire at night with like-minded riders, and not be bothered by thousands of fans, television crews or journalists. As much as they worshipped him, the locals treated him with respect and courtesy and never bothered him any further than humbly asking for an autograph. Throw in the historical sight-seeing on the way there and back, and it's easy to appreciate just why Joey loved this kind of race meeting so much. He even appreciated the Estonians' unique post-race prize presentations, as Billy Nutt explained. 'Afterwards, the prizegiving was done at the side of the road, and Joey told me later, "The cups were filled with pure vodka. It was the real thing. I want to race here more often."[67]

After taking a couple of wins at Tandragee in 1995, Joey had a relatively poor North West 200 with a best finish of second place in the 125cc event. But his sixth and tenth places in the two Superbike races gave no indication of what was to come at the TT. It had been fully seven years since Joey had won a big bike race at the TT and few thought he would ever manage to do so again. He came close in the Formula One race, despite continuing handling problems with the RC45. The bike may have worked well enough on some circuits, but it still tied itself in knots around the fast and bumpy TT course. Despite this, Joey led Phillip McCallen into the pit stops at the end of lap two but McCallen, also fighting with his own bucking and weaving RC45, regained the upper hand after fuelling and Joey was never able to regain the lead. He finished 18 seconds down, but second place was still the best finish he'd had on a Superbike at the TT since the 1991 Senior race.

After winning the Ultra-Lightweight TT for the last three years, luck deserted Joey this time around when his little RS125 seized on the opening lap and ended his race. There was better luck in the Lightweight event; his RS250 ran like clockwork and allowed Joey to take yet another TT win, with a new race record time thrown in for good measure. The 600cc Junior TT also proved Joey was getting to grips with John Harris's CBR600 as he finished fourth before setting his sights on the final race of the week – the Senior TT.

Phillip McCallen, by this point looking to break into international short-circuit racing, had elected to miss the Senior and instead flew to Italy to ride in the now defunct Thunderbike championship. His absence left Joey as the firm favourite for the race win and, apart from some early pressure from Simon Beck on his Ducati in the opening laps, Joey cruised to a trouble-free victory. It was rich reward for all the years he had spent adapting to a big bike again, but there were those who felt the victory was somewhat cheapened by McCallen's absence.

But a win is a win, and Joey could retire to the TT beer tent satisfied with his week's work. The only thing still bothering him was that he hadn't won the Formula One TT; the one he really wanted to win again. He would have to try harder; he had to find more speed, more strength, more stamina. Two months after the 1995 TT, Joey Dunlop packed up smoking for good.

With McCallen also missing the Ulster Grand Prix, Joey was left to complete a rout, taking his first treble at the meeting (both 250cc races and one of the two Superbike races) since way back in 1985. There seemed to be no stopping him now and all the younger riders could only shake their heads in disbelief and wonder what on earth they had to do to beat the old master. While riders do not lose talent with age, the willingness to use that talent usually declines; as they get older, get married and start families, riders are simply not prepared to take as many risks as they were in their youth. As former racer turned television commentator Steve Parrish says, 'When you're seventeen years old, the blinkers are on so tight that you can't see any further than the edge of the track, but eventually you start to see those barriers and you start to see those ambulances sitting trackside.'

Joey didn't seem to see them – the blinkers were still firmly in place. But in 1996 he would get yet another sharp reminder of just how close to the ragged edge he was operating.

CHAPTER 18

TRUE GRIT

**'I GOT A SIGN AT GLEN HELEN THAT I WAS 20 SECONDS DOWN
AND I JUST FLIPPED AND RODE LIKE SOMEONE POSSESSED –
SO HARD IT WAS UNBELIEVABLE.'**
Phillip McCallen

Throughout his long and distinguished career, Joey Dunlop had been extremely lucky in avoiding serious injury. Unlike some road racers he never made a habit out of crashing and, when he did, it was usually without breaking any major bones. His big Brands Hatch crash in 1989 was the exception, and he had broken his collarbone on more than one occasion, but it was still an impressive record, given the sheer amount of miles he had covered at flat-out racing speeds on many of the world's most dangerous circuits. By 1996, he had been racing for twenty-seven years and was only getting faster with age. Something had to give and, at the Riga circuit in Latvia, it did.

Having claimed another two TT wins on his 125 and 250cc

Hondas, Joey travelled out to Latvia in July to take part in a round of Billy Nutt's 'Pure Roads' series. He had already won the 125cc and Superbike races and was leading the 250cc event when he slipped off his machine and appeared to slide harmlessly to a halt. But when he got to his feet, he was supporting his left arm and was soon attended by an ambulance crew.

Once Joey got back home to Ballymoney, however, it was no longer his fractured left shoulder blade that was concerning him; it was the damage he had done to the little finger on his left hand. Most of the skin had been ground off the digit when Joey's hand became trapped under his sliding motorcycle and, on the first day of practice for his beloved Ulster Grand Prix, Joey was forced to see a specialist and underwent reconstructive surgery. Instead of taking part in the practice sessions at Dundrod he had to rest his hand, much to the disappointment of tens of thousands of fans for whom the Ulster Grand Prix meant nothing without its star attraction.

It would be nine weeks before Joey returned to racing and, when he did, it was at the Frohburg road races in Germany where he took a sixth place in the 250cc race while still struggling to operate the clutch lever properly with his damaged left hand.

While his 1996 season had been reduced by two months due to injury, it also hadn't been a vintage year as far as results went – his twentieth and twenty-first TT wins being the only major highlights. But after a winter of rest the finger was fully healed by the time the 1997 season got underway and Joey celebrated by finally sitting, and passing, his motorcycle test. Incredibly, he had never got round to earning a licence for the roads, despite all his years of racing and his testing of race bikes on public roads. It might sound easy for a five-time world champion and twenty-one-time TT winner to pass his motorcycle test, but racers do not ride like road riders do: Joey's former TT Formula One rival Rob McElnea also sat his test many years after his racing career began and failed it for getting his knee down at a roundabout!

Joey was nervous about how vulnerable he felt on two wheels in amongst busy road traffic too – and keeping to one side of the road didn't exactly come naturally to him either. 'I had to get used to the traffic and it's difficult concentrating on riding on one side of the road,' he said. 'I think I'll keep off the streets of Belfast until I get used to it.'[68]

He passed his test first time, however, and, perhaps with one eye on retirement, was safe in the knowledge that he could always have an occasional ride out once his racing career was over.

But it wasn't over yet. By 1997, Joey had made the Lightweight 250cc TT his own, having won it for the last three years, and it was beginning to eat away at Phillip McCallen, who, despite having won in almost every other class at the TT, had never won a 250 race. He was desperate to beat Joey, so desperate that he crashed out in pursuit of the old master. His description of just how hard he had to ride to try and catch the race leader speaks volumes about Joey's blistering pace – and the price others often had to pay when they tried to match it. 'I got a sign at Glen Helen that I was 20 seconds down and I just flipped and rode like someone possessed – so hard it was unbelievable,' McCallen says. 'I was a silly boy and tried to make all that time up in one section, instead of over a full lap. Going through Rhencullen the bike was right on its side; I was just holding it flat-out everywhere. Then I got a sign saying I'd pulled 9 seconds back in just a few miles. I really shouldn't have been riding that hard, but I was so mad with myself inside because I was more desperate than anything to win that 250 race.'

Always an aggressive and electrifying rider, McCallen now pulled out all the stops in pursuit of Joey. 'Coming into the first right-hander at Quarry Bends, I'd usually knock it back a gear, but I decided to hold it flat-out in top, then brake really hard and knock it down two gears for the following left. I held the throttle against the stop and tipped the bike in, flat on its side. Whether it was the camber change on the road or not, I don't know, but I just lost the front.'

Crashing at the TT is never a good idea, but crashing at 150mph and living to tell the tale is an exceedingly rare achievement. 'Everything went dead quiet – so quiet that I actually heard the crowd gasp as I slid down the road,' McCallen continues. 'When I got up, the pain was unbelievable – it was the first time I'd had a proper beating at 150mph. I had friction burns everywhere and gravel all through my legs. I got into a hot bath and my wife scrubbed the gravel out of my legs with a scrubbing brush. I had another race in two days' time, so I just had to get better.'

Unaware that McCallen was out of the race, Joey carried on leading it, smooth, calm and completely under control. He would win by almost a minute from Welshman Ian Lougher. A young John McGuinness, taking his first-ever TT podium, rounded out the top three. He had idolised Joey when he was a child and used to sneak onto the ferry in his hometown of Morecambe and sneak a free crossing to the Isle of Man to watch him race at the TT.

The rest of TT week in 1997 was disappointing for Joey. After losing more than a minute during his pit stop, he lost heart in the Formula One race and could only manage to bring Nick Jefferies' RC45 home in sixth place. 'I crashed in practice and was in hospital, so Joey asked if he could borrow my bike for the Formula One race because I had qualified second on it, so he knew it was well set-up,' Jefferies explains. 'The steering offset and weight distribution were never right on the RC45, so I set my bike up really soft and Joey said it was the best-handling RC45 he had ever ridden. That was when Joey seemed to finally have a little bit of respect for me. It was like a strange sort of Irish acceptance of me!'

Joey's Honda RS125 had been lacking horsepower all through practice week and, despite having a new barrel and piston flown in the night before the Ultra-Lightweight race, he could only manage a disappointing tenth spot in an event that had once been his own.

After posting his fastest-ever Supersport lap (118.34mph), Joey brought John Harris's CBR600 home in fifth place but never found his form in the Senior TT and limped home in seventh, while Phillip McCallen won his eleventh TT. It would prove to be his last. While competing in a British championship round at Thruxton in 1998, McCallen crashed and broke his back in three places. He would recover enough to attempt racing again, but the risk of another crash permanently damaging his spine was enough to make him quit the sport. He now owns a successful bike dealership in Lisburn.

Joey had outlasted yet another rival, but his apparent lack of commitment in the 1997 Senior TT was a sign to some that he was winding down his career and no longer had the motivation to push as hard as he needed to in order to win races. A win on the 250 at the Ulster Grand Prix was the only other outstanding result of the 1997 season. By Joey's exceptionally high standards, it hadn't been a very successful year, but a trip to Australia in the off-season appeared to refresh him and convince him that he wasn't ready to call it a day just yet.

The trip had been a present from his wife Linda to celebrate Joey's forty-sixth birthday and, by flying out there alone, he proved he had managed to come to terms with his fear of flying. The trip not only allowed him to enjoy some more Antipodean sunshine, it also added further to his legend. While having a spin on a friend's road bike, Joey went a little over the speed limit and was stopped by the Queensland police. As he was writing up a speeding ticket, the policeman asked, 'So, who do you think you are, then? Joey Dunlop?' to which, Joey removed his helmet and confessed that, yes, in fact, he was. The astonished policeman, who happened to be a huge bike-racing fan, immediately ripped up the ticket and instead asked for his hero's autograph. Despite being more than 10,000 miles from home, and despite the fact he had spent his entire career trying to avoid publicity and fame, Australia was no different to anywhere else.

After thinking he had luckily avoided a speeding ticket, Joey returned to his hotel room to find a message requesting he present himself at the local police station. It seemed the policeman had changed his mind, after all. Duly obliging, Joey turned up at the local station to face the music and was staggered to find the building crowded with policemen clutching autograph books and cameras. He spent the next hour or so posing for pictures and signing photos and posters of himself, utterly bemused that he was known on the other side of the world. He had, both literally and metaphorically, come a long, long way from his poor, rural upbringing outside of Ballymoney.

Refreshed and recharged after his Australian adventure, Joey prepared for yet another season of racing and Honda's fiftieth anniversary. The Japanese giant was pulling out all the stops at the TT and Joey Dunlop factored heavily in its plans. Honda supplied him not only with his usual RC45 but also with a two-stroke NSR500V Grand Prix bike to race in the Senior TT (the loose regulations for this invitation-only race allow for many different types of machines to race together).

It looked like being a big year, but then disaster struck. While lying in third place in the 125cc race at the Tandragee in May, Joey hit a series of bumps too fast and was thrown from his machine and landed heavily. The race was immediately stopped while an ambulance crew attended to Joey and whisked him away to hospital. Rumours immediately began to circulate that Joey had been killed and the paddock was full of shocked, numbed faces. He couldn't be. Not Joey Dunlop. He simply couldn't be. It was unthinkable.

He wasn't. But he had suffered a cracked pelvis, a broken left hand, and a broken left collarbone, though the biggest problem was that he had lost the end of his wedding ring finger. He was now an amputee, but his sense of humour at least remained fully intact. 'It's a matter of time to getting used now without it,' he said on the *Kelly* show on Ulster Television just hours after having the heavy bandaging removed from his hand. 'I've been talking to people that has lost fingers and eventually you get used to it. It's difficult – you reach into your pocket to get change and you think there's a hole in your pocket!'[69]

But it had been no joke. Doctors told Joey he was lucky to be alive and that, if he had struck something instead of simply being thrown down the road and sliding to a halt, he would almost certainly have been killed. His racing career, they told him, was over and surely even he could see that now. He couldn't, and his only regret was that he had made a mistake. 'I was a wee bit disappointed at the Tandragee because it was my own fault,' he said of the crash. 'I just lost control over the jumps and I was going far too quick.'

Although there was no hope of riding at the North West Joey set his sights on returning to racing at the TT, set to start in just three weeks' time. When he arrived on the Isle of Man looking haggard and strained, he had to undergo a medical to be passed fit to race. He was desperate to race in the one event that was now the sole focus of his career but the decision lay in the hands of the medics: if they deemed him unfit to muscle a racing motorcycle around the TT course at 190mph, he would be refused permission to take part, whether he was Joey Dunlop or not.

Ultimately, he was given permission, but it was clearly going to be a struggle and Joey announced that he would not attempt to ride any machine bigger than his 250cc Honda. 'I'll be back on a 750,' he said of the future, 'because all I want to do is a win another Formula One race.' But it wasn't going to happen that year: that year Joey would only have two chances of adding to his overall win tally – the Ultra-Lightweight 125 race and the Lightweight 250cc. In the 125cc event, run in drying conditions, Joey could only manage a ninth place, clearly exhausted and in a great deal of pain.

The man who won the race knew a thing or two about pain himself. Despite suffering those life-threatening injuries in his big TT crash in 1994, Robert Dunlop had refused to give up racing. Although his right arm and leg were now practically useless appendages, he had set to work converting his 125cc Honda – and his race gloves – to enable him to ride. Wullie Dunlop had cobbled together an ingenious right-hand glove that had springs on the backs of each finger. Since Robert was unable to grip the handlebar tightly enough – and was completely unable to use the front brake lever – the springs on the glove would assist him by offering mechanical support: as Robert tightened his grip, the springs would compress, and as he loosened it, they would recoil, allowing him to hold onto the bike's handlebars more securely.

To address the front brake problem, Robert switched the traditional brake lever for a thumb-operated brake paddle and switched it over to the left side of the handlebars. Another problem solved. Changing gears was no problem as Robert's left leg was working normally, but he couldn't use the rear brake because of the nerve damage to his right leg. Simple, Robert thought – I won't use the rear brake.

But the modifications didn't end there. He was also forced to turn the handlebars upside down to allow him to hold on more comfortably. Each of these modifications were serious compromises and many felt Robert would be a liability to both himself and others if he returned to racing. The point seemed to be proven when, attempting to ride the bike on an airfield for the first time, Robert crashed heavily and broke his arm so badly the bone was actually protruding through his jacket.

He had attempted to race at the North West 200 in 1996 but had been refused permission by race organiser Billy Nutt. Worse was to come when the Motorcycle Union of Ireland (MCUI) revoked Robert's racing licence, claiming his injuries were too serious to allow him to control a racing motorcycle, and also claiming that his heavily modified machine was not race-worthy.

Undeterred as ever, Robert launched a legal action and eventually won his licence back but Nutt continued to refuse him an entry to the two races he controlled – the North West 200 and the Ulster Grand Prix. The organisers of the TT *did* allow Robert to race and he returned there in 1997, astonishing everyone by taking a podium. He could be seen on the longer straights putting his overworked left arm behind his back to give it a break and ease himself into a more comfortable position, while hanging on with only his disabled right hand. Most spectators could only shake their heads in disbelief at the levels of drive, determination and sheer guts on display. Others saw only madness.

Three weeks before the 1998 TT, Robert had finally been allowed to compete at the North West 200 again, but probably wished he hadn't bothered. He was knocked off his bike by another rider and suffered yet another break to his right leg and another broken right collarbone. Broken again, but still not bowed, he turned up on the Isle of Man on crutches, fully intending to race.

Having somehow been passed fit by the medics, he then went on to achieve one of the grittiest victories in TT history by winning the Ultra-Lightweight race.

Had it happened in a Hollywood movie, it would have been laughable, so far-fetched did the end result seem. But it happened for real and the crowds at the prize-giving ceremony were sent into raptures when Robert took to the stage on a crutch before throwing it into the crowd and standing on his own two feet. It was the stuff of legend, and in that one race Robert Dunlop proved himself the equal of his more famous brother once and for all. No one in racing could remember seeing such a display of bravery, grit and sheer bloody-mindedness. 'This is my best TT win ever,' said an emotional Dunlop, who had also had to mount the winner's rostrum after the race with the aid of crutches. 'When I was lying in the road at the North West 200, I didn't think I'd be riding here.'

The Dunlop brothers were clearly made of very special stuff and Joey proved it yet again in the Lightweight 250 race. Nowadays, TT races are no longer held in wet conditions as it's deemed to be just too dangerous, but in 1998 they still were. And it had rarely been wetter on the Isle of Man than it was for the 1998 Lightweight race – but the appalling conditions played right into Joey's hands. During practice, the empty finger on his left glove had been flapping painfully against the still-raw stump of his amputated ring finger, so Joey had taped back the glove finger to reduce the flapping. Bravery and determination aside, it was Joey's experience and his unrivalled race tactics that would see him pull off one of his greatest ever wins.

The race was cut from four laps down to three just before the start sand most riders planned to pit after one lap for fuel. Showing years of TT experience, Dunlop gambled on doing two straight laps, believing the weather would worsen and the race would be stopped after two laps. 'It was so wet that Joey knew they were going to stop the race after two laps, but the others hadn't figured that out,' says Neil Tuxworth. 'You could only do three laps of the TT course on a tank of fuel on a 250 so, normally, with a four-lap race, riders would come in at the end of the first lap so they could have a really quick top-up and then do three straight laps. If you pulled in after two or three laps you had to take on much more fuel and that took longer. A lot of the top riders pulled in at the end of the first lap, as per usual, but Joey didn't – he went straight through because he knew they would have to stop the race. They did, and he won it. That was an exceptional race.'

Joey Dunlop won his twenty-third TT in weather conditions so bad that many of the other top riders pulled out and refused to go any further. He was, quite naturally, delighted with the victory. 'I was very pleased with the way it went, especially in the wet,' he said. 'A lot of people thinks I'm really good in the wet, but I think I'm awful! But it's the only chance, really, I had at the TT and I really went for it and it paid off. I was surprised that the doctor even said that he would gie me a chance. At the beginning of practice, I knew masel I couldn't do it. It was very, very hard – it was the hardest TT I ever rode in. Practice week and race week and the pressure that people – the pressure I had to put on myself – because I knew I wasn't fit. It was difficult. I couldn't believe it once it was all over. When that flag dropped, I was just ready for home.'[70]

And when he did get home, Joey knew it was rest he needed above all else. 'Once I come home, the doctor said I needed to give it a month to six weeks or, he says, "You'll end up wi' a bad hand." I geen it no chance whatsoever at the TT, like. I went to physio every day and everything; bathed it in boiling water every morning... You can't just keep on doing that.'[71]

Joey would race on for the remainder of the 1998 season but without any spectacular results. But it didn't matter – he had taken yet another TT win in the most difficult of circumstances and that was all he now cared about; his other outings were purely for fun. No one expected to see Joey Dunlop winning an international race on a Superbike again, not after having a finger amputated and reaching the grand old age of forty-seven in February of 1999. But six months after reaching that milestone, Joey would yet again stun the racing world with another of his greatest-ever performances. The memory of the 1999 Ulster Grand Prix is still enough to raise the hairs on the backs of the necks of those who witnessed it. On an under-powered bike, and against a new generation of ferociously fast young riders, he would once again show them who was boss.

CHAPTER 19

THE BOSS

'JOEY IS AN UNBELIEVABLE RIDER. GOING INTO FAST, BLIND CORNERS HE KNOWS WHEN TO HOLD IT FLAT OUT AND WHEN TO OPEN HER UP AT OTHER CORNERS. I JUST COULDN'T DO THAT.'

David Jefferies

By the time he lined up on the grid for the 1999 Ulster Grand Prix, Joey Dunlop had racked up twenty-three wins at the event and forty-eight around the Dundrod circuit in total. He was the undisputed master of the fast, flowing ribbon of tarmac set in the hills overlooking Belfast. But there were some who wanted to claim Joey's King of the Roads title and in the vanguard was a twenty-seven-year-old Yorkshireman called David Jefferies.

Son of TT winner Tony Jefferies, nephew of TT winner Nick Jefferies, and grandson of TT racer Allan Jefferies, it's fair to say that racing was in David's blood. A hugely popular character, David was also of a different generation to Joey Dunlop and had a very different riding style. With vast experience in 500cc Grands Prix,

World Superbikes and British championship racing, 'DJ' attacked the pure roads courses with a short-circuit aggression that no one had seen before and, in June of 1999, he had taken a hat-trick at the TT, winning the Formula One, Production 1000 and Senior races. Joey had come away from the event without a single win to his name for the first time since 1991.

Jefferies was perfectly comfortable with his bike sliding around underneath him and happy to showboat to the fans by leaving huge black lines of rubber on the track as he over-stressed his rear tyre and drifted his machine around corners. A big man, and strong with it, DJ would literally muscle his machine around any given circuit in complete contrast to Joey's classically smooth, calm and controlled riding style. When the pair raced together, it was clear evidence of one era overlapping another. 'You'd watch David Jefferies coming round a corner and he'd have the back end hanging out and he'd be manhandling the bike everywhere and fighting with it while it was tying itself in knots, as it was drifting out towards the gutter,' says TT privateer Paul Owen. 'Then Joey would come round the corner, super smooth, with about two or three feet to spare at the edge of the track. Every time he passed me – which was many times – he was so smooth and never took any chances. It just looked completely effortless and within seconds he'd be gone.'

Jefferies had made history at the TT in 1999 by beating the hugely expensive factory Honda RC45s on what was essentially a tuned-up road bike – the 1000cc Yamaha R1. The bike was a game-changer and proved that production machines were now so fast that it was no longer necessary to have an exotic factory machine to win TT races. Joey's 750cc RC45, now in its sixth year of competition, was hopelessly outclassed by comparison, but in his favour was his experience around Dundrod. While Jefferies was making his debut, Joey had won more races around the 7.4-mile circuit than anyone else. Joey was giving twenty-one years away to Jefferies in terms of age, but DJ was carrying a wrist injury, so each rider had as many advantages as disadvantages. The scene was set for a classic confrontation.

As usual, there were two Superbike races at the 1999 Ulster Grand Prix and Jefferies took a debut win on the course by emerging as the victor of the first. Joey had fought back bravely, as had Jefferies' V&M Yamaha team-mate Iain Duffus, but it looked like a new King of the Roads had arrived at Dundrod and had raised the bar completely. Although Joey had a sluggish start, he posted his fastest-ever lap around Dundrod (at an average speed of 125.14mph) to pass Jefferies and rejoin the battle. All three riders banged fairings and elbows as they fought for supremacy, but there was no beating Jefferies. This was an alien way of racing for Dunlop, and not one that he thought was safe.

Jefferies' V&M Yamaha team boss, Jack Valentine, says he heard lots of partisan Irish fans brandishing his rider 'a complete nutter' because of his riding style, but he offers an alternative explanation. 'There were a lot of Irish fans coming over and saying, "Aye, yer man's crazy." We used to get that a lot, because nobody on the road-racing scene had seen a bike with proper horsepower before and, even at the TT, David was coming out of corners leaving fucking big black lines, just power-spinning the tyres, and it was the same at the Ulster. They had never seen it, they said he was just crazy. I had a few of the regular Irish teams and team owners saying, "Your fuckin' man's crazy – slow him down" and all that. Again, it was just his handling of the bike.'

There were rumours in the paddock that, between races, Joey had approached Jefferies to warn him that his riding style was too dangerous for a circuit like Dundrod, but Jefferies' father Tony plays these rumours down. 'They didn't really have strong words,' he says. 'Dave was having to push really hard because he was on Pirelli tyres and he couldn't get the drive out of the slow corners. Joey was pulling away out of those on his Michelins, so DJ had to ride really hard to catch him up again. It was really frustrating for Dave because he knew he could go as fast as Joey, but his tyres were spinning up and he kept losing time. So, to stay with Joey, he had to pull a few moves that were pretty close. Joey was pretty philosophical about it. He was like, "Well, that's what you've got to do sometimes, I suppose." He'd had days where he'd had to do the same.'

In the Supersport 600 race that was held between the two Superbike races, Jefferies and Duffus were racing so hard that DJ actually knocked his team-mate off and sent his bike flying into a road sign. Perhaps Joey had a point, and clerk of the course Billy Nutt had a word with Jack Valentine about his riders' aggression levels and riding styles. 'This is a road circuit,' he reminded Valentine, 'They can't ride it like a short circuit.'

Joey was in a rare angry mood when he took to the line for the second Superbike race – the main race of the day. He might have been treating his racing more like a hobby in his later years, but he still had plenty of fight in him when his hackles were up, and Jefferies had most definitely raised them. Joey came out for the second leg with his 'race face' on and his thousand-yard steely gaze. He was clearly going to be a dangerous opponent and, while he didn't approve of riding so aggressively on the roads, he wanted to prove he could do it if he had to.

Dunlop fluffed the start but was soon hunting down the yellow and red V&M bikes at the front of the field. When he eventually took the lead, the partisan crowd went wild to see this silver-haired old fox taking the fight to the two wild-riding young guns. After biding his time in third place, Jefferies made his move past Duffus and set about attacking Dunlop, but even he admitted he scared himself, such was the pace the leader was setting. 'I ran wide and almost hit a telegraph pole at Budore and gave myself a big fright,' he said.

With a monumental effort, he finally caught Dunlop on the penultimate lap but had to set a new outright lap record of 126.85mph to do it – and this on his first-ever visit to the track. But Joey was having none of it and responded by lapping Dundrod quicker than he had ever done before (126.80mph) to just edge the win from Jefferies, who showed how much he had enjoyed the race by pulling a monster wheelie out of the final corner. 'I was trying and was going to pass him into Wheeler's on the last lap,' Jefferies told *Road Racing Ireland* magazine, 'but, just as I was going to, I realised I was too fast and shut it off. Then, at the hairpin, I had too much power to give it a handful coming out of the corner.'

Whatever their differences, Jefferies paid tribute to Dunlop after the race and openly admitted he simply could not find a way to beat him in such form. 'Joey is an unbelievable rider,' he said. 'Going into fast, blind corners he knows when to hold it flat out and when to open her up at other corners. I just couldn't do that.'

Fittingly, it was a draw between Jefferies and Dunlop, with each rider taking a Superbike win apiece. The older man from another era of bike racing had shown he still had the mettle to mix it with, and beat, the very best of the young road-racing hot shots, and proved he had no intention of relinquishing his King of the Roads title just yet.

o

Part of the reason for Joey's lack of success at the 1999 TT was that his Honda RC45 was too old and too slow to be able to take it to the new generation of 1000cc Superbikes. He had run David Jefferies close in the Formula One race but had shredded his tyre by having to ride so hard and could only manage second place. He was going to need a better bike for the 2000 TT if he was to achieve his dream of winning another Formula One race and, for a while at least, it was going to be a racing version of Honda's flagship road bike, the CBR900RR Fireblade. If a Yamaha R1 road bike could be turned into a racing machine so readily, Honda saw no reason why its own Fireblade could not follow suit. But things didn't turn out that way.

In late 1999, Bob McMillan had presented Joey with a rare gift on behalf of Honda: he was given his factory RC45 to keep and to do what he wished with. Joey chose to hang the bike – which would easily have fetched £500,000 at auction – from the ceiling of his pub as a decoration. It was a fine gesture by Honda to the man who had been faithful to the company for longer than any other and McMillan made no secret of his wish that Joey would now retire as he approached his forty-eighth birthday. 'I would like to see him retire now, when he is at the top and has done everything,' he said. 'We owe him so much – we can never repay him.'[72]

Joey had other ideas. He desperately wanted one last Formula One TT win, but it soon became clear that the Honda Fireblade was not going to be the bike to do it on. With development of the machine being painfully slow, and Joey dismissing the near-standard version of the machine as simply not good enough after he had ridden it, another plan was hatched. Joey phoned Bob McMillan and vented his anger, saying Honda was being made to look a laughing stock and that something had to be done. "I'll never forget it," McMillan recalled. 'He said, "This is supposed to be my last year and now it's ruined."'

McMillan, a close friend and confidante of Dunlop's, was

startled to hear Joey talking about this being his last TT. While he himself had expressed the wish that Joey would retire from racing, it was the first time he had heard Joey touting the idea. Gravely disappointed by Honda's lack of support, Joey packed a tent, jumped in his Mini, and headed off to the mountains of Donegal for three days to calm down and consider his options. It was a tried and tested exercise: whenever he needed time alone to think or just re-set himself, Joey headed for the hills with just the bare necessities needed to survive.

With the Fireblade needing much more development work, Plan B was to provide Joey with one of Honda's new SP-1 machines. To counter the supremacy of Ducati V-Twins in the World Superbike championship, Honda had built its own V-Twin in the shape of the VTR1000 SP-1. Joey would be given the same race-kitted bike used by James Toseland in the British Superbike Championship to use at the North West 200 and the TT. It was still going to be an uphill battle to fight with the much more powerful Yamaha R1s, but there was no other option – Honda didn't have any other suitable machines.

'Joey tried the Fireblade in a shakedown test at Cadwell Park but we were struggling a bit because it wasn't producing as much horsepower as we wanted,' Bob McMillan says. 'So, he decided to go for the SP-1 and raced it for the first time at the Cookstown 100 before going to the North West 200. The SP-1 wasn't as quick as it should have been either. It wasn't quite desperation, but I was keen to see if the Japanese could help us some more with our TT effort. I knew it would be good for sales if we could get the SP-1 to win. The Blade was already a top seller, so to me it was a matter of trying to improve the image of the SP-1.'

Fifth and second places on the booming V-Twin at the Cookstown seemed to offer at least some hope, but by the time

Joey had ridden the bike during practice at the North West, he knew it wasn't the weapon he needed. 'I don't know what I'm doing here,' he told journalist and author Jimmy Walker. 'The engine is just not quick enough – I may as well use an ordinary road bike.'[73]

A fifth place in the first Superbike race didn't appear to be such a bad omen, given that Joey was no longer keen on all the short-circuit style, close-quarter battle that was the new norm at the North West. But when he was black-flagged off the course in the second outing with his rear tyre burning up, things started looking ominous. The TT was just a couple of weeks away and he didn't have a bike he could win on. Something had to be done – and it was Bob McMillan who took up the fight and persuaded his Honda bosses in Japan that Joey deserved better. No one argued with him and, before he knew it, Honda had given special permission for Joey to cannibalise Aaron Slight's full factory SP-1 that he was campaigning in the World Superbike Championship. 'We ended up with Slight's engine and forks and everything else that we were legally allowed to put on the bike while keeping within the rules for the Formula One class,' McMillan explains. 'We had the top Showa suspension man come over from HRC [Honda Racing Corporation] as well. The president of HRC at the time, Nobuhiko Kawamoto, was a big TT man and he agreed to give Joey a bit of a hand.'

Joey finally had a factory machine again, just like in his 1980s heyday, and he knew that this was it: this was the best chance he was ever going to have of recapturing the glory days of old, when he dominated the Formula One TT and won it six years in a row. The only difference was time: Joey was now forty-eight years old, wore spectacles to work on his bikes, and had a full head of grey hair. In fact, his appearance left his Japanese crew slightly agog when they arrived on the Isle of Man to assist their legendary rider. 'The lads who came across from HRC in Japan were fairly bemused when they first saw Joey,' McMillan says. 'They knew about him, but had never met him, and they just saw his silver hair and must have thought, in a nice sort of way, "What's going on here?"'

That bemusement would soon turn to awe.

CHAPTER 20

NO ORDINARY
JOE

'HE WAS TO BE THE BIGGEST STAR AT THE SHOW, YET THERE HE WAS,
QUEUING TO BUY A TICKET JUST LIKE EVERYONE ELSE.'

Neil Tuxworth

While some staff members from Honda Japan were bemused at his
appearance in 2000, those who had been around for longer knew
all about Joey Dunlop and his utterly unique ways. In 1990, Neil
Tuxworth travelled to the TT for the first time as Honda Britain's
team boss and Joey Dunlop was one of his riders. He had known
Joey since 1973, so knew exactly how he operated, but he genuinely
feared for his job when asked to take a very important visitor to
Joey's garage. 'Honda Japan had sent over some very special flat
slide carburettors for Joey's RC30,' he explains. 'There were only
two sets in existence, and they were worth around £20,000 each,
which was an awful lot of money at the time, and I was told we had
to take very good care of them. It was my first year as team boss for
Honda Britain and a man called Michihiko Aika came over from

Honda Japan that year. He used to be Mike Hailwood's mechanic and was, by 1990, head of Honda Motorsports. I was told to collect him at the airport and to really look after him because he was senior Honda management. I was quite nervous about meeting him but I picked him up and asked if he wanted me to take him to the hotel or to the paddock. He said, "No, I want to go to Joey Dunlop's garage," and I just I thought, "Oh, no."'

Instead of operating out of the impressive Honda team camp in the TT paddock, Joey preferred to use a shabby little garage away from the crowds, down by the harbour quay in Douglas. Tuxworth still cringes when he recalls what happened next. 'When we got to Joey's garage, there was nobody there but the RC30 was sitting outside in the pissing rain. The cylinder head had been taken off the bike and there must have been an inch of rainwater in the top of each piston. The garage was next to a little river and Mr Aika looked over the wall and saw a twig sticking out of the wall with those £20,000 carburettors hanging off of it, dangling over the river. Mr Aika looked at me and I was shaking and must have had the fear of God in my eyes – I was certain that I had just lost my job. But he just looked at me and said, "Neil-san, please do not be concerned – we all know about Joey Dunlop"!'

It wasn't through any lack of respect for Honda that Joey treated its exotic equipment with such nonchalance; it was just his way and, as different as that was to the Japanese way of operating, they understood their rider from years of dealing with him. No other Honda rider had ever failed to return a contract to ensure he was paid and no other rider expected so little of his employer, especially when it came to spare parts. John Harris remembers Joey's completely selfless attitude when it came to accepting things from others – even when they were gladly offered. 'I remember in 1993 Joey told me the brake discs on his 600 were getting a bit worn, so

I said I'd send him a couple of new ones. He said, "Are you sure? Could you not just get a couple of second-hand ones that are in decent condition?" He could have had as many new parts for that bike as he liked, but he never wanted to take advantage of anybody. Money just never seemed to matter to him. In all the time I knew him, money was never mentioned, and I can't think of anyone else like that. Honda would have put him up in five-star hotels if he'd wanted, but he preferred to just sleep in his van.'

Neil Tuxworth also remembers being astonished by Joey's spartan way of operating. 'When Joey and Carl Fogarty were both riding for Honda, Foggy used to have a brand-new clutch in his RC30 every single week,' he says. 'He would do practice and two race starts on it and then it was wrecked, whereas Joey would use the same clutch for three years! We had spare parts budgets for all of our riders, which could run up to £100,000 each, depending on how many crashes they had in a season. Joey would use up next to nothing of his allocated budget – he just didn't use up parts.'

While other riders happily grabbed each and every free part on offer, Joey insisted on getting by with the bare minimum. 'He rung me up once and told me he was rebuilding the engine in his RC30 and asked if I could send him a set of piston rings,' Tuxworth continues. 'When I told the lads in the workshop to send Joey the rings they said, "Well, if he's rebuilding the engine, he'll need more than rings – he'll need gaskets, circlips, valves, springs…" So, they put a box of parts together and sent it over to Joey. About a week later, this box came back to us with all the parts, apart from the rings, and a note from Joey, saying, "I only wanted some fuckin' piston rings!" I mean, who else would do that? He was just unbelievable.'

While he hated to ever ask anyone for anything, or to even accept what was freely offered to him, Joey was very quick to give to others. Don Morley remembers that Joey's hospitality was so generous it was dangerous. 'I used to go over to Ireland quite a bit to do publicity shots of Joey,' he says. 'I used to dread those trips because, the moment I arrived, I had a Bushmills whisky put into my hand and the hospitality never stopped! I remember one time there wasn't a plant pot or anywhere else I could tip some of the drink into, so I had to drink it all and I was just gone – I could barely see after a while!'

Seemingly completely unaware of the esteem he was held in by others – and certainly unwilling to ever exploit the fact – Joey's incredibly humble attitude revealed itself in other ways too. 'Joey was to be guest of honour at the big annual motorcycle show at the NEC in Birmingham one year,' Tuxworth remembers. 'John McGuinness, who was also riding for us at the time, told me he turned up at 10am to go to the Honda stand and he spotted Joey in a big queue with all the punters. John asked him what he was doing, and Joey said, "I'm waiting to buy a ticket to get in." John had to explain that Joey was the guest of honour and he didn't need to wait in line to buy a ticket! He was to be the biggest star at the show, yet there he was, queuing to buy a ticket just like everyone else. That was just Joey.'

Steve Reynolds, former managing director of Aprilia Moto UK, remembers a similar situation occurring one year at the Antrim motorcycle show. 'Joey was supposed to be opening the show and was to be the guest of honour,' he says, 'but, ten minutes before the show was due to start, there was still no sign of him. People were sent all over to look for him and someone eventually found him waiting patiently in the queue to buy a ticket!'

Reynolds also remembers the demoralising effect that Joey's casual attitude to racing and fitness had on his opponents. 'I was helping our rider, Ian Newton, at the Ulster Grand Prix one year and he finished fourth, while Joey blitzed everybody at the head of the field. Most of the riders by then were teetotal and obsessed with the gym, but after the race we saw Joey walking through the paddock with a can of beer in his hand, a fag on the go, and his belly hanging out of his leathers. Ian looked at me and said, "For fuck's sake – why am I even bothering?"'

Joey simply did not understand how popular he was. Just before the 2000 TT, he agreed to help his old friend John Harris by attending a launch event for the Honda SP-1 that Harris was staging to promote his motorcycle dealership. 'Joey very kindly helped me with the promotion of the bike, despite him hating those kind of events,' Harris says. 'Some of the Honda guys were like, "How the hell did you get him to do that?" Anyway, we had the launch at a local vineyard and, as I drove Joey down the long drive that led to the vineyard, there were cars and bikes parked up everywhere, and he said, "You know a lot of people, John, don't you?" I had to explain to him "Er, no, Joey – these people have all come to see *you!*" He had no idea how loved he was.'

Bob McMillan learned that, due to Joey's idiosyncrasies, there were certain procedures to be followed if he wanted him to attend an event. 'He was a very determined character and, if he didn't want to do something, then he didn't do it,' he says. 'For example, if we were having a Honda function and I wanted Joey there, I had to send the right man to get him, or he wouldn't come! One time, when Joey didn't turn up at an event, his 250cc sponsor, Bertie Payne, told me, "Hey, Bob, ye sent the wrong boy!"

'Joey didn't care what anybody else thought – he just did what he thought he wanted to do,' McMillan continues. 'He used to do odd things because he felt it was right to do it. I don't think you could quantify him – I've never met anybody like him. He had such a skill and such a way of dealing with things, even though he was such a humble, ordinary-looking man.'

Despite his diminutive stature, his quietness and his scruffy appearance, Joey Dunlop had an aura about him that was very palpable to those who spent time in his company. 'Joey was a legend, and you knew you were in the presence of a legend when you were with him,' Ian Simpson says. 'You never hear a bad word about Joey, but how could you? How could anyone have a bad word to say about him?'

Nick Jefferies was another team-mate who was somewhat in awe of Joey. 'He was the sort of person who just touched the hearts of people, especially with his charity work with the orphanages,' he says. 'When you were in Joey's presence there was an aura about him, the same as there was with Mike Hailwood. You knew you were in the presence of greatness. Joey caused a similar reaction to Captain Tom Moore. It's all to do with latching onto something inside that human gene that touches the heart and goes right through it. Joey just had that very rare ability.'

Jefferies still laughs about the occasion when he realised just how popular Joey was, compared to any of the other riders, himself included. 'Castrol Honda made up little postcards of each of its riders every year, so we had something to sign for the fans. I seemed to be signing an awful lot in the North West 200 paddock one year and thought there must be a lot of Nick Jefferies fans in Ireland. But it turned out people were using them like trading cards and the fans needed ten of my signed cards to trade for just one of Joey's! My mechanic still laughs at that to this day.'

Despite winning five British championships, three TT races, and five North West 200 races, Ian Simpson says one of his proudest moments in his racing career was discovering that Joey had a cat that was named after him. 'He had a cat called Simmo!' he says, laughing. 'How good was that? I was walking about the paddock like a bantam cock with my chest puffed out when Joey told me that!

I think his daughter Donna named it. If people ask me what my biggest achievement in racing was, I tell them that Joey Dunlop's cat was named after me!'

That love that everyone seemed to have for Joey manifested itself in many ways and often worked in his favour, as Neil Tuxworth remembers. 'The respect that people had for him, particularly in Northern Ireland, was immense,' he says. 'I remember at the North West one year, I went up to the race organisers' office and said to Mervyn Whyte, "Practice should have started half an hour ago – what's going on?" and he said, "Oh, Joey hasn't turned up yet, so we're just waiting for him." The whole meeting was being held up just for Joey! That was the kind of respect they had for him. People just *did* things for Joey. Everybody loved him and thought the world of him.'

Joey's scruffy appearance also held huge appeal in a racing world that was growing ever more corporate – although it didn't always go down so well with team bosses. When Neil Tuxworth presented him with a wardrobe of immaculate Castrol Honda team clothing one year, he was dismayed to find out how quickly it received the Joey treatment. 'We gave him some new team clothing once – really smart Castrol Honda gear. The first night in the paddock Joey was kneeling down in the grass and mud, working on his bike, and he had this brand-new clothing all covered in mud and oil and grease! He used to frustrate the hell out of me because we would have functions and he wouldn't turn up – it wasn't that he was awkward, it's just the way he was.'

When filmmaker David Wood arranged for Joey to turn up at the studio for the on-camera interview that would be used in *V-Four Victory*, he was almost disappointed when a clean-shaven and neatly dressed Joey appeared. 'He did that himself – I wouldn't have told Joey to change a thing,' he says. 'He just turned up with

his hair all smart and a sweater and shirt on. It didn't look like Joey
– I wanted him to put some mucky old overalls on, but I thought,
"No, he's gone to all that trouble and his wife had probably told
him to smarten up for filming," so we filmed him as he was.'

While Joey was prepared to smarten up on occasion, he was
never comfortable with it, and Barry Symmons learned to dress
down in order to better communicate with his rider. 'If we were
having a planning meeting and I wanted to get any sense out of
Joey, I quickly learned to leave my tie at the door, because he didn't
trust people who wore ties.'

Symmons was shrewd enough to realise that, underneath all
Joey's quirky ways and aversion to ties, there was a very genuine
human being who understood what really mattered in life. 'A more
genuine person you could never hope to meet,' he says. 'He had his
own beliefs and his own way of doing things – which made him the
individual that he was – but he had a heart of gold, which his mercy
missions to those Romanian orphanages proved.'

Graham Sanderson also remembers just how humble Joey
Dunlop was. 'He was a man of this earth – a man rooted in just
doing everything for himself and getting his hands dirty and being
an absolute professional at what he was doing.'

John Harris got closer to Joey than almost anyone outside of the
Dunlop family, yet never once spotted any flaws in his character.
'He was utterly unique,' he says. 'A lovely man without an ego,
very cheery and just a pleasure to be with. There wasn't a bad bone
in that man's body. You won't find anyone with a bad word to say
about him, and how many people could claim that? If you have
children and want a role model in life for them, you could do no
better than Joey Dunlop – perfect on a motorcycle and perfect as a
human being.'

'There couldn't be a Joey Dunlop in today's world,' Neil

Tuxworth says. 'He was such a special guy. Money was of no interest to him at all. Honda very, very rarely paid Joey – he just wasn't bothered about being paid. I think Michael Dunlop [Robert Dunlop's son] tried to be another Joey to some degree, but times have moved on and it's a different era now. Joey goes right back to the late sixties, when most riders were living out of the back of a van – only Giacomo Agostini stayed in hotels.

'The sport has moved on,' he continues, 'and, in fairness, it *had* to move on. If it hadn't kept pace with all the other professional sports out there, we wouldn't be getting television coverage and sponsorship. I know a lot of people say the old days were better, but things had to change for racing to get to where it is now and, of course, a lot more people are earning money from the sport now. Back when I was racing in Grands Prix, very few riders were getting paid, and the mechanics were all volunteers. There's so much more money in the sport now, so all sorts of people, like the mechanics, the press, the hospitality people, are all getting paid. When more money comes into a sport and it becomes more professional, then obviously people expect a lot more from it. Joey was of his time – you just couldn't be a Joey Dunlop today. He was a very special person and very unique.'

This was the character of the man who travelled across the Irish Sea in late May of the year 2000 to take part in the race of his life.

CHAPTER 21

THE GREATEST RACE

'HE WAS UNBELIEVABLE THAT DAY. JUST OUT-AND-OUT INCREDIBLE.'
Michael Rutter

Despite having Honda's full backing, and with three Japanese engineers and a factory SP-1 at his disposal, TT practice week did not start well for Joey Dunlop in 2000. The bike, which was competitive enough on the smooth circuits used in the World Superbike championship, refused to behave itself over the tortuous bumps and jumps of the TT course and was weaving all over the road on the faster sections. 'There was one time when Joey came back to the pits and wasn't too amused that he'd been passed by a lad wearing an orange novice bib!' Bob McMillan said. 'He clearly had a lot of work to do, but Joey and the team eventually managed to get the bike sorted out. It was a lot of hard work and a lot of Joey's determination, as much as anything, that really made the difference.'

While the SP-1's engine was superb, the handling was terrible and, after making endless tweaks to the chassis and suspension, Joey and his team reached the conclusion that the problem was being caused by the tyres, so new rubber was flown in by the Tuesday night of practice week. Tyres weren't the only thing being flown in at the last minute to improve Joey's chances of success. 'Every plane that came in from London had parts,' Linda Dunlop said. 'It was just amusing, standing in the garage watching it all; them opening the suitcases, lifting the clothes out, followed by an exhaust or whatever.'[74]

With so much now invested in the TT, then Honda president Kiyoshi Kawashima flew to the Isle of Man to keep an eye on things. Honda had come through for Joey in his hour of need but with that extra support came extra pressure, though Joey wasn't showing it. In fact, he seemed more relaxed than ever. Paul Owen had raced against Joey for years and noticed that he seemed to be completely relaxed at the 2000 TT. 'Usually, at the TT, he'd look like he didn't want to talk to anybody – he was just head down and focused – but he seemed so much more relaxed that year, as if he knew it was going to be his last TT and he was just going to enjoy it. I think he was planning to retire after that year. He didn't seem to be feeling any pressure and it did feel like it was a bit of a swansong for him. I knew when I'd had enough of racing – I knew when to walk away, and maybe Joey felt the same that year.'

The question of retirement had raised its head in practically every magazine article or news story published about Joey for years by this point and, although he never directly announced that 2000 would be his final year of racing Superbikes, it was widely believed that would be the case. While he would almost certainly have continued to race his little Andy McMenemy-backed Honda RS125, or taken part in classic bikes races, Joey knew his time on Superbikes was drawing to a close – he knew how hard he'd had to ride to beat David Jefferies at the Ulster Grand Prix the year before and he knew how much more dangerous things became when racing on the absolute limit on fire-breathing Superbikes. 'I know I can't do it for much longer,' Joey himself admitted, before adding a proviso. 'So long as I feel fit, and I'm competitive, I'll keep racing… maybe I should only be riding in the smaller classes now.'[75]

While Joey never specifically mentioned retirement in his phone call to Bob McMillan (when he had called to complain about Honda's lack of support), he did say that 'this is supposed to be my last year' and McMillan took that to mean Joey had decided that the 2000 TT was to be his last. It seemed he really was planning to retire after thirty-one years of racing, which might explain why he was so eager to have a good TT and to persuade Honda to pull out all the stops to help him achieve that.

On Saturday, 3 June Joey Dunlop lined up on the Glencrutchery Road to contest the first TT of the new millennium – the Formula One. He hadn't won the race since 1988, the year before his big Brands Hatch crash. He also hadn't shown his hand in practice (Joey's usual tactic was to ride flat-out between certain timing points on the course and then throttle off for others, so as not to reveal his true pace to his competitors) and V&M Yamaha rider Michael Rutter didn't see him as a threat. 'He didn't do very well in practice, so I didn't take too much notice of him,' Rutter recalls. 'But come race day it was damp, and Joey came flying through on slick tyres like it was bone dry. I thought, "Okay, he's on it." I'd raced against Joey many times before, but he was unbelievable that day. Just out-and-out incredible.'

By the time he reached the bottom of Bray Hill on the opening lap, it was obvious to all that Joey had his 'race face' on and meant business. David Jefferies, Michael Rutter and John McGuinness chased hard, but in the patchy conditions Dunlop led the way and completed the first lap with an advantage of 0.2 seconds over Rutter. But after Rutter had several massive slides on damp patches, he lost his confidence, and with McGuinness dropping back the race became a straight fight between Jefferies and Dunlop. On laps two and three Joey held the advantage but, after posting the fastest lap of the race on lap four, Jefferies briefly snatched the lead, only for Joey to regain it with a quicker pit stop. The duo were neck and neck in the early part of the fifth lap, with both men clearly giving it everything they knew, when suddenly the race was over: Jefferies' R1 had destroyed its clutch basket and he was forced to retire.

Although their hero still had more than a lap and a half to go, Joey's fans – which meant practically everyone watching the race – sensed a fairy-tale victory was within reach. As he had roared away from his last pit stop, even rival teams had cheered him on.

As he flashed across the finish line the crowds around the grandstand area rose as one to cheer home the most unlikely star any sport had ever produced. The shy, humble folk hero of Ballymoney had achieved his last great ambition – to win back the Formula One crown that he had made his own in the 1980s when he had been a much younger man. Joey Dunlop was back where he belonged, and the tributes were universal. Four-times World Superbike champion Carl Fogarty said, 'To still be winning races at forty-eight on the hardest and most dangerous circuit in the world? Well, he's got all my respect.' Steve Hislop added, 'What he's done is a great achievement. He seems to be more up for it now than ever.' And Phillip McCallen admitted, 'When everything goes right for Joey, on his bike and in his mind, he's virtually unbeatable. There will never be another TT rider like him.'

Gracious in defeat, David Jefferies added his own tribute, saying,

'Joey is simply a miracle man. He can still show us youngsters how to handle a Superbike around the world's most demanding road circuit.'

For Bob McMillan and his hard-working Honda crew, the unfancied victory was the ultimate reward. 'Everyone was amazed when Joey won,' he says. 'It was like a dream. *I* believed he could do it, *he* believed he could do it, but not everyone believed he could do it.'

Despite McMillan's post-race confidence, Joey did admit to having had doubts beforehand. 'I never thought I'd win another F1 race,' he said, 'but I've never had a bike this good. It's the best bike I've ever ridden. I wondered during the week whether I could do six hard laps. We had some handling problems during practice and tried a load of different suspension settings, but it wasn't until we used the rear tyre we used in last year's F1 race that it started coming together. On the final lap, I eased off and I tried to be smooth.'[76]

Almost a quarter of a century after making his debut at the TT, Joey's race time for the Formula One was the fastest he had ever set. Instead of getting slower with age, he was getting faster.

Joey seemed relieved as much as anything at the end of the race and admitted, 'The pressure was really on me because of having Slight's engine, and because there were a lot of top men from Japan here. I'm just glad I could repay them for the faith they've shown.'

There were still some sceptics who felt that Jefferies would have won the race had his R1 not broken down, but Bob McMillan isn't one of them. 'Some people wondered if DJ would have won the race but when I spoke to Joey afterwards – and not many people know this – but he reckoned he would still have won it. He said he was holding the pace and was okay with it, but he could have pushed a bit harder. As always, Joey was only riding as hard as he felt he needed to. He believed he'd still have beaten DJ had he not broken down and I had no reason to doubt him.'

Nick Jefferies says his nephew was astonished at Joey's pace in the race. 'David was very impressed by how fast Joey was. He knew Joey's SP-1 was a fantastic bit of kit, but I think he was a bit shocked that Joey could be up there at the same pace as him at forty-eight years old.'

Joey was deeply grateful to everyone at Honda for coming through when he needed them most – and he surprised Bob McMillan by agreeing to make a very rare speech to show his appreciation. 'After the race, I asked Linda where Joey was, because I wondered if he would consider making a short speech to some very senior Honda people,' McMillan says. 'Linda said I didn't have much hope, but that Joey was in the beer tent if I wanted to ask him. When I did, he simply said, "Aye, what time do you want me there, Bob?" I was quite taken aback, but that's how much it meant to him; he was prepared to make one of the few speeches of his career as a way of saying thank you to Honda for all the help he had been given to win that race.'

Joey Dunlop had achieved his greatest dream by finally re-taking the Formula One TT trophy after twelve years of trying, and his daughter Donna knew just how much it meant to him. 'The Formula One – words cannot even describe it,' she later said. 'It was the only race he ever wanted again and, seeing him, it just nearly brought tears to your eyes, cos it was the one that he really wanted, and he got it.'

Remembering the bemusement of the Japanese technicians at the start of TT fortnight, Linda Dunlop said of her husband, 'He never, ever would have said anything to boost himself, even to me, but when he won the race and we went home that evening, he said, "I just wonder what they think of the wee, grey-haired man now."

He just laughed, for he just thought it was hilarious himself – that, at his age, he could do it. But he was so happy.'[77]

The men in Japan who had provided Joey with the SP-1 were happy too. Several years later, Bob McMillan was astonished to hear just how impressed senior Honda management had been with that win. 'Mr Kawashima was second-in-command to Mr Honda and, in 2003, I asked him what was the best race performance he had ever seen by a Honda rider. Bear in mind that Kawashima-san was involved with the Honda race team back in the sixties, so he had watched Mike Hailwood race and, later, riders like Freddie Spencer, Wayne Gardner, Eddie Lawson, Mick Doohan and Valentino Rossi, but he said, "Bob-san, Formula One TT. 2000. Joey Dunlop. Amazing result."

'He said that was the most amazing race he had witnessed, because it should have been impossible for a forty-eight-year-old man to jump on a bike that had never been raced on the Isle of Man, and to win on it, against riders like David Jefferies. Just think about that as a statement – that includes every ride by every Honda rider since the 1960s – and yet, Mr Kawashima rated Joey's Formula One win in 2000 as the greatest ride of them all.'

Joey, everyone believed, would surely now announce his retirement from the sport: there simply was nothing left to prove or achieve. He had done it all. But then, he still had four more races to go that week, so there was no point in packing it in just yet. Besides, he had admitted back in 1997 that he simply wouldn't know what to do with himself without his racing. 'I couldn't settle at home,' he said. 'I couldn't settle to just stay at home and work in the bar.' He was clearly a man in turmoil: he knew he had to stop, but he couldn't quite bring himself to do it.

Nine-times TT winner Charlie Williams knows how hard it is for a rider to kick the habit of road racing. 'When I retired from the TT it left a huge gap in my life,' he says. 'I've never replaced the buzz I got from riding round the mountain circuit. I was tempted to make a comeback just to get that rush again because I got terrible withdrawal symptoms for years after I stopped. I knew one former TT racer who tried sky-diving and umpteen parachute jumps but said he still couldn't replace the buzz of racing at the TT. Sadly, he missed it so much that he made a comeback and was killed.'

Two days after his historic Formula One victory, Joey lined up on the Glencrutchery Road yet again, this time on his Honda RS250. The race had been postponed and cut from four laps to three due to inclement weather, and everybody knew who the danger man was in such conditions.

The tens of thousands of fans on the Isle of Man had barely stopped celebrating Joey Dunlop's Formula One triumph when the man from Ballymoney outdid himself yet again. With such a stunning win already in the bag, Joey could have been forgiven for taking it easy in his remaining races, but he set such a pace in the Lightweight 250 event that his nearest rival, John McGuinness, destroyed his engine trying to keep up with him. Using his unrivalled knowledge of the TT course, Joey consistently found the fastest lines round the damp roads to rack up win number twenty-five. He finished 77 seconds ahead of New Zealander Bruce Anstey.

And *still* he wasn't finished. Two days later, it was time for the Ultra-Lightweight 125 race, and Joey could finally line up on his Andy McMenemy-sponsored Honda RS125 alongside his brother again. Robert Dunlop started the race at number 4, just 10 seconds behind Joey. If his plan had been to reel Joey in by having him in sight right from the start, it didn't work – Joey won yet again, while Robert could only finish third and admitted, 'There was nothing I could do to go any faster and I couldn't match him.'

In the early 1990s, it had seemed that Joey Dunlop would never match the great Mike Hailwood's all-time record of fourteen TT victories. Now, with victory over fellow Ulsterman Dennis McCullough in the Ultra-Lightweight race, he had notched up an incredible twenty-six wins. Two years shy of his fiftieth birthday, Joey Dunlop was on the best form of his life.

What made his three wins even more impressive was that they were all achieved on very different bikes. Racing flat out on different motorcycles at the TT is not easy, as Paul Owen explains. 'To jump on that SP-1 Superbike, that wasn't really handling, and beat everybody, then jump onto a 125 and beat everybody, and then jump onto a 250 and beat everybody, was just amazing,' he says. 'Jumping between different capacity bikes at the TT is very difficult. I had a 125 and a Superbike one year and I went out on the Superbike for two laps then switched to my 125. Before I even reached the end of pit lane I pulled in, complaining that the clutch must be slipping because there was just no power. My mechanics assured me there was nothing wrong with the bike – it just had 40bhp as opposed to 180bhp. So, I set off again and realised I just had to ride it very differently. But I found I was braking too early everywhere, I wasn't changing gears enough – you really have to rev a 125 – and I was making all sorts of mistakes, just because of the huge differences between the two bikes.'

Reversing the order in which he rode the bikes proved to be no easier for Owen. 'The next night I went out on the 125 first, then got on the Superbike, and it was pulling wheelies everywhere because I was giving it so much throttle, having just come off the 125, which I was riding flat out. You really have to change your mindset between bikes and it's not easy. But Joey could do it so naturally. And for such a small bloke to muscle a big Superbike around the TT course was just so impressive.'

Joey took part in two more races during that unforgettable

week and finally seemed to get the hang of John Harris's Honda CBR600 in the Junior race. 'He set off and led for about half of the first lap,' Harris says. 'I was getting really excited, but I knew he was tired because he had already won the Ultra-Lightweight race that morning, and to switch from a 125 to a 600 is very difficult too. So, a bit of tiredness set in about the beginning of the fourth lap and he ended up fourth, after running third for a while. But he enjoyed it, and we enjoyed it too. He said to me, "Next year, if they have that 600 race in the morning when I'm fresh, I could win that." He handed me the fourth-place replica, which now takes pride of place in my house. As I was preparing to take the bike back home, he said to me, "John, I think I'm finally getting a hang of these 600s!" He explained to me that across-the-frame, four-cylinder bikes require a different riding technique to the V-Fours and the V-Twin SP-1 he'd been used to riding.'

That left the Senior TT, in which Joey would ride the SP-1 again. Was it intended to be his last hurrah? Did he know this was it? According to his rival, Michael Rutter, Joey certainly rode like it was his last-ever TT race. Rutter had finished second to Joey in the Formula One race after David Jefferies' demise, but it wasn't Joey's performance in that damp F1 race that left the greatest impression on Rutter – it was his pace and aggression in the Senior, which was held in perfect conditions at the end of the week, conditions that meant the riders could race even harder. 'What shocked me the most was his performance in the Senior,' Rutter says. 'We raced neck and neck for the last four laps. The race was run in totally dry, really fast conditions, so, when I passed Joey on the road, I didn't think I'd see him again, but the next thing I knew he'd come back past me. We must have passed each other about five or six times on the last lap, and I eventually thought, "Right, there's no way he's beating me on the last lap."'

Yet, even when Rutter rode as fast as he possibly could, he still struggled to pass Joey. 'I tried to pass him going into Creg-ny-Baa and kept waiting for him to get on the brakes, but he braked so late I couldn't get past,' Rutter continues, still sounding shocked by Joey's pace, all these years later. 'So, I followed him into the Nook, and his back wheel must have been a foot off the ground because he was braking so hard. He ran a little wide and I just managed to squeeze through and beat him across the line.'

David Jefferies took the Senior win from Rutter, with Joey coming home in third place after setting the fastest lap of his entire TT career – an average speed of 123.87mph. Such was his level of sportsmanship, he let Rutter know how much he had enjoyed the battle in his own special way. 'Joey was always very quiet and didn't say much more than "Hello" to me, but after that race he bought me a pint and said how much he'd enjoyed it,' Rutter says. 'That meant so much to me. I was shocked at how fast he was on the short-circuit-style corners. I mean, I was racing in British Superbikes, so I was used to that, but I didn't expect a forty-eight-year-old man with grey hair to be so fast. He was incredible. There will never be anyone like that again.'

Once again, the TT prize-giving ceremony was all about Joey Dunlop, but this year he was bestowed with an honour above and beyond the historic and highly valuable TT silverware. David Cretney, the Isle of Man's Minister for Tourism and Leisure, presented Joey with a gold replica of the Manx Sword of State. Asking Joey to kneel while he dubbed him on each shoulder with the blade, Cretney said, 'I now present you with this honour. Not only are you king of the mountain, but you are now a knight of the Isle of Man.'

There was simply no escaping the limelight, the awards, the accolades, and the adoration of his fans now – Joey had to accept his status as the most popular motorcycle road racer of all time, and there would be more attention to deal with when he returned home to Ballymoney. As soon as he had completed his incredible TT treble, the officials of the town decided they had to mark the occasion. Having already presented Joey with the Freedom of Ballymoney in 1993, this time the local authorities honoured him with a civic reception and paraded him round the streets in an open-topped bus.

Bob McMillan was by Joey's side throughout the event. 'I made a speech at the civic reception,' he says. 'I said, "I think it's time for Joey to seriously consider retiring – he can't do any more, and he can't do any better than what he's done, and I think it's time." Nobody in that room thought it was a good idea, but Joey quietly said to me, "I'm thinkin' about it, Bob, I'm thinkin' about it." So, he *was* thinking about retirement, but only quietly – he didn't talk to anyone about it.'

Much later that night, in Joey's pub, McMillan tried again. 'I spent about an hour talking to him about retirement, and I asked him if he couldn't just run the pub or set up a shop and a Joey Dunlop museum or something like that. He said, "Aye, aye, I could do that, Bob." In other words, he *was* thinking of options by that point. We were all trying to talk him into retirement. Andy McMenemy once said to me, "Can you no have a word wi' the wee man? He'll listen to you, Bob. Tell him it's time to pack it in – he's gettin' a bit old."

The celebrations in Joey's bar continued until 4am, when Joey and his old friend Bob McMillan had their final night cap, having set the world to rights – though not having agreed on a retirement plan.

As they finally headed to their respective beds a little the worse for wear, Joey was completely unaware that McMillan had been keeping a dark secret from him all night: Joey's long-time friend and sponsor, Andy McMenemy, had driven out to a field and shot himself in the head. It was a suicide that would have far-reaching consequences. 'We all knew that Andy had killed himself, but Joey didn't know, and we couldn't tell him that night,' McMillan says. 'He was told the next day and he was absolutely shattered. He decided to go up to Donegal to do a bit of fishing and just slept in his Mini. Then, he must have thought, "I'm going to go away" and he went to Estonia. I don't think he had been planning to go there – he was down to ride at the Skerries, but then he decided to go away.'

Estonia.

CHAPTER 22

ESTONIA

**'HE WAS JUST LYING THERE, NOT MOVING. THAT WAS THE
MOMENT MY LIFE CHANGED.'**
John Harris

Andy McMenemy had been sponsoring Joey Dunlop's 125cc racing campaign for a decade and had become a very close friend during that time, so his suicide, which was attributed to him having business problems, came as a terrible shock to Joey. John Harris had attended the civic reception in Ballymoney and was with Joey when he was told about McMenemy's death. 'I stayed at Joey's house that evening, but I wouldn't really want to comment on that,' he says. 'Andy was quite a character but, why he did it, I'm not sure. But Joey was obviously very upset. When he took me back to the airport the following day, he was very quiet. It had affected him quite deeply.'

After attending McMenemy's funeral, Joey decided to drive over 2,000 miles to Estonia to get away from all the sadness and to try to clear his head. He needed something to focus on and some time on his own, and the Skerries meeting in the south of Ireland that he was due to attend would only have lasted for a weekend. But according to Lavinia Cooke (then girlfriend of racer Dave Woolams, who competed regularly in Estonia), Joey had stated his intention to race in Tallinn on the night of that year's TT prizegiving ceremony, *before* Andy McMenemy had taken his life. Joey had mistakenly believed the Estonia meeting clashed with the Southern 100 that year and so he would miss out on it, but Woolams assured him that the two meetings did not clash. 'Joey's eyes lit up and he said, "Put me down for entries",' Cooke remembered. [78]

So, while many believed that Joey only went to Estonia to escape the fallout from the tragedy that had occurred back home, it seems he had been intending to go anyway – or was at least considering it as an option. Joey had, after all, raced at the same track on several occasions since his first visit in 1995 and had always enjoyed the experience. John Harris remembers receiving the phone call that would ultimately change his life. 'Joey phoned me at work and said, "How's the 600, John?" I told him it could do with being re-jetted and I said, "Why do you ask?" He told me he was going to Estonia to race and was taking the RC45 Superbike down from the ceiling of the pub and was going to race that as well as his 125. He wanted to take my 600, too. He said to me, "You know, I think you would enjoy it in Estonia. If you feel like coming along, just phone Donna [Joey's daughter, who worked for a travel agency at the time] and we'll fix it up."

'He would never have directly asked me to come along, but he sowed the seeds in my mind, and I think Donna was half expecting me to call, and I did. So, he drove out to Estonia and I flew out to meet him there on the Friday of the race weekend.'

Unbeknown to Harris at the time, Joey had already secretly

arranged to pay for his flight. The man who wouldn't put Harris to the expense of supplying him with two new brake discs, thought nothing of paying for a return flight to Estonia for him.

Upset as he was by Andy McMenemy's death, Joey was clearly in good spirits by the time Harris arrived at Lennart Meri Tallinn Airport on Friday, 30 June. 'Joey told me that he would be waiting for me at the airport, but when I got out the front of the main building he was nowhere to be seen,' Harris says. 'I sat down and waited, then a very stern-looking guy approached me and asked if I was there to meet Mister Dunlop. When I told him I was, he said, "Would you come with me please? We have to go to the police station. Mister Dunlop is very drunk and is being held there." He asked me if I had any money and I thought I was going to have to bail Joey out, but then I looked over the road and there he was, peeking out from behind his van, grinning from ear to ear. He had completely stitched me up.'

The Pirita-Kose-Kloostrimetsa circuit is 4.2 miles long, runs through a forest of pine trees, skirts the Baltic coastline, and crosses the Pirita river twice. In many respects it's no different to the public roads courses Joey was so accustomed to racing on back home in Ireland, but the proximity of so many trees so close to the roadside did cause concern for some, including Joey's helmet supplier, Ferry Brouwer. 'I went to Tallinn in 1990 and watched the bikes from the very fast left-hander that leads onto the start/finish straight,' he says. 'I stood on the inside of the corner and looked across at the spectators, who were effectively acting as straw bales, standing just one foot away from the outside of the track. I noticed a tree with two trunks and thought, "Jesus, if somebody hits that, it's not going to be nice." It was so dangerous looking that I took a photograph of the tree. The Estonians had a very different view of safety compared to the rest of us.'

It's a fast circuit, too. On a Superbike, the top riders would be nudging 180mph, the densely packed trees just a few feet from the edge of the road, but Joey was not worried about the dangers of the circuit. 'He never mentioned that he was concerned about the proximity of the trees,' Harris says. 'He drove me around the track in the van on the Saturday evening and, apart from the seafront section, it's very densely wooded, but he never made any comment on that at all.'

What Joey *was* concerned about was getting a decent night's sleep before the first day's racing on Saturday, 1 July. 'We put wet tyres on the spare wheels on the Friday afternoon, then got our heads down for the evening in what the locals called a "summer house" – which was really just a garden shed,' Harris explains. 'It was difficult to get to sleep, because it was so noisy with lots of Finnish fans drinking and partying, so Joey told me he was going to sleep in his van on the Saturday night, away from that noisy area. So, he spent his last night alone, sleeping in his van, after we'd had a few drinks and a meal together on the Saturday.'

The weather was poor all weekend, varying between damp and fully wet, but Joey continued his run of superb form and won the Supersport 600 race on Harris's Honda CBR600 on the Saturday afternoon.

Conditions were much worse on the final race day on Sunday, 2 July. Despite heavy rainfall, Joey cruised to yet another victory, this time on the Honda RC45 that he had taken down from the ceiling of his pub. His next outing would be in the 125cc race, due to start fifteen minutes later.

By then, conditions had dried somewhat, and tyre choice became critical. While he had used full wet tyres front and rear in the Superbike race – which had been held in heavy rain – Joey opted to run a full wet front tyre and an intermediate rear in the

125cc race, due to the slightly drier conditions. 'It was never really dry on the Sunday, so me and another racer, Dave Kerby, lifted the front wheel of Joey's 125cc bike up and changed the wheel for one that was fitted with a full wet tyre,' Harris continues. 'It was raining at that point, but not heavily. Joey completed the warm-up lap, then pulled up on his grid spot and nodded to me and Dave that everything was okay. He had an intermediate tyre on the rear. And then the flag dropped and off he went.'

Even when a racetrack is just over four miles long, conditions can still vary greatly from corner to corner, and rain showers can be localised to specific parts of the track. When a sudden heavy downpour occurred in this instance, the final corner on the circuit – a 125mph left-hand bend – was the worst affected. 'At the beginning of the second lap the heavens really opened,' Harris says. 'I had a towel over my head, and I was drenched. That fast, last corner was totally different with that amount of water lying on it, compared to just a bit of water like earlier. The deluge was mainly concentrated on the last corner and the start/finish straight. When Joey came round to that corner it was totally waterlogged.'

Even with full wet tyres front and rear, a motorcycle can lose traction and aquaplane if there's enough standing water underneath it. With the reduced grip of an intermediate tyre on the rear – designed to cope with damp conditions rather than full wet conditions – Joey would have been even more vulnerable if he struck standing water. English racer Ray Hutchinson pulled out of the race after the first lap, saying conditions were too dangerous. Joey appeared to have no intention of stopping.

At the end of the second lap, chaos and confusion suddenly broke out in the paddock. Riders started making their way back to their garages, red flags came out, a siren wailed, and all the while the rain battered relentlessly down. One woman could be heard screaming hysterically, over and over. People began making their way towards the last corner on the circuit to try to establish the source of the commotion.

'I hadn't realised what had happened,' John Harris says. 'The red flag came out and I didn't think any more of it, but then I didn't see Joey returning, even though a lot of other riders were now returning. So, I put my signal board down, dried myself off a bit, and went to find the clerk of the course to see what was happening. He spoke very little English, but I asked him where Mr Dunlop was, and he pointed to the last corner and said, "He had accident – you may walk there." Little did I know. So, I started walking towards the final corner and I met Dave Kerby. I think Dave knew what had happened but didn't want to tell me right at that moment. So, I walked a little further and could see all the crowd gathered around, and there he lay…'

Harris's world collapsed. 'I just couldn't believe that the clerk of the course gave me no warning. I expected to see Joey sitting on the banking having a cigarette, nursing a shoulder injury or something like that, but he was just lying there, not moving. That was the moment my life changed.'

As he had attempted to negotiate the waterlogged last corner on the course, Joey lost control of his Honda RS125 and slid off the track. On a purpose-built short circuit, with ample run-off areas, it would have been a harmless spill and Joey would have simply slid to a halt and walked away. But this was a road race and there were no such luxuries. Joey Dunlop, five-times world champion, twenty-six times a TT winner, and widely considered the greatest road racer of all time, had finally run out of luck. His body struck the very tree that his friend Ferry Brouwer had been so concerned about ten years earlier. He was killed instantly.

o

More than 2,000 miles away, most of the British motorcycle racing community was at Silverstone in Northamptonshire for a round of the British Superbike Championship, when word started to come through. It was met with shocked disbelief. 'I was at Silverstone and Roger Burnett walked into the garage and said, "Have you heard?",' says Roger Marshall. 'I said, "Heard what?" And he told me. I was absolutely stunned. Absolutely gutted. After all those years racing with him... I just admired him for the way he carried on racing for so long, and to win a big race at the TT again at forty-eight? I was so proud of him after that. What an achievement, and yet, a few weeks later, he was gone. But racing was Joey's life, and I don't think he ever wanted to stop.'

Neil Tuxworth was also at Silverstone. 'I got a call from Roger Harvey, who looked after Honda's motocross efforts. It was just unbelievable. I was absolutely stunned. Joey was one of those guys you never thought it would happen to. I mean, you never think it's going to happen to anybody, or none of us would ever race, but it was just so sad that it had to end that way for Joey.'

Nick Jefferies simply didn't believe what he was being told when the news came through. 'I was sitting with my mum watching Wimbledon, round at her house, and a mechanic friend contacted me and said, "Joey's gone. Joey's dead." I will never forget it. Terrible. It was just disbelief. I mean, Joey just wasn't a crasher – I think he only crashed once at the TT in all those years. I didn't believe it, so I had to ring someone else to get it confirmed. It took a while to sink in.'

Ian Simpson was equally devastated. 'I was at Silverstone and just felt terrible when I heard the news,' he says. 'Nobody ever expected that with Joey because he was so safe on a bike.

News of Joey's death even reached halfway up the Amazon. 'I was astonished when I heard that Joey had been killed,' says David

Wallace who directed *The Road Racers.* 'I thought "How can it happen to a guy who's been so safe for all those years?" I was doing a series called *Conquistadors*, about the Spanish conquest of South America, and I was in the Amazon at the time. My wife had heard it on the radio and, the next time I spoke to her on the phone, she told me about it. It was a huge shock. I didn't make it back in time for the funeral, but I saw pictures from it in the strangest places because it was such a momentous event.'

Following news of Joey's death, his pub in Ballymoney became a shrine to its former landlord, as thousands of mourners queued for miles to pay tribute, from early morning until late into the night, day after day, night after night. Books of condolence were opened all over Ireland and filled with hundreds of thousands of messages of love and sorrow.

Back in Estonia, John Harris found himself in a waking nightmare. In a strange country, where he couldn't speak the language, and where few others spoke English, he found himself practically alone, trying to deal with all the formalities and legal procedures, struggling to contact Joey's wife to inform her of the devastating news. There were very few Brits at the meeting, but Harris at least was supported by Dave Woolams and his girlfriend, Lavinia Cooke, who helped with making the necessary arrangements.

Yet Harris had no mobile phone and no one else had travelled out to Estonia with him – Joey's entire team had consisted of just Joey and John. And all the while, amidst the whirlwind of arrangements that had to be made, Harris was having to come to terms with the loss of his friend and hero. 'I lost somebody so very special – I worshipped him, really,' he says, the deep sadness in his voice still apparent some two decades later. 'There was so much going on in my head at the time. How do I get hold of Linda? How do I do this, and how do I do that? I couldn't find the interpreter, and I was just trying to gather my thoughts. I didn't have a mobile phone with me, but I knew I had to somehow phone Ballymoney police station, because I knew the Dunlop family had friends in the local police. But sadly, before I could get hold of a number and a phone, someone had already told Linda.

'I don't know to this day how that person found out so quickly. I wanted someone with respect and a bit of stature to go and break the news, so the police were my first thought. I was very, very sorry that Linda found out the way she did. I managed to make contact with her later that day, but I forget what I said to her. I really can't remember that conversation at all.'

Bob McMillan was in his garden at home in Eccleshall, enjoying the sunshine, when his phone rang. It was his Honda colleague, Roger Harvey. To this day, McMillan struggles with his emotions as he recalls that grim moment. 'Roger said, "Bad news, Bob – Joey's gone. Estonia." My brain just simply didn't process that. Roger was at Silverstone, so I started asking him how his riders were doing. I thanked him for calling, hung up, then went outside to the garden, where my wife Sandra was pottering, and I told her that Joey was dead. And at that moment, having actually said it out loud, I just completely broke down. I sat on a rock in the rockery, just absolutely sobbing my heart out. My brain had finally engaged and told me what Roger had meant, and I'm not afraid to admit the effect it had on me. Bad things happen in the bike world and we've all been involved in a lot of bad things – good friends of mine have lost their lives on bikes. You have a lot of things in your life that happen, but that really hit me hard.'

As soon as he had composed himself sufficiently, McMillan rang Linda Dunlop. 'The first thing I did was phone Linda and I asked her if she wanted to come with me to Estonia, or should I take Robert, or what did she want me to do?" She said, "You go, but just make sure that you don't bring him back in two boxes." She had heard that in the old Russia, they used to take the head off a corpse and put it in a separate box. That might be total nonsense, but that's what she had heard, so I assured her that I would bring him back in one piece. So, I got the first flight out to Estonia and John Harris met me at the airport.'

'Bob flew over on the Monday evening,' says Harris. 'I was struggling on the Monday, I must confess.' The pair could at least console one another and found some solace in a bottle of whisky to numb the pain. 'We drank and laughed and cried until about 4am then, at 8am, we were at the British Embassy, working out how we could bring Joey back,' McMillan says.

On the Wednesday, McMillan and Harris flew back to Gatwick airport with Joey's body. 'Once we had got Joey on the aeroplane, underneath us, I was carrying his helmet in a bag and I refused to put it on the floor,' McMillan remembers. 'You couldn't put it in the overhead rack so I sat with it on my knee and, all the time, when they came round to give us drinks and food, I had to pass Joey's helmet to John to hold, and then he would pass it back to me so that he could eat. We passed it back and forth during the whole flight because neither of us would put it on the floor.'

'We stopped at Gatwick and Bob got off, then I flew on to Dublin with the body,' Harris continues. 'It had to be Dublin, because it was an Aer Lingus flight, and that was the only airline that could accommodate the coffin.'

When Harris arrived at Dublin airport with Joey's body, he was met by a hearse and driven north to Ballymoney. Word had already spread throughout Ireland and he was astonished to see the streets were lined with people, all standing by the side of the road, having waited for hours for the chance to pay their last respects. 'I think we set off from Dublin airport at about seven o'clock in the evening;

just Joey, myself, and the undertaker. Word had got around so, all the way from Dublin, we were followed by a ribbon of motorcycles. There were people standing on roundabouts, they were lining the streets, all saying their goodbyes to Joey in a very respectful way, as we slowly drove back to Ballymoney.'

Such was the universal respect for Joey in Ireland, even the Loyalist and Republican stand-off at Drumcree was briefly put on hold. 'We heard that there had been a bit of a clash and a stand-off between Loyalists and Republicans somewhere on the route but, out of respect, there was a bit of a truce until Joey's body was brought through,' Harris continues. 'July was a sensitive time in Ireland, with all the marches, but even that was put aside for Joey. It was a long, long journey – we didn't get to Ballymoney until three o'clock in the morning. I stayed the night with Robert Dunlop and his wife and then, in the morning, I walked round to see Linda. She was wonderful; very caring and very kind to me, and I tried to be as kind to her as I could.'

Ballymoney's favourite son was back home for good, his last lap completed. The night before the funeral, Bob McMillan went to see his old friend one last time. 'Me and my wife stayed at the Bushmills Hotel and, that night, about eleven o'clock, Robert and Jim Dunlop came to see us and had a drink or two,' McMillan says. 'Then they took me and Sandra to Joey's house to see him laid out in his coffin in the bedroom, surrounded by flowers. By now it was about one o'clock in the morning, but the house was packed with people. Sandra tried to go in to see Joey, but she couldn't do it, so I went in to see him on my own. I went up to him and just looked at him and said, "Well, you've fucking done it now, haven't you?" Those were my exact words. I was in tears, but I kissed him on the forehead and came out.'

o

No one could have predicted the turnout for Joey's funeral on 7 July. From very early in the morning, all roads leading into Ballymoney were clogged with thousands upon thousands of motorcycles. While the family had expected that around 3,000 people would turn out for the open service, the RUC estimated that more than 50,000 people packed the one-mile stretch of road between Joey's house and Garryduff Presbyterian Church, where the service was to be held. Many had been in position since before dawn.

'It was just astonishing,' Bob McMillan says. 'It was like the funeral for Princess Diana, but you're talking about a little man from Ireland, with dirt under his fingernails, who just worked on his bikes in a shed. It was just unbelievable, really, the outpouring of grief and support.'

The 50,000 mourners all fell respectfully in behind the hearse as it made its slow, dignified passage to Joey's final resting place. The hearse was led by five police motorcycle outriders and flanked by race marshals from the North West 200, wearing their customary orange overalls and acting as a guard of honour. They had watched over Joey before; they would do it one final time.

The hearse was followed by Joey's shattered wife and children, his parents Wullie and May, his brothers Robert and Jim, with 50,000 people in support, right behind them, sharing their pain, lost in grief. Joey may never have known just how loved he had been by so many, but the hard evidence was there for everyone to see at his funeral.

'I was told that only Princess Diana's funeral had more people at it,' Neil Tuxworth says. 'It was just unbelievable. So many people had so much respect for him. I'm proud to have known Joey Dunlop, and to have ridden with him, and to have managed him for so long. I have tremendous respect for him – there will never be another Joey Dunlop.'

The funeral was covered live on Irish national television, the sombre silence of the mass of mourners punctuated only by the sounds of grown men crying as they covered every square inch of the very road on which Joey had so often illegally tested his racing machines.

They came from north and south of the border, Catholics and Protestants, old and young, bike fans and non-bike fans, grandmothers, grandfathers and children, men in suits, ladies in hats, tattooed bikers in leathers and chains, Loyalists and Republicans... it didn't matter; they all shared a love and respect for the humble humanitarian who had conquered the world in his own quiet way. The sadness and sense of loss was palpable as the service was relayed by a PA system outside the thronged church. There were people everywhere.

John Harris was astounded. 'We knew there would be a good number at the funeral but 50,000-plus? It was astonishing,' he says. 'When you looked back up the road from the church at Garryduff, there were people as far as the eye could see. I don't think Ireland had ever seen anything like it – there were grown men in tears everywhere.'

The service was led by the Reverend John Gilkinson, assisted by Joey's friend and the former reverend of Garryduff Presbyterian church, the Reverend John Kirkpatrick. Bob McMillan read a tribute and Joey's daughter Donna read out a poem she had written for her father. 'Joey touched millions of people with his modesty, his humility and his humanity,' McMillan read out. 'And yet I'm sure he never knew how great a star he was.'

Men who had spent their entire careers trying to beat Joey Dunlop now sat silent in the crowded pews to pay their final respects: men like Ray McCullough, Brian Reid, Mick Grant, Phillip McCallen, Johnny Rea, Eddie Laycock and Steve Cull. Government ministers from London, Belfast, Dublin and the Isle of Man attended the service, including the Reverend Ian Paisley, Irish Sports minister Jim McDaid, Deputy First Minister Seamus Mallon of the Northern Ireland Assembly, the Isle of Man's Minister of Tourism, David Cretney, and the UK's Minister for Sport, Kate Hoey, who had presented Joey with his trophies at the TT just a few short weeks before. 'He didn't have a lot of words,' Hoey said in tribute. 'But he was someone who, if you ever met him once, you never forgot it, because he had that capacity to sort of make you feel he was just a really ordinary person doing extraordinary things.'

Sportsmen from other disciplines, accustomed to being mobbed by fans wherever they went, melted into the background on this day. Boxer Barry McGuigan, and Formula 1 drivers Eddie Irvine and David Coulthard were just some of the major stars who humbly paid their respects to the most reluctant and unlikely of sporting heroes.

Joey fans travelled from as far away as Canada, Japan, South Africa and New Zealand to be in attendance. It seemed impossible that such a quiet, self-effacing, publicity-shy man from a quiet backwater in County Antrim could possibly have commanded so much respect on such a global level.

Raido Rüütel, the director of racing in Estonia, who had done so much to help in the aftermath of the tragedy, also flew over to pay his respects. 'Northern Ireland has not just lost a great sporting hero; the world of racing has lost its leader,' he said. 'The Estonian people will miss him badly. Ireland will miss him. The world will miss him. We have lost a master – nothing less.'

In paying his own tribute, the Reverend John Kirkpatrick said of Joey, 'In every generation there appear those who achieve greatness against all the odds. Joey was such a one.'

But it was the heartfelt tribute written by Joey's daughter Donna that really hit home and reminded everyone that, while they might have lost a friend, a rival or simply a sporting hero, the real hurt would be felt by the family Joey left behind. Between them, they had lost a husband, a father, a brother and a son. 'To people, you were number one,' Donna read out with great bravery whilst choking back tears. 'To me you were a daddy.'

Joey's wife Linda and his children, Julie, Donna, Gary, Richard and Joanne, his brothers and sisters, Robert, Jim, Helen, Margaret, Virginia and Linda, and his mother and father, May and Wullie, had all lost the centre of their universe. Yet, while Joey's wife Linda was utterly devastated at her loss, she refused to blame the sport of road racing and, in fact, defended it. 'You can be angry now, but you can't be angry for the past thirty years,' she said sometime later. 'Joey picked his sport. Unfortunately, it took his life, but it gave him and us thirty great years.'[79]

As the service ended, the quiet dignity that had endured throughout suddenly erupted into a celebration and appreciation of Joey Dunlop's life as one mourner began to clap and was joined by another and then another. Soon, that single mourner was joined by 50,000 others, as a raucous applause spread all the way down the Garryduff Road and out over the fields and pastures of the surrounding countryside that had produced a home-grown hero who had touched hearts around the world.

After the service, Joey was buried in a private family ceremony in the cemetery behind Garryduff Presbyterian Church.

David Wallace, who had first brought Joey to the attention of the wider world with his documentary film in the 1970s, went on to make many more successful documentaries and television series, but Joey Dunlop had never been far from his mind, and a poignant thought struck him when he was working on a series called *In the Footsteps of Alexander the Great*. 'There's a wonderful Greek song about Alexander at the end of the film that says, "Alexander, you conquered the whole world, but you lost your soul",' he says. 'That's one thing you could never say about Joey – he conquered the world, but he absolutely kept his soul.'

Joey himself had once been asked how he would like to be remembered. His response spoke volumes about the man and how he lived his truly remarkable life: 'I never wanted to be a superstar – I just wanted to be myself. I hope people remembers me that way.'

EPILOGUE

'JOEY DUNLOP, WITHOUT DOUBT, IS THE BEST ROAD RACER THAT THE
WORLD HAS EVER SEEN AND, I THINK, EVER WILL SEE.'
Roger Burnett

Mather's Cross, North West 200 circuit,
Thursday, 15 May 2008

Robert Dunlop had decided to race on after his brother's death and
his sons, William and Michael, had also decided to try their hands
at the sport that had taken their uncle Joey's life – and very nearly
their father's.

During the 250cc practice session for the 2008 North West 200,
on the Thursday before race day, Robert's Honda TSR250 started
puffing out clouds of dirty smoke. It was the first time he had
ridden a bigger 250cc bike since his massive TT crash fourteen years
earlier. William Dunlop, who was also taking part in the practice
session, saw the problem and tried desperately to intervene. 'I saw

smoke coming out of the back of my dad's bike,' he said. 'I tried to pass him to warn him, but he was too quick for me.'[80] At forty-seven years of age, Robert Dunlop was still too fast to catch.

On the approach to Mather's Cross – the very same corner where Mervyn Robinson had been killed twenty-eight years before – Robert realised his bike was about to seize, so he attempted to do the only thing that would prevent a catastrophic accident: he tried to pull in his clutch, so that he could coast to a halt. But on his heavily modified bike, the clutch wasn't where it should have been and, in that one moment of pure reflexive instinct, Robert accidentally pulled hard on his front brake lever instead. So hard, he was thrown over the handlebars of his machine while travelling at 160mph and was then struck by another rider as he slid down the track. Michael Dunlop came upon the scene moments later, threw his bike away, and ran to his father's side. Robert Dunlop was still alive as his son held his hand and waited for medical assistance, but he had suffered massive trauma to the chest and died on route to the Causeway Hospital in Coleraine.

Two days later, Michael and William Dunlop shocked everyone by turning up on the grid for the 250cc race at the North West 200. The race stewards had decided the brothers were in no fit mental state to race and would not be permitted to take part but, when Michael and William sneaked onto the start line, the stewards felt it would create too much of a scene to physically force them off the grid. They had no option but to let the boys take part. While William suffered machine problems and was forced to pull out of the race, Michael did something so extraordinary it had never been seen in racing before. Just two days after his father had been killed – and before the funeral had even taken place – he rode like a man possessed to take his first-ever international road race win, in honour of his father. It was, quite simply, beyond belief. The following day, Michael and William Dunlop buried their father next to their uncle Joey.

o

Since the deaths of Joey and Robert Dunlop, their memories have been kept alive in so many ways, and the tributes to them are ongoing. A memorial garden was established in Ballymoney, close to Joey's Bar, that features statues of both men, Robert garlanded and holding a bottle of victory champagne, Joey sat astride the Honda SP-1 that took him to his greatest victory. An identical statue of Joey also looks over his beloved TT course on the Isle of Man. A simple, yet elegant, stone memorial stands on the spot where Joey lost his life at the final corner of the former Pirita-Kose-Kloostrimetsa circuit in Tallinn, Estonia. It is no longer used for racing.

On 27 August 2000, the Isle of Man government organised a tribute lap of the course in memory of Joey. More than 10,000 people turned up on motorcycles and rode the hallowed 37.73-mile course in tribute to their fallen hero. The throng of motorcycles was some seventeen miles long, and thousands more cheered and applauded from the roadside.

Charity work continues in Joey's name through The Joey Dunlop Foundation, which raised the funds to build a house for disabled race fans right on the TT course, so they can stay there in comfort and enjoy the racing.

Also in 2000, Joey was awarded the Segrave Trophy, which is awarded to a British subject who accomplishes the most outstanding achievements on land, in the air or on water. The only other time the honour was bestowed posthumously was for Sir Donald Campbell. Joey was also posthumously voted Man of the Year by readers of *Motor Cycle News* in 2000, some sixteen years after first taking the much-coveted title, and was also named Sportsperson of the Millennium by *The Irish Post*. Other awards poured in – he was named the Guild of Motoring Writers Rider of the Year, *Road Racing Ireland*'s Rider of the Year, Enkalon Rider of the Year, BBC Sports Star of the Year (Belfast) and Texaco Sports Stars' Rider of the Year (Dublin), all in 2000. Everyone, it seemed, wanted to honour the man who had won 26 TT races, 13 North West 200 races, 24 Ulster Grand Prix races, 31 Southern 100 races, 119 Irish national races, and 23 Irish road race championships. It's a phenomenal record by any standards, and one that is unlikely to ever be beaten.

In 2014, Hollywood movie star Liam Neeson narrated what is already considered a classic racing documentary called *Road* that chronicled the lives of two generations of the Dunlop Dynasty – Joey and Robert, and William and Michael. It was a huge success.

One year later Joey was voted Northern Ireland's greatest sports star ever by readers of the *Belfast Telegraph*, ahead of such luminaries as George Best, Rory McIlroy and Alex 'Hurricane' Higgins.

Commemorative Joey Dunlop coins and stamps have been produced, songs have been written about him (most notably by Irish rock band Therapy?), replica motorcycles, helmets and leathers have been produced, and new documentaries continue to be produced about his astonishing life and tragic death.

The Dunlop name has kept on winning in Joey and Robert's absence, too. To date, Michael Dunlop has won nineteen TT races and was responsible for raising the bar at the event, just as his uncle Joey had done decades before. William Dunlop won four North West 200 races and seven Ulster Grand Prix races, solidifying the dominance of the next generation of Dunlops on the world's most dangerous road courses.

Then, on 7 July 2018, tragedy struck yet again. During practice for the Skerries race in the Republic of Ireland, William Dunlop was thrown from his machine after it had leaked oil onto his rear wheel. He was killed instantly. His partner Janine Brolly gave birth to their baby daughter two months later. She named her Willa, in honour of the father she never got the chance to meet. William Dunlop was laid to rest, alongside his father and uncle Joey, in Garryduff Presbyterian Church on 11 July 2018.

Michael Dunlop, with nothing left to lose, continues to race.

JOEY DUNLOP CAREER RESULTS

Compiled by Ivan Davidson, Motorcycle Union of Ireland (MCUI)

1969

Tandragee 100
200cc race: 10th

Cookstown 100
200cc race: 8th

Carrowdore 100
200cc race: 5th

1971

Maghaberry
200cc race: 3rd

Kirkistown
200cc race: 4th

Tandragee 100
200cc race: 2nd

Cookstown 100
200cc race: 3rd

1972

Maghaberry
200cc race: 6th

Maghaberry
200cc race: 3rd

Lurgan Park
200cc race: 5th

Mid Antrim 150
200cc race: 5th

1973

Maghaberry
200cc race: 6th

Tandragee 100
350cc race: 6th

Kirkistown
350cc race: 5th

Mondello Park
Grade B race: 6th
Handicap race: 3rd
Monarch of Mondello race: 4th

Maghaberry
350cc race: 5th

Mid Antrim 150
350cc Handicap: 1st
500cc Handicap: 2nd

Ulster Grand Prix
350cc race: 19th

Maghaberry
350cc race: 6th

Fore
350cc race: 4th

Maghaberry
350cc race: 6th

Maghaberry
350cc race: 4th
Embassy race: 4th
Over 250cc Club Members race:
3rd

Maghaberry
350cc race: 2nd

1974

Kirkistown
350cc race: 4th
Embassy race: 3rd

Maghaberry
350cc race: 2nd
Embassy race: 3rd

Tandragee 100
350cc race: 5th

Leinster 200
350cc race: 2nd
Unlimited race: 4th

Cookstown 100
500cc race: 4th

Kirkistown
350cc race: 4th

Killinchy 150
350cc race: 4th

Kirkistown
350cc race: 2nd
Embassy race: 3rd

Maghaberry
350cc race: 3rd

Fore
350cc race: 2nd

Mondello Park
350cc race: 6th

Carrowdore 100
350cc race: 4th

Maghaberry
350cc race: 1st
Embassy race: 2nd

Kirkistown
350cc race: 4th
Embassy race: 4th

Maghaberry
350cc race: 4th

1975

Kirkistown
350cc race: 6th

Aghadowey
350cc race: 2nd
Embassy race: 3rd

Tandragee 100
350cc race: 2nd

Leinster 200
350cc race: 1st
Unlimited race: 1st

Mondello Park
Invitation race: 2nd

Kirkistown
350cc race: 5th
King of Kirkistown/Embassy race:
1st

Killinchy 150
350cc race: 2nd

Mondello Park
Grade A race: 2nd
Monarch of Mondello: 1st
Fleetwood Handicap race: 4th

Skerries 100
350cc race: 2nd
Shell Sport race: 2nd

Aghadowey
350cc race: 1st
500cc race:1st
Embassy race: 2nd

Temple 100
500cc race: 1st

Mondello Park
350cc race: 1st
500cc race: 1st
Invitation race: 1st

Mid Antrim 150
500cc race: 1st

Carrowdore
350cc race: 1st
500cc race: 1st

St Angelo
350cc race: 1st
Ace of St Angelo: 1st

Aghadowey
350cc race: 1st
500cc race: 1st
Embassy race: 3rd

Mondello Park
Unlimited race: 1st
Christy Clarke Memorial race: 2nd

Kirkistown
350cc race: 3rd
500cc race: 1st
Embassy race: 2nd

1976

Mondello Park
350cc race: 1st
Invitation race: 1st

St Angelo
350cc race: 1st
500cc race: 1st
Embassy race: 2nd

Aghadowey
350cc race: 3rd
500cc race: 1st
Embassy race: 3rd

Kirkistown
350cc race: 1st
500cc race: 1st
Embassy race: 2nd

Tandragee 100
350cc race: 1st
500cc race: 1st

JOEY DUNLOP CAREER RESULTS

Leinster 200
350cc race: 1st
Unlimited race: 1st
Invitation race: 1st

North West 200
250cc race: 3rd
750cc race: 7th

Cookstown 100
250cc race: 3rd
350cc race: 2nd
500cc race: 2nd

Isle of Man TT
Junior TT: 16th
Senior TT: 18th

Killinchy 150
350cc race: 2nd
500cc race: 1st

Mondello Park
250cc race: 1st
350cc race: 1st
Grade A race: 1st

Skerries 100
350cc race: 2nd
Unlimited race: 2nd
Shell Sports Skerries 100 race: 1st

Munster 100
350cc race: 1st
Unlimited race: 1st
Munster 100 race: 1st

Southern 100
250cc race: 3rd
350cc race: 2nd
750cc race: 2nd
Solo Championship race: 1st

Aghadowey
350cc race: 3rd
500cc race: 1st
Embassy race: 2nd

Temple 100
350cc race: 2nd
500cc race: 3rd

Fore
350cc race: 5th
500cc race: 1st

Phoenix Park
O'Reilly Memorial race: 1st

Mid Antrim 150
250cc race: 3rd
500cc race: 2nd

Mondello Park
250cc race: 1st

350cc race: 1st
Unlimited race: 1st
Invitation race: 1st

Ulster Grand Prix
250cc race: 8th
350cc race: 5th
500cc race: 2nd

Carrowdore 100
250cc race: 2nd
350cc race: 2nd

Aghadowey
350cc race: 2nd
Embassy race: 1st

Kirkistown
250cc race: 1st
350cc race: 1st
500cc race: 1st
Embassy race: 3rd

Aghadowey
350cc race: 1st
500cc race: 1st
Unlimited Handicap race: 1st

1977

Mondello Park
250cc race: 1st
350cc race: 1st

Unlimited race: 1st
North Dublin Invitation race: 1st

Kirkistown
250cc race: 1st
350cc race: 1st
750cc race: 1st

St Angelo
250cc race: 2nd
350cc race: 1st
Unlimited race: 1st

Aghadowey
250cc race: 1st
350cc race: 1st
Embassy race: 1st
Ace of Aghadowey: 1st

Leinster 200
250cc race: 1st
350cc race: 1st
Invitation race: 1st
Leinster 200 race: 1st

Tandragee
250cc race: 3rd
350cc race: 1st
Unlimited race: 1st

North West 200
250cc race: 2nd
Superbike race: 9th

JOEY DUNLOP CAREER RESULTS

Cookstown 100
250cc race: 2nd
350cc race: 2nd
500cc race: 1st

Isle of Man TT
Classic: 7th
Senior: 4th
Junior: 10th
Jubilee: 1st

Kirkistown
250cc race: 1st
350cc race: 1st
Unlimited race: 1st
King of Kirkistown race: 1st
Embassy race: 1st

Skerries 100
350cc race: 5th
Unlimited race: 1st
Skerries 100 race: 1st

Southern 100
250cc race: 1st
750cc race: 1st
Solo Championship race: 1st

Temple 100
250cc race: 2nd
350cc race: 2nd
750cc race: 2nd

Killinchy 150
250cc race: 2nd
350cc race: 3rd
1000cc race: 3rd

Aghadowey
250cc race: 1st
350cc race: 6th
Embassy race: 1st
Enkalon Trophy race: 2nd

Fore
250cc race: 4th
350cc race: 2nd
500cc race: 1st

Ulster Grand Prix
250cc race: 1st
350cc race: 5th

Kirkistown
350cc race: 1st
750cc race: 1st
Embassy race: 1st

Aghadowey
350cc race: 2nd
750cc race: 1st
Embassy race: 1st

Mondello Park
Monarch of Mondello,
leg one: 2nd

Monarch of Mondello,
leg two: 1st
Fleetwood Handicap race: 4th

Kirkistown
250cc race: 3rd
500cc race: 2nd
750cc race: 1st
Embassy race: 1st

Aghadowey
250cc race: 2nd
350cc race: 2nd
750cc race: 1st
Sunflower Trophy race: 1st

Aghadowey
250cc race: 1st
350cc race: 2nd
750cc race: 1st
Up to 250cc Handicap race: 2nd
Unlimited Handicap race: 2nd

1978

Kirkistown
250cc race: 1st
750cc race: 1st
Embassy race: 1st

Mondello Park
Unlimited race: 3rd
Invitation race: 1st

Aghadowey
750cc race: 1st
Ace of Aghadowey race: 1st

Kirkistown
250cc race: 1st
350cc race: 1st
750cc race: 1st
Embassy race: 1st

Tandragee 100
250cc race: 4th
350cc race: 2nd
750cc race: 1st

Cookstown 100
350cc race: 1st
500cc race: 2nd

Isle of Man TT
Formula 2: 5th
Junior: 11th

Killinchy 150
250cc race: 4th
350cc race: 1st
500cc race: 4th

Aghadowey
500cc race: 2nd
Embassy race: 5th

JOEY DUNLOP CAREER RESULTS

Skerries 100
Unlimited race: 2nd

Southern 100
1300cc support race: 1st
1300cc race: 1st

Kirkistown
500cc race: 1st
Embassy race: 2nd

Temple 100
250cc race: 1st
350cc race: 2nd
750cc race: 1st

Ulster Grand Prix
350cc race: 6th
1000cc race: 8th

Kirkistown
350cc race: 3rd
500cc race: 1st
750cc race: 1st
Embassy race: 1st

Carrowdore 100
250cc race: 1st
350cc race: 1st
750cc race: 2nd

Aghadowey
250cc race: 5th

500cc race: 1st
750cc race: 2nd
Embassy race: 2nd

Kirkistown
250cc race: 3rd
350cc race: 2nd
750cc race: 1st
Embassy Grand Final race: 1st

Aghadowey
250cc race: 1st
350cc race: 4th
500cc race: 1st
750cc race: 1st
Sunflower Trophy race: 1st

Mondello Park
250cc race: 3rd
350cc race: 4th
Unlimited race: 3rd

1979

Aghadowey
250cc race: 4th

Kirkistown
250cc: 3rd
350cc: 1st

Tangragee 100
350cc: 1st

Cookstown 100
250cc: 2nd
350cc: 1st
500cc: 1st

North West 200
Match Race: 1st
350cc: 5th
500cc: 5th
North West 200: 1st

Isle of Man TT
Schweppes Classic: 6th

Killinchy 150
250cc: 1st
350cc: 1st
1000cc: 1st

Aghadowey
250cc: 1st
350cc: 1st
750cc: 1st
Ace of Aghadowey: 1st

Kirkistown
250cc: 1st
350cc: 2nd
500cc: 1st
Unlimited cc: 1st
Rothmans Top 20: 1st

Skerries 100
250cc: 1st
Skerries Shell Sport: 1st

Kirkistown
250cc: 3rd
350cc: 3rd
Unlimited cc: 2nd
Embassy race: 2nd
King of Kirkistown: 2nd

Southern 100
250cc race: 1st
350cc race: 1st
Solo Championship race: 1st

Mid Antrim 150
350cc: 1st
Unlimited cc: 1st

Ulster Grand Prix
350cc: 2nd
500cc: 1st
1000cc: 1st

Oulton Park
350cc race: 10th

Kirkistown
250cc: 8th

Oulton Park
350cc race: 10th
Marlboro Race of the Year: 10th

Aghadowey
250cc: 3rd
500cc: 2nd
Unlimited cc: 1st
Unlimited cc Handicap race: 6th

Brands Hatch
1000cc race: 8th

1980

Aghadowey
250cc: 5th
250cc Handicap race: 9th
501-1000cc: 2nd
351-1000cc: 4th

Kirkistown
250cc: 2nd
500cc: 3rd
Wills Challenge Trophy: 3rd

North West 200
350cc: 4th

Cookstown 100
500cc: 3rd

Isle of Man TT
Senior: 9th
250cc Junior: 12th
Classic: 1st

Killinchy 150
250cc: 1st
350cc: 4th
500cc: 1st
1000cc: 1st

Mondello Park
250cc: 4th
251-500cc: 1st
501-1000cc: Formula 1: 4th

Kirkistown
250cc: 2nd
350cc: 1st
Rothmans Top 20 race: 7th

Aghadowey
250cc: 3rd
501-1000cc: 1st

Skerries 100
250cc: 1st

Southern 100
250cc race: 1st
350cc race: 1st

Kirkistown
250cc: 2nd
350cc: 7th
500cc: 1st
501-1000cc: 2nd
Embassy race: 2nd
King of Kirkistown: 1st

Silverstone
TTF1 race: 2nd

Ulster Grand Prix
250cc: 1st
Unlimited cc: 1st
TT Formula 1: 2nd

Donington Park
TTF1 race: 2nd

Carrowdore 100
Unlimited cc: 1st

Cadwell Park
TTF1 race: 9th

Mondello Park
250cc: 2nd
350cc: 1st
351-1000cc: 1st
Race of the Year: 1st

Kirkistown
250cc: 2nd
350cc: 1st
500cc: 1st
501-1000cc: 1st
Embassy Grand Final: 1st

Aghadowey
500cc: 1st
201-1000cc: 1st

Brands Hatch
TTF1 race: 5th

1981

Cadwell Park
Forward Trust TT F1
championship race: 7th

Donington Park
Forward Trust TTF1
championship: 6th
MCN/Shell Streetbike
championship: 2nd
ITV World of Sport Superbike
Challenge: 6th

Brands Hatch
Transatlantic Trophy Race 1: 13th
Transatlantic Trophy Race 2: 10th

Mallory Park
Transatlantic Trophy Race 1: 12th
Transatlantic Trophy Race 2: 11th

Oulton Park
Transatlantic Trophy Race 1: 9th
Transatlantic Trophy Race 2: 7th

North West 200
Feature race: 1st

Isle of Man TT
TT Formula 1 (world
championship round): 3rd

Mallory Park
MCN/Shell Streetbike
championship: 3rd

Killinchy 150
Unlimited cc: 1st

Donington Park
Daily Mirror Superbike race: 2nd

Silverstone
Forward Trust TTF1
championship: 3rd

Ulster Grand Prix
Feature race: 5th
Unlimited cc: 5th
TT Formula 1 (world
championship round): 5th

Donington Park
MCN/Shell Streetbike
championship: 8th

Oulton Park
Forward Trust TTF1
championship: 8th
MCN/Shell Streetbike
championship: 6th

Mallory Park
Forward Trust TT F1
championship: 6th
MCN/Shell Streetbike
championship: 6th

Brands Hatch
Forward Trust TT F1
championship: 7th
MCN/Shell Streetbike
championship: 8th
MCN/Shell Superbike race: 7th

1982

Cadwell Park
British TTF1 championship: 5th
MCN Superbike championship:
10th
MCN/Shell Oils Streetbike
championship: 4th

Brands Hatch
MCN/Shell Oils Streetbike
championship: 5th

Mallory Park
MCN/Shell Oils Streetbike
championship: 4th

Oulton Park
MCN/Shell Oils Streetbike
championship: 3rd

Donington Park
British TTF1 championship: 6th
MCN Superbike championship,
leg one: 8th
MCN Superbike championship,
leg two: 10th
MCN/Shell Oils Streetbike
championship: 3rd

North West 200
Classic 1000 race: 2nd
TTF1 race: 2nd

Isle of Man TT
TT Formula 1 (world
championship round):
2nd

Killinchy 150
501-1000cc: 5th

Aghadowey
501-1000cc: 1st
Formula 1: 1st
John Player Race of the Year: 1st

Vila Real
TT Formula 1 (world
championship round): 2nd

Snetterton
MCN/Shell Oils Streetbike
championship: 3rd

Race of Aces: 8th

Silverstone
British TTF1 championship: 7th

Mid Antrim 150
501-1000cc: 1st

Ulster Grand Prix
TT Formula 1 (world
championship round): 2nd
1000cc: 2nd

Donington Park
British TTF1 championship: 6th
MCN Superbike championship:
8th
MCN/Shell Oils Streetbike
championship: 1st
ITV World of Sport Production
race: 3rd
John Player Anglo-Dutch
Superbike race: 7th

Assen
Anglo-Dutch Superbike race: 5th

Aghadowey
350cc-1000cc: 3rd
Production Bike: 1st
Sunflower Trophy: 5th

Mondello Park
Unlimited cc/Formula 1: 5th
Production Bike: 1st
Fingal Race of the Year: 1st

Oulton Park
MCN/Shell Oils Streetbike
championship: 3rd

Oulton Park
MCN Superbike championship,
leg one: 10th

Brands Hatch
British TTF1 championship: 6th
Marlboro Powerbike International:
6th

* FIM TT Formula 1 world
champion

1983

Donington Park
1000cc British championship: 4th
Cadwell Park

MCN Masters championship: 9th
Shell Oils TTF1: 4th

Thruxton
Shell Oils TTF1: 8th

Oulton Park
1000cc British championship: 6th

Donington Park
1000cc British championship:
10th

Oulton Park
MCN Masters championship: 5th
Shell Oils TTF1: 3rd

Aghadowey
501-1000cc: 2nd
Formula 1: 1st
Russell Menagh Race of the Day:
2nd

Brands Hatch
MCN Masters championship: 9th
Shell Oils TTF1: 10th

Tandragee 100
500-1000cc: 1st

North West 200
500cc: 1st
Superbike: 3rd
North West 200: 1st

Isle of Man TT
TT Formula 1 (world
championship round): 1st
Senior Classic: 3rd

Mondello Park
351-1000cc: 1st
Leinster 200: 7th

Killinchy 150
1000cc: 1st
Invitation race: 1st

Assen
TT Formula 1 (world
championship round): 2nd

Donington Park
Shell Oils TTF1: 4th
ITV World of Sport Superbike
challenge: 10th

Snetterton
MCN Masters championship: 8th
Shell Oils TTF1: 6th

Silverstone
Shell Oils TTF1: 4th

Ulster Grand Prix
TT Formula 1 (world
championship round): 1st
500cc: 3rd

Aghadowey
Unlimited cc: 1st
John Player Race of the Year, leg
one: 1st

John Player Race of the Year, leg
two: 1st

Mondello Park
First 125cc/200cc: 2nd
Second 125cc/200cc: 1st
Unlimited cc: 1st
Race of the Year: 1st

Aghadowey
Unlimited cc: 1st
Embassy: 1st
Sunflower Trophy: 3rd

Oliver's Mount
MCN Masters championship:
3rd
Shell Oils TTF1: 2nd
1000cc Race: 6th

Kirkistown
125cc: 3rd
Unlimited cc: 1st
Embassy Championship: 3rd

Brands Hatch
Shell Oils TTF1: 4th
Powerbike International: 7th

* FIM TT Formula 1 world
champion

1984

Cadwell Park:
500cc race: 6th

Thruxton
Shell Oils TTF1: 4th
500cc race: 4th

Cadwell Park
MCN Masters championship: 3rd
500cc race: 3rd

Donington Park
ITV World of Sport Superbike
Challenge: 9th

Brands Hatch
1300cc race: 3rd
F1 Four-Strokes race: 1st

Aghadowey
500cc: 1st
501-1000cc: 2nd
Ace of Aghadowey: 1st

Oulton Park
Shell Oils TTF1: 2nd
500cc race: 1st

Oliver's Mount
Ken Redfern Trophy race: 1st
500cc race: 1st

Snetterton
Shell Oils TTF1: 3rd
North West 200
MCN Masters race: 1st

Isle of Man TT
TT Formula 1 (world
championship round): 1st
Classic: 2nd

Killinchy 150
250cc: 1st
1000cc: 1st
Invitation race: 1st

Assen
TT Formula 1 (world
championship round): 2nd

Vila Real
TT Formula 1 world
championship (world
championship round): 2nd

Silverstone
Shell Oils TTF1: 3rd

Ulster Grand Prix
TT Formula 1 (world
championship round): 1st
250cc: 1st
500cc: 1st

Zolder
TT Formula 1 (world
championship round): 2nd

Oliver's Mount
MCN Masters championship: 8th

Killalane
250cc: 1st
351-1000cc: 1st

Mondello Park
250cc: 1st
351-1000cc: 3rd
Hutchinson Trophy & AGV race:
1st

Aghadowey
351-1000cc: 2nd
John Player Race of the Year, leg
one: 2nd
John Player race of the year, leg
two: 2nd

* FIM TT Formula 1 world
champion

1985

Cadwell Park
250cc British championship: 8th

Aghadowey
250cc: 2nd
351-1000cc: 4th

Aghadowey:
250cc: 1st
351-1000cc: 3rd

Tandragee 100
250cc: 1st
351-1000cc: 1st

North West 200
First 250cc race: 1st
North West 200: 1st

Isle of Man TT
TT Formula 1 (world
championship round): 1st
250cc Junior: 1st
Senior: 1st

Killinchy 150
351-1000cc: 1st
Invitation race: 1st

Assen
TT Formula 1 (world
championship round): 1st

Vila Real
TT Formula 1 (world
championship round): 1st

JOEY DUNLOP CAREER RESULTS

Montjuich Park
TT Formula 1 (world
championship round): 1st

Ulster Grand Prix
TT Formula 1 (world
championship round): 1st
250cc: 1st
500cc: 1st

Kirkistown
First 250cc race: 1st
Second 250cc race: 3rd
351-1000cc race: 5th
Race of the Day: 1st

Mondello Park
250cc race: 8th

Hockenheim
TT Formula 1 (world
championship round): 1st

Kirkistown
250cc race: 1st
First Invitation race: 3rd
Second Invitation race: 7th

* FIM TT Formula 1 world
champion

1986

Aghadowey
351-1000cc race: 3rd
250-1000cc race: 8th

Kirkistown
250cc race: 1st
351-1000cc race: 4th

Hockenheim
TT Formula 1 (world
championship race): 1st

North West 200
Second Superbike race: 1st

Isle of Man TT
TT Formula 1 (world
championship round): 1st
Production Class C: 4th
Senior: 4th

Killinchy 150
250cc race: 1st
Invitation race: 2nd

Aghadowey
351-1000cc race: 1st
John Player Race of the Year, leg
one: 1st
John Player Race of the Year, leg
two: 1st

Assen
TT Formula 1 (world
championship round): 1st

Jerez
TT Formula 1 (world
championship round): 5th

Vila Real
TT Formula 1 (world
championship round): 1st

Imatra
TT Formula 1 (world
championship round): 1st

Fore
250cc race: 3rd
351-1000cc race: 5th

Ulster Grand Prix
TT Formula 1 (world
championship round): 2nd
250cc race: 4th
1000cc race: 1st

Mid Antrim 150
250cc race: 1st
1000cc race: 1st

Mondello Park
First 250cc race: 6th
Second 250cc race: 4th

351-1000cc race: 4th
AGV race: 2nd

* FIM TT Formula 1 world
champion

1987

Aghadowey
351-1000cc race: 5th

Misano
TT Formula 1 (world
championship round): 3rd

Hungaroring
TT Formula 1 (world
championship round): 8th

North West 200
240-350cc race: 4th
First Superbike race: 1st
North West 200 Superbike race:
1st
400-750cc Production race: 1st

Isle of Man TT
TT Formula 1 (world
championship round): 1st
Junior: 8th
Senior: 1st

Aghadowey
John Player Race of the Year, leg
one: 1st
John Player Race of the Year, leg
two: 3rd

Temple 100
351-1000cc race: 3rd

Fore
351-1000cc race: 5th
Production Superstock race: 3rd

Killalane
Enkalon Grand Final race: 1st

Hockenheim
TT Formula 1 (world
championship round): 4th

Donington Park
TT Formula 1 (world
championship round): 3rd

Kirkistown
351-1000cc race: 3rd
Neil Robinson Memorial race, leg
one: 1st
Neil Robinson Memorial race, leg
two: 1st

1988

Donington Park
World Superbike championship,
race one: 3rd
World Superbike championship,
race two: 6th

Hungaroring
World Superbike championship,
race one: 6th

Hockenheim
World Superbike championship,
race one: 7th
World Superbike championship,
race two: 5th

North West 200
250-350cc race: 3rd
401-750cc race: 1st
North West 200 race: 2nd

Isle of Man TT
TT Formula 1 (world
championship round): 1st
Production Class B: 5th
Production Class C: 11th
Junior: 1st
Senior: 1st

Killinchy 150
250-350cc race: 2nd

351-1000cc race: 2nd
Kevin Martin Memorial race: 1st

Assen
TT Formula 1 (world
championship round): 8th

Vila Real
TT Formula 1 (world
championship round): 4th

Kouvola
TT Formula 1 (world
championship round): 3rd

Ulster Grand Prix
TT Formula 1 (world
championship round): 7th
First 250/350cc race: 4th
Second 250/350cc race: 1st
Senior race: 2nd

Donington Park
TT Formula 1 (world
championship round): 11th

1989

Fore
125/200cc race: 8th

Munster 100
125/200cc race: 5th

Ulster Grand Prix,
TT Formula 1 (world
championship round): 20th

Mid Antrim 150
125/200cc race: 3rd
250cc race: 10th

Carrowdore 100
125/200cc race: 3rd
1000cc race: 6th

Killalane
125/200cc race: 4th

Kirkistown
125cc race: 5th
Senior race: 12th
Sunflower Trophy race: 13th

1990

Mondello Park
125cc race: 5th

Kirkistown
125cc race: 7th
250cc race: 12th

Aghadowey
125cc race: 16th
250cc race: 13th

Kirkistown
250cc race: 12th

Cookstown 100
125/200cc race: 4th
250/350cc race: 1st

Tandragee 100
125/200cc race: 7th
Tandragee 100 race: 8th

Kirkistown
250cc race: 9th

North West 200
125cc race: 4th
250/350cc race: 13th
Superbike race: 4th

Isle of Man TT
TT Formula 1 (TTF1 Cup
round): 8th
Senior: 16th

Killinchy 150
125/200cc: 4th
First 250/350cc race: 5th
Second 250/350cc race: 3rd
Invitation race: 3rd

Vila Real
TT Formula I (TTF1 Cup
round): 3rd

Milverton (Skerries)
125/200cc race: 1st
First 250/350cc race: 3rd
Second 250/350cc race: 3rd
Grand Final race: 6th

Kouvola
TT Formula (TTF1 Cup round):
5th

Munster 100
125/200cc race: 2nd
First 250/350cc race: 3rd
Second 250/350cc race :1st
750cc race: 3rd
Munster 100 race: 7th
Temple 100
125cc race: 2nd
250cc race: 1st

Ulster Grand Prix
125cc race: 2nd
Junior Prince of the Roads race:
3rd
TT Formula 1 (TTF1 Cup
round): 1st

Mid Antrim 150
125cc race: 1st

Mondello Park
First 125cc race: 7th
First 250/350cc: 13th

Senior race: 12th
Second 125cc race: 6th
Second 250/350cc race: 9th

Carrowdore 100
125cc race: 2nd
750cc race: 6th

Killalane
125cc race: 1st
First 250/350cc race: 7th
Second 250/350cc race: 4th
750cc race: 3rd

Aghadowey
Over 80cc-200cc race: 5th
750cc race: 8th

1991

Aghadowey
First 125cc race: 1st
Second 125c race: 2nd
First 250cc race: 2nd
Second 250cc race: 4th

Nutts Corner
125cc race: 5th
250cc race: 8th

Mondello Park
First 125cc race: 9th
Second 125cc race: 8th
250/350cc race: 8th

Aghadowey
125cc race: 2nd
250cc race: 2nd
750cc race: 1st
Enkalon Trophy race: 4th

Kirkistown
125cc race: 3rd
First 250cc race: 1st
Second 250cc race: 5th
First 750cc race: 3rd
Second 750cc race: 2nd
King of Kirkistown race: 2nd

Nutts Corner
125cc race: 12th
750cc race: 6th
First Aid charity race: 8th

Cookstown 100
125cc race: 2nd
250-750cc Senior race: 9th

Tandragee 100
125cc race: 2nd
250cc race: 2nd
Tandragee 100 race: 2nd

Kirkistown
125cc race: 5th
750cc race: 1st
Norman Brown Memorial race:
1st

JOEY DUNLOP CAREER RESULTS

North West 200
125cc race: 2nd
250/350cc race: 4th
North West 200 Superbike race:
2nd

Isle of Man TT
Ultra-Lightweight 125: 2nd
Junior: 5th
Supersport 600: 6th
Senior: 2nd

Killinchy 150
125cc race: 2nd
250/350cc race: 4th
750cc race: 1st

Aghadowey
125cc race: 2nd
750cc race: 4th
John Wallace Memorial race: 5th

Skerries
125/200cc race: 1st
First 250/350cc race: 3rd
Second 250/350cc race: 2nd
Senior race: 3rd

Fore
First 125/200cc race: 2nd
Second 125/200cc race: 2nd
First 250/350cc race: 3rd
Second 250/350cc race: 3rd

Southern 100
Senior Founders race: 1st
Junior Founders race: 1st
Junior race: 1st
Senior race: 1st
Solo Championship race: 1st
125cc race: 1st

Dundalk
250/350cc race: 3rd

Ulster Grand Prix
125cc race: 2nd
First Superbike race: 1st
Second Superbike race: 1st

Mid Antrim 150
125cc race: 1st
250cc race: 2nd
250-750cc race: 2nd

Carrowdore 100
125cc race: 1st
250cc race: 7th
750cc race: 3rd

Killalane
First 125/200cc race: 1st
Second 125/200cc race: 1st
250-750cc race: 3rd

Kirkistown
125cc race: 3rd
Senior race: 8th

1992

Nutts Corner
Regal 600cc race: 14th

Nutts Corner
125cc Enkalon race: 18th
Regal 600cc race: 12th

Aghadowey
125cc race: 5th
Regal 600cc race: 9th
750cc race: 5th
Enkalon Trophy race: 7th

Kirkistown
125cc race: 11th
Regal 600cc race: 8th
Imperial Tobacco Challenge race:
10th
First 750cc race: 5th
Second 750cc race: 7th

Tandragee 100
125cc race: 2nd
Regal 600cc race: 8th
750cc race: 3rd
Classic bike race: 10th

Cookstown 100
125cc race: 3rd
Regal 600cc race: 5th
750cc race: 2nd
Classic bike race: 10th

Bishopscourt
125cc race: 8th
750cc race: 5th
Regal 600cc race: 6th

North West 200
125cc race: 3rd
600cc race: 4th
Superbike race: 8th

Isle of Man TT
TT Formula 1: 3rd
125cc Ultra Lightweight: 1st
Junior: 9th

Steam Packet Races
125cc race: 1st
250cc race: 3rd
750cc race: 1st

Skerries 100
125/200cc race: 3rd

Temple 100
125cc race: 9th

Dundalk
First 125/250cc race: 6th
Second 125/250cc race: 10th

Mid Antrim 150
125/250cc race: 3rd
750cc race: 5th

Ulster Grand Prix
125cc race: 1st

Killalane
125/200cc race: 3rd
Supersport 600cc race: 5th
750cc race: 4th

Kirkistown
125cc race: 18th

1993

Aghadowey
125cc race: 7th
First 250cc race: 2nd
Second 250cc race: 1st
Supersport 600/750cc race: 5th

Aghadowey
First Shell 125cc race: 9th
Second Shell 125cc race: 9th
1000cc race: 13th

Kirkistown
First Shell 125cc race: 4th
Second Shell 125cc race: 2nd
First 1000cc race: 7th
Second 1000cc race: 3rd

Cookstown 100
250/350cc race: 2nd
Regal 600cc race: 1st
Senior race: 1st

Tandragee 100
125cc race: 2nd
250/350cc race: 1st
Regal 600cc race: 1st
Senior race: 1st

North West 200
125cc race: 5th
250/350cc race: 6th
Regal 600cc race: 3rd
First Superbike race: 3rd
Second Superbike race: 5th

Billown Road Races
125cc race: 1st

Isle of Man TT
TT Formula 1: 14th
125cc Ultra-Lightweight: 1st
250cc Lightweight: 3rd
Senior: 11th

Dundrod 150
125cc race: 16th
Regal 600cc race: 5th

Skerries
First 125/200cc race: 2nd
Second 125/200cc race: 2nd
Supersport 600cc race: 3rd
1000cc race: 1st

Southern 100
250/350cc race: 1st
600cc race: 1st
Solo Championship race: 1st

Fore
125/250cc race: 2nd
First 250/350cc race: 1st
Second 250/350cc race: 1st
Supersport 600cc race: 1st
1000cc race: 1st

Temple 100
125/200cc race: 1st
250/350cc race: 2nd
Regal 600cc race: 3rd
Open Senior race: 4th

Ulster Grand Prix
125cc race: 3rd
250/400cc race: 5th
250/1000cc race: 2nd

Mid Antrim 150
125/200cc race: 2nd
250/350/400cc race: 2nd
Regal 600cc race: 1st
250-1000cc race: 5th

Dundalk
First 125/200cc race: 1st
Second 125/200cc race: 1st
250/350/400cc race: 5th
250-1000cc race: 6th

Carrowdore 100
125/200cc race: 2nd
250/350/400cc race: 1st
Regal 600cc race: 1st
250-1000cc race: 3rd

Killalane
125/200cc race: 1st
250/350/400cc race: 3rd
Supersport 600cc race: 5th
First 250-1000cc race: 3rd
Second 250-1000cc race: 3rd

1994

Aghadowey
First 125cc race: 6th
Second 125cc race: 7th
First 250cc race: 7th
Second 250cc race: 8th
Senior race: 7th

Cookstown 100
125cc race: 2nd
250cc race: 1st
Cookstown Senior race: 3rd

Kells
First 125/200cc race: 2nd
Second 125/200cc race: 1st
250cc/Junior race: 1st
Grand Final race: 3rd

North West 200
250/400cc race: 4th
Supersport 600cc race: 5th
Superbike race: 4th

Tandragee 100
125cc race: 1st
Senior race: 1st

Billown Classic TT
250/350cc race: 3rd

Isle of Man TT
TT Formula 1: 3rd
125cc Ultra-Lightweight: 1st
250cc Lightweight: 1st
Junior: 7th
Senior: 3rd

Dundrod 150
125cc race: 1st
250cc race: 1st
Senior race: 3rd

Skerries
First 125/200cc race: 23rd
Second 125/200cc race: 1st
250cc/Junior race: 1st
1000cc race: 1st

Kells
250cc race: 8th

Southern 100
Senior Founders race: 1st
Junior Founders race: 1st
250/350cc race: 1st

Mid Antrim 150
125cc race: 1st
250cc race: 1st
Senior race: 1st

Ulster Grand Prix
125cc race: 1st
First 250/400cc race: 3rd
Second 250/400cc race: 2nd
Superbike race: 1st

Dundalk
250cc/Junior race: 2nd
Senior race: 7th

Killalane
First 125/200cc race: 6th
Second 125/200cc race: 7th

1995

Aghadowey
First 125cc Superkings race: 5th
Second 125cc Superkings
race: 11th
250cc Enkalon race: 6th

Tandragee
125cc race: 1st
Open race: 2nd
Senior race: 1st

North West 200
125cc race: 2nd
First 250GP/Supersport 400cc
race: 5th
Second 250GP/Supersport 400
race: 7th
Regal 600cc race: 10th
First Superbike race: 10th
Second Superbike race: 6th

Isle of Man TT
TT Formula 1: 2nd
250cc Lightweight: 1st
Junior: 4th
Senior: 1st

Steam Packet Road Races
125cc race: 1st
250/400cc race: 2nd

Dundrod 150
125cc race: 4th
Open race: 6th

Kirkistown
First 125cc Superkings race: 2nd
Second 125cc Superkings race: 3rd
First 250GP/Supersport 400cc

race: 6th
Second 250cc Enkalon race: 4th

Skerries
First 125/200cc race: 1st
Second 125/200cc race: 1st
250cc/Junior race: 2nd
Senior race: 3rd
Castrol Grand Final race: 3rd

Mettet Road Races
125cc race: 11th
250cc race: 5th

Mid Antrim 150
125/200cc race: 1st
Open race: 3rd

Ulster Grand Prix
125cc race: 4th
First 250GP/Supersport 400cc
race: 1st
Second 250GP/Supersport 400cc
race: 1st
Supersport 600cc race: 7th
Superbike race: 1st

Carrowdore 100
125/200cc race: 1st
Open race: 3rd
Carrowdore 100 Senior race: 3rd

Tallin Road Races
125cc race: 1st
250cc race: 1st
Superbike race: 1st

1996

Aghadowey
First 125cc Superkings race:
7th
Senior race: 8th
Enkalon Trophy race: 9th

Cookstown 100
125cc Superkings race: 1st
Open race: 6th
Senior race: 10th

North West 200
125cc race: 9th
First 250/350cc race: 8th
Second 250/350cc race: 2nd
First Superbike race: 5th
Second Superbike race: 6th

Isle of Man TT
TT Formula 1: 7th
250cc Lightweight: 1st
125cc Ultra-Lightweight: 1st
Senior TT: 2nd

Steam Packet
125cc race: 2nd
250cc race: 1st

Dundrod 150
125cc race: 4th
Open race: 3rd
Dundrod 150 Senior race: 2nd

Riga Road Races
125cc race: 1st
Senior race: 1st

1997

Aghadowey
First 125cc race: 5th
Second 125cc race: 1st
First Senior race: 6th
Second Senior race: 8th

Cookstown 100
125cc Superkings race: 5th
Open race: 1st
Open Senior race: 11th

North West 200
First 250cc race: 9th
Second 250cc race: 14th
Supersport 600cc race: 10th
Superbike race: 6th

Isle of Man TT
TT Formula 1: 6th
Lightweight 250: 1st
Ultra-Lightweight 125: 10th
Junior: 5th
Senior: 7th

Louth Road Races
125/200cc race: 7th
250cc/Junior race: 5th
Open race: 4th

Dundrod 150
125cc Superkings race: 3rd
Regal 600cc race: 6th

Temple 100
First Open race: 8th
Second Open race: 5th

Mid Antrim 150
125cc Superkings/200cc race: 5th
Open race: 5th

North Monaghan Road Races
125/200cc race: 8th
250cc/Junior race: 4th
Open Senior race: 5th
Grand Final race: 5th

Ulster Grand Prix
125cc race: 2nd
First 250cc/Junior race: 1st
Second 250cc/Junior race: 3rd
600cc race: 4th
Superbike race: 3rd

Killalane
125/200cc race: 7th
Open race: 5th

Carrowdore 100
Open race: 4th
Carrowdore 100 Senior race: 4th

1998

Aghadowey
125cc Superkings race: 17th

Kirkistown
First 125cc Superkings race: 13th
Second 125cc Superkings race:
14th
250/350cc Junior race: 10th
First Senior race: 7th

Cookstown 100
125cc Superkings/200cc race: 5th
Open race: 4th
Tandragee 100
125cc Superkings/200cc race: 3rd

Isle of Man TT
Lightweight 250: 1st
Ultra-Lightweight 125: 9th

Mid Antrim 150
Open race: 11th

Kells
125/200cc race: 11th
Open race: 10th
Grand Final Senior race: 8th

Monaghan Road Races
First 125cc race: 8th
Second 125cc race: 10th
250cc/Junior race: 10th
Grand Final race: 11th

Ulster Grand Prix
250/400cc race: 12th
First Superbike race: 10th
Second Superbike race: 6th

Carrowdore 100
125cc Superkings/200cc race: 8th
Open race: 13th
Senior race: 3rd

Killalane
Open race: 7th

1999

Aghadowey
125cc Superkings/200cc race: 8th
Regal 600cc race: 13th
Enkalon Trophy race: 13th

Kirkistown
125cc Superkings/200cc race: 7th
Regal 600cc race: 6th
Lambert & Butler Open race: 1st

Cookstown 100
125cc Superkings/200cc race: 6th
Regal 600cc race: 13th

Lambert & Butler Open race:
16th

Tandragee 100
Regal 600cc race: 11th
Lambert & Butler Open race: 3rd
Tandragee 100 Senior race: 7th

North West 200
Supersport 600cc race: 11th
Superbike race: 7th

Isle of Man TT
Formula 1: 2nd
Lightweight 250: 5th
Ultra-Lightweight 125: 27th
Junior: 5th
Senior: 5th

Dundrod 150
125cc Superkings/200cc race: 2nd
Regal 600cc race: 5th

Dundalk Road Races
125/200cc race: 6th
Supersport 600cc race: 8th
Open race: 1st
Senior race: 1st

Skerries
First 125/200cc race: 3rd
Second 125/200cc race: 4th
250cc/Junior race: 4th

Supersport 600cc race: 5th
401-750cc race: 1st
Grand Final Senior race: 1st

Southern 100
Senior Founders race: 1st
Solo Championship race: 1st

Monaghan Road Races
125cc Superkings race: 9th
125/200cc race: 5th
250cc/Junior race: 3rd
Regal 600cc race: 8th
First Lambert & Butler Open race: 1st
Second lambert & Butler Open race: 6th

Ulster Grand Prix
125cc race: 2nd
250cc race: 6th
Supersport 600cc race: 5th
First Superkings Open race: 3rd
Second Superkings Open race: 1st

Carrowdore 100
Lambert & Butler 250cc/Junior race: 7th

Killalane Road Races
First 125/200cc race: 3rd
Second 125/200cc race: 4th
250cc/Junior race: 3rd

Supersport 600cc race: 4th

2000

Aghadowey
First 250cc race: 2nd
Second 250cc race: 2nd
First Senior race: 12th
Second Senior race: 9th

Aghadowey
First 125cc Superkings race: 6th
Second 125cc Superkings race: 5th
First Regal 600cc race: 10th
Second Regal 600cc race: 11th
Lambert & Butler Open race: 14th

Kirkistown
First 125cc Superkings race: 3rd
Second 125cc Superkings race: 6th
First Regal 600cc race: 14th
Second Regal 600cc race: 9th

Cookstown 100
125cc Superkings race: 2nd
Regal 600cc race: 4th
Lambert & Butler Open race: 2nd
Cookstown Senior race: 5th

North West 200
125cc race: 4th
Supersport 600cc race: 5th

JOEY DUNLOP CAREER RESULTS

First Superbike race: 5th
Second Superbike race: 25th

Tandragee 100
125cc Superkings race: 1st

Isle of Man TT
TT Formula 1: 1st
Lightweight 250: 1st
Ultra-Lightweight 125: 1st
Junior: 4th
Senior: 3rd

Tallin Road Races
Supersport 600cc race: 1st
Superbike race: 1st

Author's note: While this does not claim to be an exhaustive list of Joey Dunlop's career results, it is the most comprehensive list I am aware of. Many of the results from smaller meetings that Joey took part in were never published and may be lost to the record.

ENDNOTES

1   From *King of the Road*, a Terry Smyth Production in association with Ulster Television, 9 June 1991

2   From *King of the Road*, a Terry Smyth Production in association with Ulster Television, 9 June 1991

3   From *King of the Road*, a Terry Smyth Production in association with Ulster Television, 9 June 1991

4   From 'Living Legends: Joey Dunlop: King of the Road', produced and directed by Terry Smyth, BBC Northern Ireland, 1997

5   Walker, Jimmy: *Just Joey: The Joey Dunlop Story* (CollinsWillow, 2001) p34

6   McDiarmid, Mac: *Joey Dunlop: His Authorised Biography* (Haynes, 2001) p20

7   McDiarmid, Mac: *Joey Dunlop: His Authorised Biography* (Haynes, 2001) p20

8   McDiarmid, Mac: *Joey Dunlop: His Authorised Biography* (Haynes, 2001) p21

9   From a YouTube interview by Gavin Caldwell/Road Racing Ireland, 2020

10 McDiarmid, Mac: *Joey Dunlop: His Authorised Biography* (Haynes, 2001) p23

11 From an interview in *Joey Dunlop: A Tribute*, BBC Northern Ireland, 13/09/2000

12 From an interview in 'Living Legends: Joey Dunlop: King of the Road', produced and directed by Terry Smyth, BBC Northern Ireland, 1997

13 Walker, Jimmy: *Just Joey: The Joey Dunlop Story* (CollinsWillow, 2001) p44

14 McDiarmid, Mac: *Joey Dunlop: His Authorised Biography* (Haynes, 2001) p27

15 From an interview in 'Living Legends: Joey Dunlop: King of the Road', produced and directed by Terry Smyth, BBC Northern Ireland, 1997

16 From an interview in *V-Four Victory*, directed by David Wood, 1983

17 From an interview in *Joey Dunlop: A Tribute*, BBC1 Northern Ireland, 13 Sep 2000

18 Walker, Jimmy: *Just Joey: The Joey Dunlop Story* (CollinsWillow, 2001) p49

19 From an interview in *Joey Dunlop: A Tribute,* BBC Northern Ireland, 13 Sep 2000

20 From an interview in *Joey, Ray & Rivals*, directed by Anna Masefield, 2011

21 From an interview in *Joey Dunlop: A Tribute,* BBC Northern Ireland, 2000

22 From an interview in *King of the Road,* a Terry Smyth Production in association with Ulster Television, 9 June 1991

23 Walker, Jimmy: *Just Joey: The Joey Dunlop Story* (CollinsWillow, 2001) p100

24 Walker, Jimmy: *Just Joey: The Joey Dunlop Story* (CollinsWillow, 2001) p87

25 'Sporting Lives and Times', Roy Harris, www.belfasttelegraph.co.uk, 20 July 2019

26 Walker, Jimmy: *Just Joey: The Joey Dunlop Story* (CollinsWillow, 2001) p178

27 Clifford, Peter (ed.): *Motocourse 1984–85* (Hazleton Publishing, 1984) p179

28 McDiarmid, Mac: *Joey Dunlop: His Authorised Biography* (Haynes, 2001) p76

29 Clifford, Peter (ed.): *Motocourse 1984–85* (Hazleton Publishing, 1984) p180

30 From an interview in *Joey Dunlop: A Tribute,* BBC Northern Ireland, 2000

31 From an interview by Póilín Ní Chiaráin, RTÉ Archives

32 From an interview in *Joey Dunlop: A Tribute,* BBC Northern Ireland, 2000

ENDNOTES

33 From an interview in *Joey Dunlop: A Tribute,* BBC Northern Ireland, 2000

34 Knight, Ray: *Joey Dunlop: A Tribute*, (Mortons Motorcycle Media Ltd), 2000, pp94–95

35 Walker, Jimmy: *Just Joey: The Joey Dunlop Story* (CollinsWillow, 2001) pp216–17

36 From an interview in *The Mecca of Motorcycling: The TT 80 Years On*, BBC2, 31 May 1988

37 From an interview in *The Mecca of Motorcycling: The TT 80 Years On*, BBC2, 31 May 1988

38 From an interview in 'Living Legends: Joey Dunlop: King of the Road', produced and directed by Terry Smyth, BBC Northern Ireland, 1997

39 'Joey Dunlop Was Just Loved by Everyone', *Belfast Telegraph*, 12 May 2010

40 'Totally and Utterly Fearless: The Legacy of Antrim Icon Joey Dunlop', Shane Hannon, OTB Sports, 15 July 2020

41 Walker, Jimmy: *Robert Dunlop: Life and Times of a Legend* (Gill & Macmillan Ltd, 2008), p30

42 From an interview in *The Mecca of Motorcycling: The TT 80 Years On*, BBC2, 31 May 1988

43 Walker, Jimmy: *Just Joey: The Joey Dunlop Story* (CollinsWillow, 2001), p240

44 McDiarmid, Mac: *Joey Dunlop: His Authorised Biography'* (Haynes, 2001) p102

45 Walker, Jimmy: *Just Joey: The Joey Dunlop Story* (CollinsWillow, 2001), pp244–5

46 McDiarmid, Mac: *Joey Dunlop: His Authorised Biography* (Haynes Publishing, 2001), p110

47 McCook, Alastair: *Days of Thunder: The History of the Ulster Grand Prix* (Gill & Macmillan Ltd, 2004), p116

48 McCook, Alastair: *Days of Thunder: The History of the Ulster Grand Prix* (Gill & Macmillan Ltd, 2004), p116

49 McCook, Alastair: *Days of Thunder: The History of the Ulster Grand Prix* (Gill & Macmillan Ltd, 2004), p116

50 From 'Living Legends: Joey Dunlop: King of the Road', produced and directed by Terry Smyth, BBC Northern Ireland, 1997

51 From 'Living Legends: Joey Dunlop: King of the Road', produced and directed by Terry Smyth, BBC Northern Ireland, 1997

52 Walker, Jimmy: *Just Joey: The Joey Dunlop Story* (CollinsWillow, 2001), p288

53 From an interview in *Joey Dunlop: No Ordinary Joe: The Man Behind the Legend*, directed by Anna Masefield, Duke Video/Waldovision, 2011

54 From an interview in *Joey Dunlop: A Tribute*, BBC1 Northern Ireland, 13 Sep 2000

55 From an interview in *King of the Road*. A Terry Smyth Production in association with Ulster Television, 9 June 1991

56 From an interview in *Joey Dunlop: No Ordinary Joe: The Man Behind the Legend*. Director Anna Masefield, Duke Video/Waldovision, 2011

57 *Reluctant Superstar: Remembering Joey Dunlop*, Peter Crutchley, www.bbc.co.uk, 6 July 2015

58 From an interview in *Road*, directed by Michael Hewitt/Diarmuid Lavery, Doubleband Films for NNC Northern Ireland, 2014

59 From an interview in *Road*, directed by Michael Hewitt/Diarmuid Lavery, Doubleband Films for NNC Northern Ireland, 2014

60 McDiarmid, Mac: *Joey Dunlop: His Authorised Biography* (Haynes Publishing, 2001), p150

61 From an interview in 'Living Legends: Joey Dunlop: King of the Road', produced and directed by Terry Smyth, BBC Northern Ireland, 1997

62 From an interview in 'Living Legends: Joey Dunlop: King of the Road', produced and directed by Terry Smyth, BBC Northern Ireland, 1997

63 Beckett, Liam: *Robert Dunlop, Road Racing and Me* (Blackstaff Press, 2016), pp114–115

64 From an interview in *The Robert Dunlop Story*, Ulster Television, 2001

ENDNOTES

65 Knight, Ray: *Joey Dunlop: A Tribute* (Mortons Motorcycle Media Ltd, 2000), p147

66 From an interview in 'Living Legends: Joey Dunlop: King of the Road', produced and directed by Terry Smyth, BBC Northern Ireland, 1997

67 Walker, Jimmy: *Just Joey: The Joey Dunlop Story* (CollinsWillow, 2001), p300

68 Walker, Jimmy: *Just Joey: The Joey Dunlop Story* (CollinsWillow, 2001), pp317–18

69 From an interview on the *Kelly* show, Ulster television, May 1998

70 From an interview in *Joey Dunlop: No Ordinary Joe: The Man Behind the Legend* directed by Anna Masefield, Duke Video/Waldovision, 2011

71 From an interview in *Joey Dunlop: No Ordinary Joe: The Man Behind the Legend* directed by Anna Masefield, Duke Video/Waldovision, 2011

72 Walker, Jimmy: *Just Joey: The Joey Dunlop Story* (CollinsWillow, 2001), p324

73 Walker, Jimmy: *Just Joey: The Joey Dunlop Story*, CollinsWillow, 2001, p20

74 From an interview in *Joey Dunlop: No Ordinary Joe: The Man Behind the Legend* directed by Anna Masefield, Duke Video/Waldovision, 2011

75 McDiarmid, Mac: *Joey Dunlop: His Authorised Biography* (Haynes Publishing, 2001), p155

76 McDiarmid, Mac, *Joey Dunlop: His Authorised Biography* (Haynes Publishing, 2001), p16

77 From an interview in *Joey Dunlop: No Ordinary Joe: The Man Behind the Legend* directed by Anna Masefield, Duke Video/Waldovision, 2011

78 Walker, Jimmy: *Just Joey: The Joey Dunlop Story* (CollinsWillow, 2001), p344

79 McDiarmid, Mac: *Joey Dunlop: His Authorised Biography* (Haynes Publishing, 2001), p173

80 Walker, Jimmy: *Robert Dunlop: Life and Times of a Legend* (Gill & Macmillan Ltd, 2008), p135

BIBLIOGRAPHY

Books

Barker, Stuart: *David Jefferies: The Official Biography*, Haynes Publishing, 2009

Barker, Stuart: *TT Century: 100 Years of the Isle of Man Tourist Trophy*, Century, 2007

Beckett, Liam: *Robert Dunlop, Road Racing and Me*, Blackstaff Press, 2016

Clifford, Peter (ed.): *Motocourse 1984–85*, Hazleton Publishing, 1984

Davison, Stephen: *Joey Dunlop: King of the Roads*, The Obrien Press Ltd, 2000

Dunlop, Michael: *Road Racer: It's In My Blood*, Michael O'Mara Books Ltd, 2017

Hislop, Steve with Barker, Stuart: *Hizzy: The Autobiography of Steve Hislop*, CollinsWillow, 2003

Kneale, Peter and Bill Snelling *Honda: The TT Winning Years*, Amulree Publications, 1998

Knight, Ray: *Joey Dunlop: A Tribute*, Mortons Motorcycle Media Ltd, 2000

McCallen, Phillip and Woods: Phil: *Supermac*, Aureus Publishing Ltd, 2000

McCook, Alastair: *Days of Thunder: The History of the Ulster Grand Prix*, Gill & Macmillan Ltd, 2004

McCook, Alastair: *The Power and the Glory: The History of the North West 20*, Appletree Press Ltd, 2002

McDiarmid, Mac: *Joey Dunlop: His Authorised Biography*, Haynes Publishing, 2001

Walker, Jimmy: *Just Joey: The Joey Dunlop Story*, CollinsWillow, 2001

Walker, Jimmy: *Robert Dunlop: Life and Times of a Legend*, Gill & Macmillan Ltd, 2008

Wilson, Ian: *Shipwrecks of the Ulster Coast*, Impact Amergin, 1979

Documentaries and Films

Big Frank: A Tribute, directed by Colin James, produced by Colin White, 2019

Champion Joey Dunlop: Profile of a Legend, Duke Marketing, 2013

Isle of Man TT Official Reviews: 1985 – 1999, Duke Video Box Set, 2005

King of the Road, a Terry Smyth Production in association with

BIBLIOGRAPHY

Ulster Television, 9 June 1991

The Last Lap: In the Footsteps of Joey Dunlop, produced and directed by Karen McGrath, Independent Pictures, for BBC Northern Ireland, 2003

Living Legends: Joey Dunlop: King of the Road: Produced and directed by Terry Smyth, BBC Northern Ireland, 1997

Mervyn Robinson: Ace of Armoy, directed by Colin James, produced by Rowland White, a Waldovision Production, 2020

Joey: 1952–2000, a UTV Video Production in association with Duke Video, 2000

Joey: The Man Who Conquered the TT, a film by John Mathews, Bigger Picture Films, 2013

Joey Dunlop: No Ordinary Joe: The Man Behind the Legend, directed by Anna Masefield, Duke Video/Waldovision, 2011

Joey Dunlop: The North West 200 Wins, a Duke DVD Production, produced by Colin James and Anna Masefield, 2014

Joey, Ray & Rivals, a Duke DVD Production, produced by Waldovision, 2011

Joey Dunlop: A Tribute, BBC1 Northern Ireland, 13 September 2000

Joey Dunlop: The TT Wins, a Duke DVD Production, 2009

Raining Champions: Road Racing Highlights from 1975 and 1976, a Duke DVD Production. Produced by Waldovision, 2009

Road, directed by Michael Hewitt/Diarmuid Lavery, Doubleband Films for NNC Northern Ireland, 2014

The Road Racers, produced and directed by David Wallace for BBC Northern Ireland, 1980

The Robert Dunlop Story, Ulster Television/Duke Video, 2001

The Title Trail: The Dramatic Story of the 1974 Ulster 350 Championship, a Duke DVD Production. Produced by Waldovision, 2009

TT 2000, Duke/Greenlight Television, 2000

V-Four Victory, produced and directed by David Wood, a CH Wood Production, 1983

ACKNOWLEDGEMENTS

I would like to sincerely thank the following people for granting me fresh interviews for this book. It was an absolute pleasure and a privilege to listen to all of your stories:

Tony 'Slick' Bass, Ferry Brouwer, Carl Fogarty, John Harris, Nick Jefferies, Roger Marshall, Bob McMillan, Stéphane Mertens, Don Morley, Hector Neill, Paul 'Moz' Owen, Johnny Rea, Steve Reynolds, Graham Sanderson, Ian 'Simmo' Simpson, Barry Symmons, Neil Tuxworth and David Wood.

For granting me previous interviews (excerpts of which I have re-used in this book), I would like to thank the following:

Jim Dunlop, Mick Grant, the late, great Steve Hislop, Paul Iddon, Tony Jefferies, Phillip McCallen, Rob McElnea, Martyn Ogborne, Phil Read, Michael Rutter, Jack Valentine, David Wallace and Charlie Williams.

Thanks also to John Murray, Mark Browne, and Jim Brown of Portaferry RNLI for talking me through the sinking of the *Tornamora* and providing eye-witness accounts of that dramatic night.

A very special thanks must go to Ivan Davidson of the Motorcycle Union of Ireland (MCUI) for allowing me to publish his comprehensive listing of Joey Dunlop's career race results. I must also thank Lisa Tams for not only keying in those results but for doing so much else while I had my head buried in my work.

I'm extremely grateful to Carl Fogarty, MBE, for sharing his memories of Joey Dunlop with me and for writing the foreword for this book.

I would like to thank my agent, David Luxton, and Rebecca Winfield of David Luxton Associates for helping to make this book happen, and huge thanks are also due to all those at John Blake/ Bonnier Books who have worked so hard on my behalf – James Hodgkinson, Nikki Mander, Sophie Nevrkla and Stella Giatrakou.

Thanks also to my mum and dad, Josie and Jim Barker, for taking me to road races when I was a kid and sparking my interest in Joey Dunlop at such an early age. Jimmy Dunbar, Martin Lambert, Tim Davies and Ben Purvis were a great help to me during my research, so I'm very grateful for their assistance, too.

For spotting and nurturing my creative side, I will always be grateful to my English Literature teacher at Stranraer Academy, Jack Hunter, who sadly passed away during the writing of this book. Thank you, Jack – your teachings have not been forgotten.

INDEX

INDEX

351

INDEX

INDEX

INDEX

INDEX